Wayne R. Besen

Anything but ⦚
Unmasking
the Scandals and Lies
Behind the Ex-Gay Myth

HPP

Harrington Park Press®
An Imprint of The Haworth Press, Inc.
New York • London • Oxford

Anything but Straight
Unmasking
the Scandals and Lies
Behind the Ex-Gay Myth

THE HAWORTH PRESS
Titles of Related Interest

Rough News—Daring Views: 1950s' Pioneer Gay Press Journalism by Jim Kepner

Reclaiming the Sacred: The Bible in Gay and Lesbian Culture, Second Edition by Raymond Jean-Frontain

Gay/Lesbian/Bisexual/Transgender Public Policy Issues: A Citizen's and Administrator's Guide to the New Cultural Struggle by Wallace Swan

One of the Boys: Masculinity, Homophobia, and Modern Manhood by David Plummer

Straight Talk About Gays in the Workplace, Second Edition by Liz Winfeld and Susan Spielman

Male to Male: Sexual Feeling Across the Boundaries of Identity by Edward J. Tejirian

Trailblazers: Profiles of America's Gay and Lesbian Elected Officials by Kenneth E. Yeager

Gay Men at Midlife: Age Before Beauty edited by Alan L. Ellis

Before Stonewall: Activists for Gay and Lesbian Rights in Historical Context edited by Vern L. Bullough

Acts of Disclosure: The Coming-Out Process of Contemporary Gay Men by Marc E. Vargo

Scandal: Infamous Gay Controversies of the Twentieth Century by Marc E. Vargo

Anything but Straight
Unmasking the Scandals and Lies Behind the Ex-Gay Myth

Wayne R. Besen

HPP

Harrington Park Press®
An Imprint of The Haworth Press, Inc.
New York • London • Oxford

Published by

Harrington Park Press®, an imprint of The Haworth Press, Inc., 10 Alice Street, Binghamton, NY 13904-1580.

TR: 1.7.03

PUBLISHER'S NOTE
The development, preparation, and publication of this work have been undertaken with great care. However, the publisher, employees, editors, and agents of The Haworth Press are not responsible for any errors contained herein or for consequences that may ensue from use of materials or information contained in this work. The opinions expressed by the author(s) are not necessarily those of The Haworth Press, Inc.

Cover design and interior graphics by Jennifer M. Gaska.

Cover and frontispiece: Photographs of John Paulk by Wayne Besen; "Gay for Life?" cover, *Newsweek,* August 17, 1998, reprinted with permission.

Library of Congress Cataloging-in-Publication Data

Besen, Wayne R.
    Anything but straight : unmasking the scandals and lies behind the ex-gay myth / Wayne R. Besen.
        p. cm.
    Includes bibliographical references and index.
    ISBN 1-56023-445-8 (alk. paper)—ISBN 1-56023-446-6 (pbk. : alk. paper)
        1. Church work with gays—United States—History. 2. Homosexuality—Religious aspects—Christianity—History of doctrines. 3. Gays—Pastoral counseling of—United States—History. 4. Gays—Counseling of—United States—History. I. Title.
BV4437.5 .B47 2003
261.8'3577—dc21
                                                                                            2002013857

In loving memory of Penrhyn "Pen" Jorgensen
and in honor of my parents,
Neil and Sydney Besen,
whose support, encouragement, and love sustained me
through this project

F I C T I O N

Mr. P's, Washington, DC's oldest gay saloon

F A C T

Ex-gay leader John Paulk running from Mr. P's

CONTENTS

FOREWORD ix
PREFACE xiii
ACKNOWLEDGMENTS xix

ACT I: THE EX-GAY MINISTRIES

Candi's Bathroom Break 3
Undercover 23
A Trilogy of Tragedy 61
Founding Follies 81
The Propagandists 99

ACT II: REPARATIVE THERAPY

Historic Injustice 119
Nicolosi's Nonsense 133
Radical Richard 161

ACT III: THE POLITICS OF CONVERSION

The Puppeteers 195
Political Science 227

ACT IV: THE ENCORE

Future Follies and Failures 245

APPENDIX: RESOURCES 275
NOTES 279
BIBLIOGRAPHY 295
INDEX 299

FOREWORD

For many years, I have admired Wayne Besen's courage and creativity as an activist and now as an author. In *Anything but Straight,* Mr. Besen examines one of the great heresies of our time. The notion that homosexuals can and should be "changed" is an insult to God, who loves variety in all things, including sexual orientation. As a proud, gay man who has served the Christian church as a pastor, seminary professor, filmmaker, author, and a lifelong student of the Bible, I can say without a shadow of a doubt that God created gay, lesbian, bisexual, and transgender people and loves us exactly as we were created. For me, that debate is over. The verdict is in. Homosexuality is neither a sickness nor a sin.

In *Anything but Straight,* Mr. Besen makes clear that the entire ex-gay enterprise is founded on the tragic belief that homosexuality is a sin and thus all "practicing" homosexuals are sinful. Also, though many ex-gay ministries do not believe that homosexuality can be "cured" or that homosexuals can become heterosexuals, most ex-gay therapies begin by asking their "clients" to seek God's forgiveness.

Ex-gay therapy continues (often for a lifetime) through a painful, sometimes pathological process of trying to "overcome one's sinful same-sex attraction" through prayer, Bible study, personal discipline, the support of the Christian community, and (in many cases) getting married and having children. Televangelists love to feature ex-gays (with their wives and families) who are "succeeding" in the process, but they never share the tragic stories of those whose desperate tries end in failure, guilt, self-hatred, and even death. I know, because I too was a victim of "reparative therapies" and I've spent the last ten years

of my life working to bring hope and healing to thousands of other
ex-ex-gay victims ("Dos Equis") across America.

Sadly, most people who decide *not* to act upon their same-sex attractions still make their decisions out of fear and guilt. These victims
of biblical misuse believe sincerely that homosexuality is a "sin," and
most (if not all) ex-gay ministries, too, are motivated by that tragic
untruth. The real evil at the heart of the ex-gay ministries is not the
villains, such as James Dobson, Elizabeth Moberly, Joseph Nicolosi,
Exodus, NARTH, or even Paul Cameron (a man who has spent his
lifetime fabricating false "studies" used by fundamentalist Christians
to "prove" their antigay hyperboles, half-truths, and lies). The real
evil at the heart of the ex-gay movement flows out of misusing the Bible to declare homosexuality a "sin."

Unfortunately, the ex-gay movement refuses even to consider the
fact that homosexual orientation, too, is a gift from God. Therefore, I
stand with Wayne Besen in wholeheartedly condemning the ex-gay
movement (in spite of all the sincere and loving people who work
within that movement).

The people associated with ex-gay ministries sin when they support ancient antihomosexual bigotry by quoting six or seven biblical
texts with no real interest in pursuing their historic or linguistic
meaning. They sin when they refuse to consider the current scientific,
psychological, historical, pastoral, and even biblical evidence that
homosexual orientation, too, is a gift from God. They sin when they
ignore the personal witness of tens of thousands of gay, lesbian, bisexual, and transgender people who live deeply spiritual lives. They
sin, too, when they make TV commercials featuring men and women
who are still in the unfinished process of living their ex-gay lives as
examples of the only way to be good, right, and holy.

I want ex-gay leaders and volunteers who read this book to know
that the author and I agree that most of you are loving, committed
people who sincerely believe that homosexuality is a "sin" and who
are equally sincere in your belief that you are saving sinners through
your ex-gay work. You are sincere, but you are sincerely wrong. In
spite of your good motives, you are doing great harm to God's gay
children. A friend of mine was equally sincere when he allowed doctors to lobotomize his eldest son to cure his headaches and fits of depression. In spite of all the experts who recommended this procedure,
the surgery turned out to be a tragic mistake that destroyed his son's

life and, in the process, left the father in endless grief and guilt. It is most likely that one day you will look back upon the days of your sincere ex-gay ministry and also feel terrible grief and guilt for what you have done.

To the villains featured in *Anything but Straight,* I confess that for awhile I struggled with writing this foreword because the author portrays you differently than I might have. I believe in the "soul force" principles of nonviolence as taught by Jesus, Gandhi, Dorothy Day, and Martin Luther King Jr., and in many ways, the author critically scrutinizes your work. Forgive him if you feel unjustly accused but then examine your actions against God's lesbian, gay, bisexual, and transgender children and see for yourself if he may be right on target with his accusations. Jesus, too, was a man of peace, but he drove the money changers out of the temple with a whip. They were cheating God's little ones out of their birthrights and so are you!

Whatever good it may or may not do, the ex-gay movement has been hijacked by fundamentalist leaders who are using their antigay rhetoric to raise money and mobilize volunteers. How often I've seen Pat Robertson, Jerry Falwell, James Dobson (and the rest of them) feature ex-gay testimonials to support their false and inflammatory accusations against God's gay children. How long will ex-gays and their leaders allow themselves to be used by fundamentalists who accuse gay people of "destroying the family, undermining national values, abusing, recruiting, and molesting children"? Even ex-gays know that their fundamentalist friends are telling lies about gay people and misusing ex-gay testimonials to support those lies.

The ex-gay movement has also been hijacked by mainstream Protestant and Catholic leaders to get them through their current fundamentalist crises. They know that fundamentalists within their own faith communities are using homosexual ordination and marriage as a wedge issue to divide and conquer their denominations. They know that if they take a stand for the full acceptance of God's gay children that they may suffer the loss of members and money and could cause their denominations (and even their local congregations) to splinter into warring factions. To avoid this loss, they sacrifice the truth and even support the introduction of ex-gay ministries into their own denominations even when they know better.

At this moment in time, the ex-gay movement is *not* simply a loving effort to help homosexuals to "overcome" their sexual "sin." It has become a major political force in the fundamentalist takeover of the Christian churches in America. It is impossible for gay Christians to discuss with leaders of the ex-gay movement how we might one day work together, when they have lost control of their own movement to fundamentalist leaders who give them massive financial support in exchange for their cooperation.

In *Anything but Straight,* Wayne Besen condemns the ex-gay movement, and so do I. Nevertheless, we both share the belief that most ex-gay volunteers are sincere people who mean well. It is our hope that one day those sincere ex-gays might work together with those of us who have accepted our homosexual orientation as a gift from God. This is a must-read book for people on all sides of the debate. Besen does a masterful job of making both gays and ex-gays alike contemplate ways to reexamine all our assumptions, restate all our conclusions, and, in the process, extricate ourselves and our issues from the hijackers who are using gay, lesbian, bisexual, and transgender people to frighten and divide the nation and control the churches.

Mel White
Lynchburg, Virginia
www.soulforce.org

PREFACE

When I came out to my parents in 1988, I saw firsthand how propaganda from the "ex-gay" ministries can seduce vulnerable, desperate people with fraudulent claims of changing one's sexual orientation from gay to straight.[1]

At the age of eighteen, I sat my mother and father down in our living room and told them I had something very important to tell them. They could see that something was terribly wrong by my serious demeanor and the uncontrollable shaking of my hands.

"Is your girlfriend pregnant?" My mother nervously asked.

Oh, how her nightmare scenario would soon seem a pleasant dream.

"No," I said, as I took a deep breath and somehow found the inner strength to blurt out, "the fact is, I'm gay."

Both parents stared in stunned silence for what seemed an eternity. Finally, my mother spoke.

"No, no, no, no," she robotically intoned.

My father eventually broke his deafening silence.

"You still like sports, don't you?"

It was clear by their initial reactions that acceptance of my sexual orientation would require time and education. Although they said they still loved me, for months the house felt like a funeral parlor, with my parents mourning the death of their dreams for my life. Overnight, we went from an extremely close, happy family to one with devastated parents who sometimes spoke of committing suicide.

The situation didn't improve after I returned home one Saturday evening from a late night of clubbing. Readying myself for bed, I emerged from the bathroom to find my father shuffling out of his bedroom on his way downstairs to read the Sunday paper.

"What's that on your neck?" he snapped.

"What are you talking about?"

I went back into the bathroom, looked in the mirror, and saw my first hickey. When I came out, my father looked at me and winced in disgust.

"We can't let Mom see it. It would be the end of her."

He made me to go to the drugstore to buy some makeup to conceal the purplish mark. I returned home and was applying the cover-up when my mother unintentionally stumbled into the bathroom, where I was staring into the mirror while holding a Cover Girl makeup kit.

"Oh, my God, not only are you a homosexual, you're a drag queen!" She wailed in horror.

Dad mercifully eased her pain with the "good news" that I was not the next RuPaul. I was simply trying to cover up a hickey planted on my neck at the Copa, a local gay bar.

A few weeks later, my mother happened upon an item in a bookstore in a local Fort Lauderdale mall that offered her great hope and joy. The cause of her newfound exhilaration was a subliminal and self-hypnotic tape titled *Gay and Unhappy.*

"But, Mom, I am happy," I protested, as she took the tape to the cash register, nervously looking around to make sure she knew no one in the line.

I walked into my bedroom later that evening and saw the tape sitting on my pillow, along with a Sony Walkman. I put on my headphones and began listening. On the subliminal side of the tape was comforting New Age music, while on the self-hypnotic side a man with a deep, monotone voice tried to transport me back to my childhood to determine how I became gay. The voice asked me to remember when I first felt rejected by my parents and became estranged from them.

The problem was that I had always had a close relationship with my parents, at least until I came out. I listened to the tape twice and realized that absolutely nothing on it applied to my life. It was attempting to establish a cause-and-effect relationship that did not exist, as if the tape were trying to drive a wedge between my parents and me by having me *manufacture* a traumatic event from my past to explain my present "situation."

I tried listening to the ridiculous ex-gay tape a third time but knew I was wasting my time. This was nothing more than a product made to profit off of my parents' misery and desperation. I removed the surreal tape and replaced it with real gay men's therapy—Madonna.

The next morning the three of us were seated around the kitchen table having breakfast and reading the newspaper. My father looked to see which section I grabbed first. I really wanted to see the latest college football scores, but just to irritate him I picked up the Style section and turned to the theater page.

"So, how did it go with the tape last night?" my father asked, while my mother's eyes glowed with anticipation.

"Dad, it was great. All I've got to do to become straight, according to the tape, is figure out when you and Mom became lousy, distant parents."

That was the last subliminal ex-gay tape they bought me.

Although some of the moments surrounding my coming out may seem humorous in retrospect, the underlying harsh fact is that thousands of desperate people are willing to embrace the quackiest of measures to cure homosexuality in themselves or in loved ones, and this is anything but funny.[2] It is tragic and has torn apart many families and ruined numerous lives, ironically, in the name of family values.

If my liberal, college-educated, Jewish parents were despondent and desperate enough to seek solace in a product influenced by the Christian ex-gay ministries, imagine how alluring these ministries must seem to those raised in evangelical or fundamentalist families.

The ex-gay ministries and "reparative therapy" are truly a testament to how the power of belief can be twisted in a distorted and deranged manner to take advantage of the weakest people in our society.[3] They are really no different from the sundry faith healers that grace our television sets offering miracle cures for money. These crafty swindlers forcefully lay their hands on the heads of the feeble and forlorn and yell, "Healed!" Miraculously, those with maladies ranging from blindness to paralysis to cancer fall back, truly believing they have been cured and condemning skeptics. They are convinced they have been subject to a divine miracle and gladly turn over their hard-earned paychecks.

Reality, however, soon sets in. The blind person still cannot drive a car. The disabled person cannot suddenly break dance. The cancer patient ends up returning to the hospital ward. The only difference is they are now poorer, both financially and spiritually, for succumbing to the lies of false, for-profit prophets.

Similar to the televangelist faith healers, the ex-gay ministries and reparative therapists prey upon the vulnerable and the gullible, luring them with promises of celestial healing and divine intervention. For a time, the power of belief can lead some people genuinely to feel they have become heterosexual. This temporary leap of faith brings a brief period of euphoria and explains why some ex-gays offer loud declarations of their newfound heterosexuality.

To help supplement the divine healing, the ex-gay ministries offer behavior modification courses that include lipstick application seminars to help some lesbians become more feminine and touch football games to butch up some of the more effeminate homosexual men.

So, in essence, for the most part, an ex-gay individual is an actor playing a role. A person may become very good and convincing in his or her part, and, for a time, through faith and mental repression, a person may even believe he or she has become the straight person being portrayed. In the end, however, the play always ends, with the final curtain of reality crashing down, and the ex-gay actor must take off the costume and rediscover his or her true self again.

Human sexuality is extremely complex, and I would not rule out the remote possibility that, in some very rare circumstances, a few people may be comfortable and honestly function as if they have changed their sexual orientation. If a person claims to have changed and is happy, who am I or anybody else to condemn him or her? Sexual decisions are best left to individuals, and, in this country, people have the freedom to pursue whatever path they want to take in life, the right to declare themselves gay, ex-gay, or asexual without fear of discrimination or punitive repercussions.

Through my extensive experience I have learned that the extraordinary claims made by ex-gay groups are without merit and the efficacy of their programs is dubious, at best, and harmful, at worst. Of the few people I found who were satisfied with the ex-gay ministries, most successfully used these faith-based groups to overcome sexual addiction or chemical dependency. Free from destructive addictions—which they erroneously blame on gay life—these rare people are happier today than they were when they lived out of the closet. They seem to thrive under the strict authoritarian rules that only fundamentalism can truly provide. Interestingly, even most of the satisfied customers will say they are not "healed," but still "struggling."

Most important, until we live in a world that no longer discriminates, it will be difficult to ascertain whether a person is truly healed or is claiming change simply to avoid societal persecution. Many people who once claimed change and now rebuff these ex-gay groups explain that they were motivated by fear of rejection and the desire to be loved. They admit to fooling themselves into embracing these desperate measures only to find acceptance and make family members proud.

The more one learns about these groups, the clearer it is how dysfunctional they are. *Anything but Straight* shows how these groups are revolving doors with a higher defection rate than the Cuban national baseball team. The most these deceptive entities can usually accomplish is teaching fearful people how to repress natural feelings, at the risk of grave psychological harm, which is really no accomplishment at all.

I am often asked, "Why can't gay activists simply leave ex-gay groups alone and let them go about their business?" This is exactly what happened for nearly three decades while ex-gay groups labored in near anonymity. All this changed recently, however, when the ex-gay groups aligned themselves with the antigay political agenda of the religious right. With ex-gays added to their arsenal, the right could disingenuously claim to love gay people and offer them "hope for change," while simultaneously fighting for punitive legislation. Their insidious message: Since gays and lesbians can change, no laws are needed to protect them from arbitrary prejudice. Thus, the political radicalization of the once apolitical ex-gay ministries has made refuting their claims an imperative for all Americans who believe in equal rights.

Anything but Straight is a one-of-a-kind book that explores

- the historical failure of the ex-gay ministries and reparative therapy,

- the dangerous quack psychology of the lucrative reparative therapy industry, and
- how the unholy alliance between the religious right and ex-gay groups threatens the civil rights of all Americans.

Anything but Straight also offers hope to those who are stuck in a lifestyle that demeans, diminishes, and dehumanizes them for who they are. This book shows the way out of this circle of shame and celebrates the possibility of being both Christian and gay, gay and happy—which reparative therapy and the ex-gay ministries claim is impossible.

The ex-gay ministries and reparative therapy will unfortunately be around as long as prejudice toward and discrimination against gays and lesbians exist. Although most of the people involved in the ex-gay movement are good, sincere individuals, they are nevertheless hurting thousands of families. This book is intended to educate people about these futile programs so they can make their decisions armed with all the facts, for only the truth can prevent suffering people, such as my parents and others, from being seduced by the specious ex-gay illusion.

ACKNOWLEDGMENTS

First, I would like to express my gratitude for living in America, an amazing country where we are free to express opinions on controversial topics. Special thanks go to The Haworth Press, Inc., for believing in this book and for their continued support in publishing authors who reflect America's diversity. I also thank *Sissyphobia* author Tim Bergling for introducing me to Haworth.

Most important, I would like to acknowledge how much I appreciate the unwavering support of my loving parents, Neil and Sydney Besen. Their sage advice, wisdom, enthusiasm, and encouragement—not to mention my mother's editing skills—have been invaluable while writing this book. I am truly blessed with the world's greatest mother and father.

I thank Elizabeth Birch and David M. Smith of the Human Rights Campaign for giving me the opportunity to serve the gay, lesbian, bisexual, and transgender community. It is a dream come true, and not a day passes that I am not grateful for this chance to make a difference in our struggle for equality. I also thank the wonderfully talented, dedicated staff at HRC for all the remarkable work that they do.

Daryl Herrschaft deserves special kudos for spotting John Paulk in the gay bar Mr. P's and for his perspicacious handling of the situation. Herrschaft, you were simply brilliant. Joel Lawson also played a crucial role in the unmasking of Paulk. I thank Lawson for his help in this matter and for his longtime friendship.

Richard Davis and Sabri Ben-Achour were my undercover angels, secretly penetrating the ex-gay ministries to offer vivid reports that helped shatter the ex-gay myth. Ben-Achour also deserves special mention for serving as my research associate.

Thanks to the superactivists who have inspired me to fight for justice: Elizabeth Birch, David Mixner, Reverend Troy Perry, Donna Red Wing, Michelangelo Signorile, William Waybourn, Reverend Mel White, and so many others.

Acknowledgment also goes to my friends who played key roles in my first activist group, Sons and Daughters of America: Brian Chase, Norm Kent, Richard Shapiro, Donald DeCarlo, Scott Denny, Brian Trageser, Brian McManamon, and Reverend Jerry Stephenson. Dan Hall, thanks for your friendship and helping to launch my activist career through your most generous financial support. I'll never forget how you were there for me.

I want to recognize all of those who submitted to interviews: Brent Almond, Elizabeth Birch, Dr. Ralph Blair, Chandler Burr, Michael Bussee, Alan Chambers, Leslie Chambers, Richard Cohen, David Cruz, Natalie Davis, Dr. Jack Drescher, John Evans, Pam Freyd, Joan Garry, Dr. Harold Lief, Simon LeVay, Dr. Elizabeth Loftus, Jeremy Marks, Scott Melendez, John Napoli, Jack Pantaleo, Reverend Troy Perry, Kent Philpott, Reverend Michael Piazza, Wade Richards, Caitlin Ryan, Tracey St. Pierre, Clint Trout, and Reverend Mel White.

I thank Keith Blackburn, Lisa Fels, and Steve Wilkins for their special friendship and unique sense of humor.

I would also like to thank Larry Warmoth, for producing an incredible promotional video, and Bob Arden, for lending his renowned voice to the project.

May this book help those in turmoil find peace, and may it give hope to the hopeless who are misled by people who cannot accept them for who they are.

AUTHOR'S NOTE

For the past four years, I have intimately examined the ex-gay ministries and reparative therapy. I have done hundreds of hours of research, attended ex-gay and right-wing conferences, and visited various ex-gay ministries undercover. I have interviewed or met nearly every major ex-gay leader in the nation, and, in a one-year period, I photographed the nation's leading ex-gay at a homosexual saloon and helped bring two leading ex-gay spokespersons out of the closet. I have also appeared multiple times on network and cable television shows to debate this issue.

Anything but Straight tells the story of reparative therapy and the ex-gay ministries from a historical perspective. Much of the narrative unfolds through profiling the zany characters who run these programs. The information is gleaned from dozens of interviews, undercover work, attending ex-gay and reparative therapy conferences, countless hours of research on Nexis, scouring ex-gay sites such as <www.exodus-international.org> and <www.narth.com>, and reading mounds of ex-gay literature (see individual chapter notes as well as the bibliography for details).

I also present some scenarios in the book that are reconstructed conversations based on interviews, undercover work, chance meetings, and phone calls; these are identifiable from the context of the narrative. Some of these conversations were not taped because while the ex-gay group leaders agreed to let me sit in on their sessions, they were uncomfortable with these sessions being recorded, as it made some of their "clients" uneasy.

Through the comprehensiveness of this diligent, investigative approach, a thorough and honest portrait will emerge that finally cuts through the antigay right-wing spin. Although those in the ex-gay movement may consider many of these findings to be unpleasant, they are an accurate reflection of the ex-gay world. If there is one consistent theme throughout the book, it is that the most damning and damaging material lies in the actual words and actions of the ex-gay leaders themselves.

ABOUT THE AUTHOR

Wayne Besen began serving as the Human Rights Campaign's Associate Director of Communications in April 1998. His responsibilities include media relations as well as monitoring the so-called "ex-gay" ministries. Besen has been interviewed by national and local television, radio, and print media, including *NBC Nightly News with Tom Brokaw, The Roseanne Show, CNN's Talk Back Live* and *The Point, The Washington Post, USA Today, MSNBC News,* and the Fox News Channel's *O'Reilly Factor.*

Besen previously worked in television production at the NBC affiliate in Fort Myers, Florida, and as a news reporter at the CBS affiliate in Bangor, Maine. In 1996, Besen was press secretary for state Senator Sean Faircloth, a Maine Democrat, in his bid for the U.S. Senate. Later, Besen moved to Washington, DC, and worked for Edelman Public Relations Worldwide where he specialized in media relations.

ACT I

THE EX-GAY MINISTRIES

Candi's Bathroom Break

I was readying myself for bed late one Tuesday evening when my phone rang. Exhausted from the long, busy day, I barely had enough energy to answer it by the third ring. What I heard, however, immediately jolted me out of my prebedtime trance and electrified my imagination in excitement and disbelief. Daryl Herrschaft, my colleague at the Human Rights Campaign (HRC), frantically yelled into the receiver, "Wayne, get down here now. Now! I'm not 100 percent sure, but I think John Paulk is in Mr. P's," a well-known gay bar in Washington's heavily gay Dupont Circle area.[1]

"No way. You've got to be joking!" I exclaimed.

It must be a case of mistaken identity, I thought. Why would the undisputed crown jewel of the so-called ex-gay movement be foolish enough to frequent a gay dive in Washington, DC, home to nearly every national gay organization in the country? As head of HRC's efforts to unmask the ex-gay ministries, I was intrigued, to say the least.

If it really were Paulk, this discovery would rock the ex-gay ministries and their religious right sponsors to the core. In 1998, a coalition of fifteen religious right organizations launched the "Truth in Love" ad campaign featuring ex-gays with headlines such as "We're Standing for the Truth That Homosexuals Can Change." The full-page ads appeared in major daily newspapers such as *The New York Times, USA Today,* and *The Wall Street Journal.* Paulk and his wife, Anne, a self-described ex-lesbian, were prominently featured in these ads, which gave them a platform from which to launch their full-time careers as America's most prominent professional heterosexuals.

For a time, they had become ubiquitous figures on the talk show circuit, appearing on CBS's *60 Minutes* and ABC's *World News Tonight, Good Morning America,* and *The Oprah Winfrey Show.* The pinnacle of Anne and John's success came when they graced the cover of *Newsweek* magazine under the bold headline "Gay for Life?"

Later that year, Paulk published his first book, *Not Afraid to Change: The Remarkable Story of How One Man Overcame Homosexuality.* The autobiography vividly explains how he transformed himself from an alcoholic, acid-dropping, sex-addicted, transvestite prostitute named Candi into a married fundamentalist Christian through the power of Jesus Christ.

Reverend D. James Kennedy of Coral Ridge Ministries said of the book, "John Paulk has the most hopeful and promising message for gay men that I have ever read."[2]

Conservative syndicated columnist Cal Thomas raved, "In his book, . . . you will find blessing and hope, especially if you are one who has been living in darkness, but longing to find the way to the light."[3]

After the book was published, Colorado Springs–based Focus on the Family hired Paulk to head their newly formed Homosexuality and Gender Department for Public Policy. In addition, he was already chair of Exodus International, the largest ex-gay support group, which serves as a worldwide umbrella organization for the ex-gay ministries.

Riding high with his new book and blossoming career, Paulk, a celebrity in fundamentalist circles, was clearly going places with the religious right. He kicked off the new millennium for Focus by launching the nationwide "Love Won Out" tour, which was a traveling road show to enlighten conservative audiences on the secrets of "leaving homosexuality behind"—as Paulk boasted he had done in 1987.

"We say God did not intend anyone to be this way—to be gay or lesbian," Paulk bellowed at North Heights Lutheran Church while on the Minneapolis leg of his Love Won Out tour. "I accepted Christ into my life and realized I could leave homosexuality. I learned that homosexuality was reversible. Through faith in Christ and counseling and support, over a four-year period, my homosexuality greatly subsided."[4]

Like a rock star, no matter where he offered his heart-wrenching testimony, he received thunderous applause. Although he was no longer a drag queen, he still hadn't lost his touch as a performer—albeit his audience had definitely changed.

I knew I had only a small window of opportunity to catch the alleged Paulk, so I grabbed my camera, threw on my baggy jeans, and sprinted to Mr. P's, about a half mile from my Dupont condo.

Meanwhile, Herrschaft engaged the suspected Paulk in casual conversation, asking the man questions that should have sent him galloping toward the exit like a 100-meter Olympic sprinter, if he were indeed Paulk.

"What is your name, and where are you from?" asked Herrschaft.

"John, from Colorado Springs," the gentleman calmly replied.

"What is your last name?"

"Clint. John Clint is my name."

"Are you sure it is not Paulk?"

"Yes, I'm sure," he replied.

Fortunately, Herrschaft bought me valuable time because the robust man in question began to fancy him. Apparently twenty minutes was not enough time for this man to enjoy his gay bar experience, so he continued to talk to his pushy inquisitor.

"Would you like a drink? It's on me," Paulk said to Herrschaft with a flirtatious twinkle in his eyes.

"Are you gay?" asked Herrschaft, persisting with his cross-examination.

"Yes," the man serenely responded.

Herrschaft continued to engage the man in conversation, revealing, among other things, that Paulk was a Democrat.

Panting and drenched with perspiration, I continued my full-out dash down New Hampshire Avenue toward the dark, dingy bar. As I reached the intersection of Dupont Circle and Massachusetts Avenue, I had to stop briefly after a speeding taxi almost flattened me. The fuming driver rolled down his window and called me what I suspected was the Arabic equivalent of "asshole" as he pealed out.

The adrenaline was kicking and I could hear my heart thumping as I reached P Street, only a few blocks from my final destination. I stopped momentarily to catch my breath before putting my head down and rumbling toward the hole-in-the-wall bar, which was now within my sights.

Standing at the shabby entrance of Mr. P's, I briefly rehashed my plan. I would furtively enter the joint, look for the alleged Paulk, and, if it were he, slip outside and call gay press reporters on my cell phone. Then, hopefully, they would race down to break a major story by photographing Paulk flirting and imbibing. Of course, breaking it in the mainstream press would have been optimum, but it was highly unlikely a *Washington Post* or *New York Times* reporter would bolt to a third-rate gay bar in the middle of the night to take paparazzi-style photographs of an ex-gay leader.

Mr. P's was the oldest standing gay bar in Washington, having been around since the mid-1970s. The foreboding gray exterior, punctuated by pitch-black-tinted windows, made the bar an intimidating place to those not acquainted with it—and those who were acquainted with it were probably too drunk to notice. The bar was known for its drag shows, cheap booze, and dim, cruisy atmosphere. Around the corner was the "P Street Beach," a heavily wooded area, Washington's most notorious gay cruising spot. If Paulk was looking for a clandestine sexual liaison or for a place where he could quietly find mischief, then he was in the right spot.

Imbued with curiosity, I slowly opened the creaky, paint-chipped door and entered the bar, trying to go undetected. Within five feet of the entrance I saw a man who from the back resembled John Paulk. He was wearing khaki pants and a long-sleeved shirt covered by a sleeveless cream-colored sweater. His prodigious love handles extended over his pants' waistline and his hair was neatly coifed.

The gentleman, whoever he was, seemed to be having a gay old time, laughing it up with several inebriated patrons while expertly nursing his half-empty cocktail. This man looked extraordinarily comfortable, as if born and raised in a gay bar. In the adjacent room, a raucous drag show of female impersonators delighted the roaring crowd.

A tall, scrawny, prune-faced drag queen with a Camel cigarette dangling out of an empty slot in her mouth where a tooth used to be sashayed right in front of the potential Paulk. If the man in question were not completely at ease in his surroundings, the sight of this drag queen would have sent him running for the nearest exit. It was evident, though, that he had no intention of leaving the scene anytime soon. He was clearly in his element, just another man with bad taste in gay bars enjoying a night on the town.

With my head down, I stealthily angled my way to a clear frontal view of the man, positioning myself where I could positively identify him. I had met the man personally on two occasions, once at a press conference in Washington and once in 1999 when I went undercover for an HRC intelligence-gathering mission at the Center for Reclaiming America for Christ conference in Fort Lauderdale. While sleuthing, I even had my picture taken with my arm around his wife, Anne. So if it were actually the world's most notorious ex-gay, I was more than qualified to recognize him. Now standing nearly three feet away and directly in front of him, I gradually lifted my head. It *was* Paulk!

My heart stopped. I could no longer hear the pulsating music and the world moved in slow motion. There he stood, his carefully crafted fifteen-year lie about to be uncovered. I was absolutely floored, in a state of total shock. If he tried this risky stunt in Washington, I thought, how many other times in his travels had he gone straight from an antigay conference to a gay establishment? The scene reminded me of a passage I had once read in his book:

> One night, I suddenly had an overwhelming urge to go to a gay bar and pick up someone. I almost experienced real physical pain as I resisted. Finally I got down on the tile floor in my bathroom and cried, "God, I beg you, keep me from going to a bar! I can hardly resist. . . ." Somehow I found the strength to stay home.[5]

Unfortunately for Paulk, tonight God wasn't on ex-gay patrol and was probably working on less pressing issues, such as ending world hunger or assisting Mideast peace talks.

At this point I was desperately afraid I would be recognized. With HRC I had done several national television shows on the ex-gay topic, including appearing on NBC's *The Roseanne Show.* I also had conceived and edited a publication only three months earlier titled *Finally Free—Personal Stories: How Love and Self-Acceptance Saved Us from the "Ex-Gay" Ministries,* which included people who had been through the ministries speaking out about their negative experiences. Only two weeks before this unlikely encounter, Paulk had personally called me to request a copy of this publication for Focus. During our brief telephone conversation I had said, "I will send you one and hopefully it will help you come out of the closet."

"Been there, done that. I don't think so," he had replied.

Well, he may have been there and done that, but on this night he *was there* and *doing that* once again.

Then he saw me, put two and two together, and pandemonium consumed the smoky dive. Raw terror filled Paulk's widening, panic-stricken eyes as he gasped in horror. My careful plan now foiled, I had no choice but to photograph him. With nothing to lose, I blurted out, "John Paulk, is that you?"

As I tried to capture his mug, Paulk swiftly turned his back and covered his face with his finely manicured hands. This must have been a weird experience for Paulk, for this was probably the first camera in fifteen years that the self-promoting ex-gay leader hadn't embraced.

As the flash lit up the shadowy, smoke-saturated watering hole, the bouncer and manager simultaneously screamed, "No photographs in the bar." The short, barrel-chested bouncer quickly jumped between us and blocked my camera lens. I was yelling at them, trying desperately to explain the situation, but with the loud music and all of the confusion, they could not comprehend what I was saying or understand the significance of the occasion. With the bouncer serving as a muscle-bound buffer, Paulk aggressively lunged for my camera and tried to confiscate it, but he was unable to seize it. To separate myself from him, I gave him a solid push, which created some space between us. The bouncer had seen enough and ejected me from the gay saloon.

In this moment of truth, I'm sure the befuddled Paulk didn't know what his next move should be. If he left the bar, he likely reasoned, I would be waiting, camera in check. However, if he lollygagged, the gay media might arrive to place him at the scene. Paulk's only hope was to abscond through a side exit, so he beckoned bar owner John Mako and asked about another way out—he told Mako he needed to escape because his "life was in danger"—but there was no covert exit, so Paulk had to face the music.[6]

As this drama unfolded, I was anxiously waiting outside Mr. P's while desperately trying to reach gay reporters by cell phone. I first tried to reach *The Advocate*'s Chris Bull, but the operator erroneously told me that his home number was unlisted. I frantically dialed the phone numbers of *Washington Blade*'s Lou Chibbaro and *Southern Voice*'s Joel Lawson, a Washington correspondent for the Atlanta-based newspaper chain and a longtime friend. Neither one was home, so I left messages.

About five minutes later, the rickety door flew open, and out scurried Paulk, ducking and veiling his contorted face with his trembling hands. I snapped another picture, but the flash was so slow that I photographed the back of him. What came over me next was a mix of indignation and fury. This was a man whom I believed may have ruined many lives and profited from his lies through his job with Focus on the Family. I confronted him, yelling at the top of my lungs.

"How many young men and women have committed suicide because of you? How many parents refuse to speak to their gay children because you have convinced them their kids can change when they cannot? Your work is killing people, yet you have the chutzpa and audacity to go to a gay bar? Your gig is over! Let us help you come out, so you can undo all of the damage you have done!"

A terrified Paulk broke out in a cold sweat and quickly slithered down P Street toward Dupont Circle. I followed close behind him and continued to take him to task for his antigay sins. Soon he was in full gallop, but his well-nourished body made it easy to keep up with him. Onlookers on P Street watched in curiosity as this bizarre tabloid-style brouhaha unfolded. When Paulk finally reached the circle, I could do nothing more, so I halted the chase and watched him disappear into the night.

I arrived home to phone messages from Lawson and Chibbaro. Chibbaro seemed moderately interested. Lawson, on the other hand, immediately grasped the importance of what had transpired and fully understood the gravity of the moment.

Lawson's interest was critical due to the nature of the newspaper in which he could publish the story. Although primarily an Atlanta newspaper, *Southern Voice* shared news content with sister papers in Houston and New Orleans. Joel was friends with William Waybourn and other investors who had bought the *Southern Voice* in 1997 through their company Window Media. In a few short years, Waybourn, along with editor Chris Crain and business partner Rick Ellsasser, had transformed the Atlanta newspaper into one of the more aggressive gay news outlets in the nation. *Southern Voice*'s connection with other papers in Houston and New Orleans meant my Paulk news could reach a print readership of over 200,000, as well as be blasted across the Internet to even more. However, though *Southern Voice* and the other Window Media papers had grown into a regional force, they were still widely unknown outside of the South.[7] Lawson knew that this story was an opportunity to gain *Southern Voice* national recognition.

"Wayne, let me come over to your house right now, tonight," said Lawson on the phone. "I really want to break this story and let the whole world know where John Paulk was hanging out tonight."

I was reluctant to hand the story to this regional publication, but I trusted Joel and knew he was aggressive and determined enough to follow through and write a more comprehensive story than anyone else. "Sure, how soon can you be here?"

"I'm already on my way," said Lawson. "First, I'll interview you. Then, the two of us should go to Mr. P's and I'll interview the bar patrons and employees while the incident is still fresh in their minds. Or, considering the place, until they pass out and forget the whole thing happened. We're in a race against Jack Daniels."

I arose early on Wednesday morning with feelings of excitement and uncertainty—excitement for having helped unmask Paulk at a gay bar, and uncertainty because I was unsure if any publication, including *Southern Voice,* would have enough physical evidence to name Paulk as the ex-gay spotted at Mr. P's. At the moment it was Paulk's word against a couple of gay activists, which made for tantalizing gossip, but not much of a legitimate news story. All I had for sure was the truth, a few witnesses, and an undeveloped roll of film.

The quality of the pictures was key, but I was highly skeptical that they would contain anything better than a shot of Paulk's rump. I had given my camera to Joel the night before so he could take the film in for development early in the morning. Feeling apprehensive, I called him the moment I got to work to see how the photos had turned out.

"The good news is that it is definitely him," said Joel. "The bad news is you have three pictures of his ass."

Joel came over to HRC's downtown headquarters to plan our next moves. We huddled in my office and explored different scenarios that might get Paulk to admit he had visited a homosexual bar.

"The first thing we need to do is establish that Paulk was in DC," I said. "Let's call Focus on the Family's Colorado Springs headquarters."

Joel made the call to Focus and was put through to Paulk's personal secretary.

"It's a glorious morning to praise the Lord," she chirped.

"Good morning, I have an important fax to send to Mr. Paulk and I was wondering if he is still in Washington."

"Oh, yes, he is still doing the Lord's work in our nation's capital. He'll be at a profamily conference until Thursday."

Now that we had proof Paulk was in Washington, our next move was to try to bluff him into admitting he was at the bar. If he came clean, Joel would have enough hard evidence to run with the story. We decided that I would call Paulk's Colorado Springs office and leave a message asking him to call me. The object was to spook him into revealing the truth.

"John, this is Wayne—we met last night in a homosexual bar in Dupont Circle," I said in a monotone voice on Paulk's answering machine. "I want to discuss with you what happened last night." I paused for effect and noisily hung up the phone.

I wasn't sure Paulk was going to call back, or if he did, I expected him to take his time. I was probably the last person in the world with whom he wanted to speak. Within ten minutes, however, the phone rang.

"Hi, this is John Paulk," intoned a jittery, high-pitched voice. The strain in his voice was palpable and he sounded a bit delirious, from what I guessed was a lack of sleep.

"We need to discuss what happened last night. I have witnesses. I've got pictures. Are you ready to come out of the closet, John?"

"I'm not gay," he warily replied. "I had just finished dinner at a nearby Italian restaurant. Afterward, I was walking and had to go to the bathroom, and I stopped into Mr. P's to use the facilities. There were men and women in the place, so I had no idea it was a gay bar."

I couldn't believe it! He was actually admitting that he had been in the bar. He could have simply denied it and waited for the pictures to hit the press to see if I had captured his mug—which I had not. Instead, to my astonishment, he offered this bathroom story—the equivalent of "The dog ate my homework"—one only the most gullible people in America would buy.[8]

"John, there were no women in that bar," I snapped. I was incredulous. "Those were drag queens. They were not even attractive ones. They were more like female imposters. You were once a glamorous female impersonator. You know the difference. You knew it was a gay bar and that's why you were there."

"I honestly had to use the bathroom. That's the only reason I was in there."

"Since when does it take nearly an hour to use the bathroom? Since when does using the bathroom require flirting with patrons and offering them cocktails?"

"I was there for only twenty minutes."

"Witnesses say you were there forty minutes to an hour."

"They are lying."

"Again, John, we've got witnesses. We've got pictures," I yelled. I felt somewhat remorseful about this hostile interrogation, but playing hardball was a necessary evil to finagle the truth out of him.

"I'm not gay. I have a wife and kids. You can't take that away from me. I urge you. I beg you. Please don't destroy everything I have worked for."

"Don't blame me for the fact that you were caught living a double life. No one pushed you onto the set of *Oprah*. I didn't catapult you onto the set of *60 Minutes* or the cover of *Newsweek*. You have no one to blame but yourself."

"Wayne, you can try to hurt me all you want, but you can never take away my wife and kids."

"But I can stop you from destroying other peoples' families. John, all you've ever had was the supposed integrity of your testimony and you no longer have that."

"Don't do it. I beg you, don't do it."

"I won't *do* it. It's already been *done*. The game is up," I stated in an icy tone.

"I told my wife and she supports me, as does Focus on the Family."

I knew this was untrue because Focus's high-priced public relations (PR) team would never have let him talk to me, and they certainly would have come up with something better than this ridiculous bathroom alibi.

Having accomplished what I wanted, I ended the conversation on a conciliatory note. "John, I know this is a difficult time for you. If you are ready to come out, I'm here to help you."

"But I'm not gay," he protested. "I'm married. I'm straight and married. I'm straight and married." The tense conversation came to a close with him repeating this mantra over and over. Sadly, it sounded as if he was trying to convince himself as much as me.

About an hour later I went to Joel's office building at the corner of Nineteenth and L Streets to give him background news clips on Paulk's career. He was on the telephone when I entered his office suite. As I was about to speak, he held up his hand, signaling for me to keep quiet. He smiled and wrote down on a piece of paper that he was interviewing Paulk. I sat and listened in absolute ecstasy and wonder as Paulk repeated to Joel the same story he had told me. It was unfathomable that Paulk had actually confessed to a journalist, but he did!

We had now moved from a gossip story that would have read, "Activists reportedly saw well-known ex-gay," to a story that would read, "Paulk admits he was in gay bar." We had hit the jackpot!

The next morning, the breaking story hit the *Southern Voice* Web site. Soon, shockwaves of excitement and bliss rapidly spread through the gay and lesbian community. On the other side, the religious right was in full retreat, the news rocking them hard, shaking their very foundations. Their entire antigay strategy was unraveling faster than they could say, "The devil made him do it." The following is how the scoop began:

Ex-gay leader confronted in gay bar

A prominent ex-gay leader once featured as "going straight" on the cover of *Newsweek* magazine was confronted and photographed by activists Tuesday night patronizing a gay bar in Washington, DC.

John Paulk, board chair for the umbrella ex-gay group Exodus International, admitted in an interview with *Southern Voice* that he was in Mr. P's, a gay bar in Washington's Dupont Circle neighborhood, but said his only intention was to use the bathroom.

Southern Voice
Thursday, September 21, 2000

The story was circulating on the Internet at warp speed. Within hours I was getting calls and e-mails from around the world and even from ex-boyfriends I never thought—or hoped—I'd hear from again. The forwarding of this story was so ubiquitous that it wasn't uncommon for people to say they had received it from five or more friends in one day. By the end of the week, *Southern Voice*'s Web site, which averages no more than a few thousand hits per day, had more than a half million hits. The response to the story was overwhelming, clearly touching a nerve within the gay and lesbian community. Within a week, the Paulk episode was on the front page of nearly every major gay and lesbian publication in America. Even though the power of the gay press and the Internet was on full display, however, this did not guarantee that the mainstream media would cover the story, and this was crucial to bringing down Paulk.

To my surprise, ABC's *Good Morning America* called and said they wanted to do a story on the topic, but only if they could get to interview Paulk. The story was canceled, though, after Focus officials told the producer that Paulk had been sent on "vacation." I suggested to the producer, tongue in cheek, that he should check Provincetown or Fire Island for Paulk because that's where gay men often like to spend their holidays.

Although Paulk had been whisked away to a clandestine hideaway somewhere in ex-gay Siberia, through a lucky break, the news did hit the mainstream media by the end of the week. The fortuitous moment came when the *Colorado Springs Gazette* reported on the incident. Not only did this get the story in the mainstream press, it also put pressure on Focus officials in their own backyard, forcing them to make a public statement.

Tom Minnery, that group's vice president of public policy, confirmed the bathroom story and told the *Colorado Springs Gazette* that Paulk used "extraordinarily bad judgment." On September 21, 2000, Focus released the following statement:

> There have been several Internet stories about a visit made by one of our employees, John Paulk, manager of Focus on the Family's homosexuality and gender division, to a gay bar in Washington D.C. earlier this week. Paulk did visit the bar, although the story is being embellished by some of the gay activist Web sites. Here is what happened, in John's own words:

"The true story is simple. Needing to use a restroom while walking in D.C., I went into a tavern. Seeing men and women there, I mistook the establishment as a safe environment. I soon realized I was in a gay bar. I had not been in one in fifteen years and I was curious, because I speak frequently about the gay bar experience. I stayed for a while. That was my mistake. As I attempted to leave, I was accosted by several people who recognized me—including a gay activist. He immediately began snapping pictures as I left. He was screaming, 'John Paulk, you are guilty of murdering thousands of people with your message' and continued to chase me down the street. I feared for my safety.

"My intentions were innocent, but my actions were unwise. This situation constituted a lapse in judgment, not a lapse in heterosexuality. Unfortunately, the gay community has begun twisting this around to say that I have returned to homosexuality. Both my wife and I, along with thousands of others, are testimonies of real transformation through Christ and we fully intend to continue sharing the message that for those who want it—change is possible."

The *Gazette* article combined with Focus's statement gave the news legitimacy and provided the local Associated Press bureau the cover they needed to run with the story. Unfortunately, the national Associated Press did not pick it up for several weeks. However, a *Newsweek* writer—who felt somewhat obligated to write a story, considering Paulk had once graced the magazine's cover—penned a short article. Later in the year, the ABC newsmagazine *20/20* did a devastating segment on the ex-gay ministries that featured Paulk's demise. The truth was now out in the open and on the big stage for all to see. No longer could Paulk say with credibility that he was "living proof" that "change" is possible.

In his years as a member of the religious right, Paulk surely did go through many life changes, both positive and negative. He undoubtedly changed his religion, marital status, and philosophy. He admirably changed his decadent lifestyle riddled with drug abuse and prostitution. And by leaving Candi behind, his drag queen alter ego, he even changed his wardrobe. Despite his loud and very public protestations, however, Paulk never changed his sexual orientation. John Paulk is now "living proof" that changing sexual orientation is highly

unlikely—and certainly not through the ex-gay ministries or reparative therapy. Hopefully, one day the truth will set him and other like-
minded people free, leaving them able to live as out, proud, gay and
lesbian Americans.

From Board Chair to the Electric Chair:
Exodus Defrocks Paulk

In Paulk's Focus statement he accused gay activists of "twisting
this around," but it soon became apparent that it was he who was
playing a game of Twister with the truth. On October 3, 2000, Exodus
International removed Paulk as board chair, punishing him for entering Mr. P's and then lying about whether he knew it was a gay establishment. Clearly, Exodus was not buying the bathroom story. According to Exodus, Paulk would still be allowed to remain on the
board under probationary status, but he would not be allowed to attend meetings or vote.[9]

In disciplining Paulk, Bob Davies,[10] North American Director of
Exodus International, released a blistering statement that appeared to
be intended to devastate Paulk's chances of rehabilitating himself as
the supreme spokesperson in the ex-gay movement. According to an
October 3 Exodus press release:

> "John's actions represent a serious lapse in sound judgment. His
> decision to enter a gay establishment for any reason opens him
> up to all kinds of speculation and questions by both other Exo-
> dus leaders and also the gay community.". . .
>
> Initial public statements issued by Exodus and repeated by
> director Bob Davies to the media were based on John's false
> claim that he had unknowingly entered Mr. P's. "That statement
> was widely doubted by both other Exodus leaders and by the
> gay community," Davies said. "John's unwillingness to tell the
> truth from the beginning was most unfortunate, as it has further
> undermined his public credibility."
>
> . . ."We believe that John's actions—to spend time socializing
> in a gay bar, and then to mislead both the public and Exodus
> leaders—merit some form of disciplinary action."[11]

Within ex-gay circles was constant gossip about how Davies was
jealous of Paulk's media attention, so it was no surprise that Davies

was not content simply to discipline Paulk. He made it a point to humiliate the man and his family publicly. In one interview, Davies maliciously lowered the pickaxe by speculating why Paulk had entered Mr. P's.[12]

"I believe he was enjoying a temporary escape from the responsibilities of the rest of his life," said Davies in the *Southern Voice* interview. "That was his pattern for years in the gay community." Davies went on to hypothesize that in Paulk's years in "the gay lifestyle," Paulk often fled his troubles by going out in drag as "Candi, the female impersonator that men all loved and adored."[13]

Clearly Davies was sticking it to Paulk. As fundamentalists often do, however, Davies, who declined to be interviewed for this book, cloaked his treachery in the guise of Christian love. According to the October 3 press release:

> "The bigger picture here is that we want to demonstrate a balance of compassion and justice". . . . "John has demonstrated genuine remorse over his behavior and the negative impact that it has had on the credibility of Exodus." . . .
>
> "We as a board wish to express our ongoing love, support and commitment to John as a beloved brother in Christ who has invested deeply in our organization for over a decade."[14]

The backbiting nature of the ex-gay ministries could also be witnessed in the initial reaction of Anthony Falzarano, America's second most notorious ex-gay, when he found out Paulk had been disgraced. Within hours of the news hitting the Internet, Falzarano—who knew me from ex-gay conferences I had monitored—called me to gloat about Paulk's fall from grace.

"Wayne, I can't believe this," he breathlessly blurted out. "This means I am the *biggest* ex-gay left standing. I need to make sure the press knows I'm available to comment."

Three weeks later I ran into Falzarano in Dupont Circle where he was handing out ex-gay fliers. Predictably, he was in convoluted spin mode, pretending that he was genuinely upset by Paulk's demise.

"I can't believe what you did to John and his wonderful Christian family," he said. "You are terrible even to insinuate that John is gay just because he was in a gay bar. If I see you in a straight bar, does that mean you are straight?"

"You're right, Anthony. Going out alone for a drink and a drag show at a seedy gay bar on a Tuesday night while out of town on business is perfectly normal behavior for a married man. What could I have been thinking?"

When Reality Is Out of Focus

When most people think of the religious right, they probably think of the Tinky Winky–bashing Reverend Jerry Falwell or the Christian Coalition's Pat Robertson. Perhaps the religious right's most powerful figure, however, is the lesser-known James Dobson, founder and potentate of Focus on the Family.

Focus is an enormous fundamentalist and evangelical empire nestled in the majestic Rocky Mountains. The Focus kingdom consists of five cavernous buildings, with 1,350 employees, and runs on an annual budget of $116 million.[15] To get some perspective on the power of Focus, compare their budget with the $18 million annual budget of the Human Rights Campaign, the nation's largest gay and lesbian advocacy group.

Focus receives more than 12,000 letters, calls, and e-mails a day—such a large volume that they have been given their own zip code (80935, in case you were wondering). Dobson is less well-known to the public because he usually operates below the radar, often shunning the mainstream press. He is, however, enormously popular with right-wing evangelicals and fundamentalists, reaching millions of loyal followers every day through ownership of his right-wing media empire. His television and radio broadcasts are heard by more than 28 million people each week and can be heard in ninety-five countries, including 1,900 U.S. and Canadian stations.[16] Dobson's daily Focus on the Family radio show alone has more than 4 million listeners per day.

One way Focus became so powerful was by using divisive social issues, such as homosexuality, to scare money out of their followers. In fact, according to Focus officials, the seventh most common reason people call is "difficulty with homosexuality."[17] Thus, one can appreciate how the discovery of Paulk in a gay bar created huge political problems for an organization that had long claimed it knew the "cure" for homosexuality. Paulk's unmasking hurt the organization's credibility, and it had the potential to disrupt its fund-raising efforts. In fact, only months after the Paulk incident, Focus had to take the rare step of sending out a special plea for money, claiming the ministry was coming up unexpectedly short of funds.

Focus officials faced a real political quandary. If they fired Paulk, critics would see the action as a tacit admission that their so-called cure had failed, but keeping Paulk on staff and in charge of the Love Won Out road show would be a risky venture that could very well backfire. Quite simply, they were faced with the prospect of having to continue to invest the organization's money and prestige in a person they could not trust. They knew Paulk had lied. They knew he had lied about his lies, and then he had lied about the lies he had lied about. Clearly, this was not the kind of employee most employers would protect.

In the end, Focus officials likely figured that firing the failed ex-gay was too politically explosive, so, instead of acting with moral integrity, they behaved as a typical big corporation, calling in their slick, high-priced PR guns to put their spin machine into high gear. On October 11, 2000 (ironically National Coming Out Day), Paulk emerged from ex-gay Siberia to appear on Dobson's radio show and pull off his best imitation of Jimmy "I have sinned" Swaggart.[18]

On the program, his wife, Anne, who served as a great prop to elicit sympathy, joined him. John cried, prayed, apologized, and repeatedly begged for forgiveness. He did everything, in fact, but tell the truth. The interview with Dobson and his sidekick Mike Trout consisted of a series of glaring contradictions and convoluted dissembling that showed precisely why most thinking people dismiss the ex-gay ministries.

In the interview, Paulk reached for his sympathy card by telling a sob story of how he supposedly became gay as a result of a "very bad relationship with my father." Moments later, though, Anne unwittingly contradicted her husband's unsubstantiated cause-and-effect association between poor family relationships and homosexuality: "I grew up in a fairly secure family," said Anne. "My parents are married to this day."

The subject turned to Anne's coming out as a lesbian: "It took until college to say, 'Yes, I'm a lesbian.' And then Jesus found me within six months. He got a hold of me and that was the end of that."

Her miraculous exit out of lesbianism made becoming straight seem simply a matter of convincing Jesus to wave his magic wand. Presto! From gay to straight faster than one can cook minute rice.

Amen. John, however, described quite a different scenario for becoming hetero than his wife's spectacular encounter with divine intervention: "It is very difficult to overcome homosexuality," John said. "It takes a committed group of Christian supporters to walk alongside of a man or woman who is . . . walking through the *years* it takes to come out of this."

So, John and Anne, which one of your tales should we believe? Does becoming straight take many difficult years of prayer and therapy, or can one overcome homosexuality through an immediate transformation through divine intervention?

John then went on to describe his years on the gay bar scene: "I was in it very heavily for six years until I was twenty-four. I just felt very depressed and just the fact that there was nothing to live for. I spent the majority of my life in gay bars and I think when you don't manage the stress, and I live under a great deal of it dealing with the gay agenda, and everything I had to deal with at Focus," he continued. "I wasn't managing my stress well and I think I walked right into Satan's trap."

What actually lured this stressed-out ex-gay into Satan's trap? "I think it had something to do with the easy camaraderie that I used to experience," Paulk explained to Dobson and Trout.

It seems odd that when faced with stress, John ran to a gay bar, the type of place he swore made him "depressed" and gave him "nothing to live for." If gay life was so bad, as he described it, why then did he extol gay bars for their "easy camaraderie"?

Furthermore, Paulk contradicted himself by saying he had spent "the majority of my life in gay bars." He had stated not long before this that he had spent only six of his thirty-seven years frequenting gay bars. This was really a small slice of his life in comparison to the fifteen years of his marriage. Most important, Paulk had an added incentive not to go into Mr. P's that fateful evening: "I heard the Holy Spirit say to me, 'Turn around and run. Do not go in there.'"

I don't know about you, but if I heard the Holy Spirit personally tell me not to go into a bar, this Jew would sprint to the nearest sink, dunk my head under the water faucet, and self-baptize. Yet, a *personal* admonition from the Holy Spirit could not keep Paulk, a fundamentalist Christian, out of a seedy homosexual bar? Clearly, something very forceful was compelling him to snub the Holy Spirit and enter the gay arena that evening. It was the desire to be free, socialize, and possibly find physical intimacy with a person similar to himself.

The Moral of the Story: The Far Right Has No Morals

It was obvious by Paulk's visit to a gay bar followed by his evasive alibi that he was not the heterosexual he claimed he was, but Paulk, I believe, is as much a victim as he is a victimizer, and he deserves more pity than scorn. To borrow a phrase from the religious right, we must love the sinner, even as we hate the sins. We must not forget that Paulk is himself a pawn and a casualty of the same religious right propaganda that he gets handsomely paid to espouse. The only difference between Paulk and many other people is that Paulk never reached the point where he could accept himself. He is a man on a stationary bicycle, telling everyone that he has traveled a great distance, when he has actually gone nowhere. For this reason, we should pity the man of many masks who has yet to acknowledge that the final curtain in his life's drama has come crashing down.

Whereas Paulk's act is somewhat forgivable because it is rooted in shame, Focus on the Family's behavior is unforgivable because it is based on the shameless. If patients keep dying after taking a certain medicine, an ethical practitioner would stop administering the deadly treatment. If a company's product proves harmful, such as with asbestos, an ethical corporation would reevaluate the product so that people stop getting sick.

Not once after Paulk's demise did Focus officials publicly question whether their so-called cure for homosexuality is defective and toxic in its own way. Today they continue to ignore mountains of evidence pointing to the failure of the ex-gay ministries because the truth interferes with their presumably biblically inspired mandates to raise heaps of money and deny gay people civil rights. If lives are destroyed in the process, so be it.

This is an indictment of not just Focus but the entire religious right, whose members care more about politics than people. For a movement that talks incessantly about honesty, integrity, and values, the religious right clearly is not practicing the love it preaches when it comes to those suffering in the ex-gay ministries.

Candi Won Out

Though Focus, out of self-interest, has tried to revive Paulk's plummeting career, the notoriety he gained decimated any shred of credibility he once had. He is now about as effective a spokesperson for the ex-gay ministries as Reverend Jim Bakker is for heterosexual morality. In the years following Paulk's big night out, Focus downsized his role until he resigned from the organization on April 14, 2003. Paulk vowed to return with his family to the Pacific Northwest, where I believe he will not take solitary confinement very well because he is a natural-born stage horse. Hopefully he will soon come to realize that he was not a true heterosexual family man; he just played one on TV. Once the TV cameras are gone, he eventually will be too.

So, what is the world's most infamous ex-gay to do when his career is in shambles and the spotlight is unceremoniously taken away? Become the world's most famous ex-ex-gay, of course. Unless Paulk has some hidden talent that no one knows about, this will be his only hope of getting back in the public eye and receiving the media attention he craves. Instead of the Love Won Out tour, the gay and lesbian community can send him in a Winnebago across the country on the "Candi Won Out" tour.

In all seriousness, Paulk has a lot to offer the world by coming out and dedicating the rest of his life to undoing much of the damage he has inflicted on other people. I hope to sit one day with John (or Candi) and laugh about the incident, with him thanking me for helping him come to grips with reality—because the reality he now occupies is nothing short of unreal.

An Undercover Cannibal

I warily reached the end of my several-hour journey from Washington, DC, to a state in the Deep South and was less than impressed with what I found. The leaders of this city's Exodus affiliate promised me a spiritual awakening in an inspirational setting. All I saw, however, was a potholed parking lot that fronted a dusty warehouselike strip mall. I parked my red compact rental car and scanned the different cube-shaped storefronts for the ex-gay ministry. I found it, and, on approach, a strikingly effeminate man and a linebacker-sized woman greeted me at the front door with warm smiles and open arms. "You can escape the homosexual lifestyle, just like I did," said the middle-aged, gray-haired "ex-lesbian" as she clasped my hand with a grip that threatened to shatter it like a dinner plate hitting the kitchen floor.

Exodus is a very cautious organization that takes a number of measures to protect against infiltrators. For instance, to attend a support group, prospective "ex-gays" must first meet alone with a ministry leader. This undercover trip was just such a meeting.

Shortly after our cheerful introduction, the brawny woman left the room, saying their policy was to "have men meet with men to talk about masculine things." Did this mean we were to discuss the World Wrestling Federation (WWF) (now World Wrestling Entertainment) or NASCAR? I didn't know what to expect. Two years earlier I had spoken to a man who claimed to have been sexually harassed at an introductory meeting at this ministry. According to his report, after telling an elderly gentleman his story about wanting to be straight, the ministry leader allegedly told him he was "cute" and that the program "didn't work" and then fondled him and followed him to his car. The leader, according to the report, stalked the traumatized young man for the next week, even calling him at home and work before finally giving up his pursuit.

The tall, balding man I was speaking with today, however, was not the same ministry leader and had so far displayed no menacing behavior, although I did find it a tad strange that he wore hot pants that hugged his rump. After several minutes of small talk, the two of us settled in at a table in the front of an office that resembled a cheap double-wide.

"Tell me about yourself," he said, offering a generous smile. I invented a bogus story about having just ended a failed relationship and wanting to be straight because gay relationships always seem doomed.

"Do you know why they always fail?" the man asked in earnest.

"Because it's a mortal sin," I mumbled, trying not to laugh and blow my cover.

"Yes, it is a mortal sin, but the reason they fail is because homosexuality is like cannibalism."

"My boyfriend dumped me. He didn't try to eat me," I replied, disconcerted by his comparison of homosexuality to cannibalism.

"I know it sounds weird, but it's true, according to the ex-lesbian leader Leanne Payne. Do you know anything about the habits of cannibals? Do you know why they eat people?" he asked, narrowing his eyes.

"No, I've never given the subject of eating people much thought," I responded.

"Cannibals eat only those they admire, and they eat them to assume their traits. So when you engage in homosexual sex, you are really looking at the other man and trying to get a lost part of you through him. When we seek other men, we try to attain their masculinity through sex, but it can never work, and when we realize that subconsciously, we leave that partner for another—a vicious circle that never ends."

"What if I sleep with a man less masculine than myself? Clearly, I'm not looking for his masculinity."

"I'm not sure," he answered, a quizzical look on his furrowed brow. "I'll have to call Exodus headquarters in Seattle and get back to you on that one."[1]

"So, how was your relationship with your mother and father?"

"It was great. I'm very close to them," I replied.

"Oh, I see," he said and sighed, looking a bit perplexed.

"Let me guess, you were picked last for sports teams."

"Actually, I was my basketball team's MVP [most valuable player] and was voted to the All City team my senior year."

"Did you move around a lot?" he asked, exasperated.

"Yes, I did."

"That's it!" he exclaimed. "That's the trigger. I knew we would find the trigger if we kept searching and got to the root of the problem. You see, you moved around and therefore became distrustful of attaching to members of the same sex. Unable to receive their love as a boy, you now desperately hunger for same-sex affirmation through homosexual activity. But this is the wrong way to go about it. You need Christian same-sex friendships, not homosexual lovers," he declared.

"Tell me about how you became straight," I said.

"Well, I wouldn't call it straight, but I am no longer gay. I have changed my sexual identity."

"Do you like women or men?" I asked.

"I still struggle with homosexual fantasies and I am working to develop an attraction to the opposite sex, but I have been free from homosexuality for several years!"

"So, let me get this right. You aren't interested in women after years of the ex-gay ministries. You still want to sleep with men but fight it. You mean being free from homosexuality simply means stopping homosexual behavior?"

"There's more to it than that. It is stopping the behavior through an intimate relationship with Jesus. I have made him my lover because he is a lover who will never leave me. He will never desert me. And he can be your lover too!"

Sounds a bit kinky, I thought.

As the session wore on, we reversed roles and I found myself in the odd position of counseling the counselor.

"I was never really into the lifestyle," he explained. "I am a preacher's son and I always knew it was wrong. My only homosexual experience came years ago when I was secretly sleeping with a married man. We knew we were sinning and the relationship had to end."

"Do you think you will ever become heterosexual?"

"I pray and try hard to change. Sometimes if I concentrate hard enough and focus, I get minimally aroused thinking of women. I'm older now, and I need to hurry up and get married and start a family. I'm already searching for a Christian wife."

"If you still aren't interested in women, why not come out?"

"I could never come out because I'm living my life how God wants, not according to how I feel inside. For me, homosexuality isn't an option. I would rather endure celibacy, if that is my destiny, than backslide into homosexual behavior."

"Aren't you afraid you will succumb to temptation?"

"I need to be careful here," he said, a thoughtful look on his face. "I sometimes have fantasies that could, if I let them, lead to masturbation. If I allow masturbation to take place, then who knows what could happen or where it may lead."

"How do you stop the fantasies from taking over?"

"Just the other evening I had to call my accountability partner late at night to tell him I was struggling and needed support," the man said, looking as if he were about to cry. "We prayed and prayed and he really lifted my spirits and renewed my faith in the Lord. I also recite the antimasturbation prayer I learned in *The Broken Image,* a book by Leanne Payne," he continued. "Masturbation is a form of the wrong kind of self-love. Please, join me in this prayer, if you would. We can hold hands while reciting it together."

> In the name of Jesus Christ I say that this creative energy from now on shall flow in its normal channel, and it shall not overflow anymore to the right hand or to the left hand. I build high dikes on the right hand and on the left hand and in Jesus' Name I command that it shall not overflow to the left hand or the right hand, but it shall flow quietly in its normal channel.[2]

"Are you happy?" I asked, hoping for an honest answer. This question apparently snapped him out of his pity party mode and he returned to the ex-gay script.

"I've never felt so happy in my life," he exclaimed, while sniffling to hold back the tears.

Moments later, the large lesbian barreled through the door to announce the session's end. They handed me piles of ex-gay propaganda and promised me that, with hard work, I could be just like them.

"Please, come to our weekly group," they said in unison, waving good-bye as I started my car. "You are now officially an ex-gay," the woman yelled as I drove away. Maneuvering around the potholes, I exited the parking lot, rolled up my window, and headed to the nearest gay bar. After listening to that ministry leader's sad lifestyle, I needed a drink and the company of well-adjusted gay people.

Rubber Band Ridiculousness

A few months after my first trip to the Deep South, I returned to another Southern town to attend an ex-gay support group. A strikingly old reverend with a wild shock of gray, Einstein-like hair agreed to let me observe a meeting in the upscale suburb of a major city. The old man portrayed himself as a wise old guru—sort of an antigay Yoda.

The advertisements from Exodus and religious right groups promoting these ministries had long touted that they had helped hundreds of thousands of people change from gay to straight. Based on these claims, I expected a large crowd to attend this meeting, considering the proximity of a sizable metro area. To my surprise, however, only seven people attended, and this included the group leader, his assistant, and me. The old reverend, "Yoda," who claimed to be heterosexual, looked a little embarrassed by the sparse crowd and assured me that the ministry had many more followers. Well, I wondered, where are they?

I had barely finished this thought when I saw the writing on the wall—literally. A large chalkboard displayed the sloppily written names of thirty-three people. The meeting began with the group forming an intimate prayer circle to pray for the people whose names were on the chalkboard; all had dropped out of the ministry in the past year after "backsliding into the lifestyle."

Of the six other attendees, only one claimed to have "changed" into a heterosexual: Yoda's assistant, "Fred," now married. Another "straight" guy in the crowd, a lanky, slightly effeminate African American, loudly and repeatedly proclaimed that he had no "sexuality issues"; he attended the meetings only to support the ex-gays, whom he called an inspiration to his Christian walk. I asked him in front of the group if he thought it was strange for a heterosexual to spend his Tuesday evenings in an ex-gay support group. At this suggestion he became defensive and scowled at me with a look as lethal as a cyanide capsule.

Another attendee, a large, muscular, African-American man was clearly angered that change wasn't occurring. Early on, he declared that he was "in a mood" and wasn't going to contribute to the discussion. I had very recently seen him happily imbibing at a local gay pub, but tonight there was no talk of dollar Vodka night. Another "struggler" was the guy sitting next to me, a balding, grossly overweight, middle-aged, white man in outdated, shabby clothes who looked and smelled as though he had not showered since President Bush was inaugurated—Bush Senior, that is. Noticeably perspiring, he kept glancing at my crotch and then scratching his own. I couldn't tell whether he was interested or just had crabs. He told me that he had been celibate for years but still hadn't changed. He asked for my card so he could further explore the Human Rights Campaign, all the while exploring my body with his eyes.

Another person seeking help was a short, strikingly effeminate man who had more issues than a New York City newsstand. A bowling-ball-shaped former drag queen, he was in a tizzy about how, when he was "in the gay lifestyle," he could never get straight, married men to leave their wives for him. His relationships were a series of disasters; he would seduce these men, telling them he was a woman, and then end up brokenhearted after they discovered that he was actually a man. He medicated his pain with drugs and alcohol and all-nighters at gay discotheques. Not once did he take responsibility for his poor choices; he blamed all of his problems on homosexuality, with which everyone in attendance seemed to agree.

The other men were nondescript. However, it is worth noting that they still were not "healed" and tried to block their pain through substance abuse and myriad dysfunctional behaviors. Not one man in the group had a "normal" background and just happened to be gay and wanted to change. The group devolved into a marathon therapy session of problems endlessly discussed, most having nothing to do with homosexuality.

However, when the topic of homosexuality did come up, it was clear that the only person in the group who claimed to be completely "healed" was Fred, Yoda's charismatic assistant. He stood in the front of the room and preached that they could be like him if they prayed hard enough. So, the people prayed that they could be Fred and have a wife and children just as he did. Of course, this made many of the participants more depressed because they were seeing no such changes in their lives. One participant complained he wasn't becoming heterosexual, and Fred chastised him for not saying "the right prayers."

Clearly no one's sexual orientation was changing anytime soon, so the lesson plan switched to the more tangible goal of behavior modification. Fred introduced the group first to the teachings of Anne Paulk. He read a passage from John and Anne Paulk's book *Love Won Out,* in which she explained her interesting technique to "overcome" homosexuality:

> . . . I would start to experience a sexual response. . . . So I'd look out the car window and say something like, "Gosh, Lord, there's a tree out there! That tree is green, and it has leaves on it. It's got brown bark." I would fix my mind on anything and everything to distract myself. . . .
>
> Over time that process made me mentally disciplined enough to displace all lesbian thoughts, period.[3]

Next, Fred asked the group to get out their textbooks so they could read about another technique designed to help them eliminate homosexual thoughts and feelings. "Open your textbook to page ninety," he told the motley crew assembled in a semicircle. The textbook was called *Homosexual No More,* by Bill Consiglio, a well-known ex-gay ministry leader in Connecticut. Fred went around the room and handed out rubber bands and instructed each man to put one around his right wrist. Then, in unison, they read a passage on the "rubber band technique":

> Every time you catch yourself watching someone erotically or engaging in a fantasy, snap the band. This will cause a moderate stinging pain which serves as a shocking reminder of what you are doing. This should help you interrupt the "spell."[4]

Upon hearing this, the creepy guy sitting next to me gave me a flirtatious wink while no one was looking and snapped his rubber band. The rest of the group then repeatedly practiced the rubber band technique. Snap . . . Snap . . . Snap . . . filled every corner of the small room.

A former ex-gay I interviewed told me he used the rubber band technique for a year but had to stop because it was awkward at work. "Here I was, this successful businessman in a suit with an expensive watch on one wrist and a rubber band on the other," he said. "It looked really unprofessional and I stopped wearing it. Looking back, I am embarrassed, but at the time, I was so desperate to change I was willing to try anything."

The meandering therapy session lasted nearly four hours while the participants whined and moaned, complaining about their hapless lives. In the end, I concluded this was not an ex-gay ministry, but a gathering of miserable wretches who simply needed someone to listen to them. These were not healthy, well-adjusted people.

No Standards and Fuzzy Math

The account of my trips to these ministries is intended to offer a realistic snapshot of being inside these programs, not to ridicule those who are trapped in the ex-gay lifestyle. They are not the enemy. They are simply homosexuals who for a variety of reasons—usually religious—have not been able to rid themselves of shame and guilt. Most are desperate, depressed people who have decimated their lives through irresponsible choices and now find it easier to blame their sexual orientation rather than themselves. Whereas most gay people reach a time in life when they are ready for self-acceptance and personal responsibility, many ex-gays hit a seemingly impenetrable wall of oppression that they are unable to scale in their quest for inner peace and freedom.

While writing this book I spoke to hundreds of ex-gays and the majority of their leadership. Although the political groups who support them can be hateful and dishonest, the ex-gays, for the most part, are sincere. I think highly of many I have met and count a few as friends—or at least friendly acquaintances. However, their sincerity makes them only sincerely wrong, and no less a threat to the thousands of people who are manipulated, coerced, or motivated by self-loathing into entering these failed programs.

The first striking characteristic of the ex-gay ministries is that they have no uniform guidelines or professional standards. Each ministry under the Exodus umbrella is an autonomous cell that offers its own unique path for "change," and even the meaning of change is quite arbitrary, varying greatly from ministry to ministry.

As an experiment, I created seven different screen names on a Yahoo account and wrote every Exodus group to ask if they could "help me become straight" and "how long would it take." I used stereotypically gay screen names such as Madonnalvr2001 or Diskolvr01. My goals were to see whether consistency existed among the programs and to find out how honest these groups were about the possibility of becoming heterosexual through their programs. The answers varied greatly from ministry to ministry. Admirably, many of the ministry leaders were honest and told me that "change" did not necessarily mean heterosexuality, but celibacy or a relationship with Jesus Christ. Some examples:

- "I don't know if I can help you 'change' in the way you are thinking of change," wrote a ministry leader in Texas, in response to my e-mail.
- An ex-gay leader from Kansas wrote, "Our goal is not so much to overcome homosexuality as it is to be overcome by Christ."
- An ex-gay leader in the Midwest responded to my query, writing, "We don't want to mislead you. We are not able to make anyone straight. What we do is teach you and give you tools to address issues in your own life." This leader went on to say that it took him ten years to change and that "this isn't a thirty weeks and you're straight program. No one can offer you that."

None of the ministries told me I could be straight in thirty weeks, but some were in fact offering me an optimistic timetable that sharply contradicted the more cautious ministries. For instance:

- A ministry leader from Tennessee wrote, "Short answer—probably twelve to twenty-four months [to become straight]."
- "You can be free from homosexuality!!!!!!!!!" exclaimed a leader of one North Carolina ministry, clearly offering me reason to believe I would become a full-fledged heterosexual.

How could these disparate answers come from the same organization? The national leaders concede that Exodus doesn't keep statistics. Thus, individual ministry leaders can offer differing results, producing wildly inflated and inconsistent numbers that give vulnerable people false hope. For instance:

- Anthony Falzarano of Parents and Friends Ministries, who says he's counseled 500 to 600 people, estimates that 40 percent of his patients were able successfully to become heterosexual.[5]
- Melvin Wong, who is on Exodus's referral list as a therapist, boasts that his success rate of helping gays go straight is "about 90 percent, depending on how much the client puts into it."[6]
- Frank Worthen once told the Associated Press that Love in Action (LIA), which has a year-long, live-in program, has a 70 percent success rate.[7] Later he modified these numbers, telling the *Progressive* that LIA had a 50 percent rate of success.[8] Was his program faltering, or did he just arbitrarily spout off numbers, forgetting what he had told the other reporter? Worthen declined my request to be interviewed.[9]
- Bob Ragan of the northern Virginia branch of Regeneration Ministries once boasted that his thirty-week program had a 50 percent success rate.[10] That he gives such a specific number is remarkable, considering that the founder of Regeneration, Alan Medinger, has admitted that coming up with an accurate conversion rate is impossible.[11]

A bizarre product of this type of thinking is a subliminal/self-hypnotic tape that claims all you have to do is listen to the tape and the change to heterosexuality should come "easily and effortlessly." The climactic moment on the self-hypnotic side features a deep male voice that drones:

> At the count of three, your subconscious mind will make you aware of the cause of your homosexual behavior. . . . You need to form in your mind the event you have been looking for whether it was created in this or a previous lifetime. . . . Your soul records are available to you on this issue. You learn from the past and move on![12]

Presto! You are straight. This is not an Exodus product, but as the lead organization promoting "change," Exodus remains embarrassingly silent about the efficacy of such products while desperate people get bilked. That the company who made this tape also sold another product called *Stop Loss of Hair Music* should have raised red flags at Exodus.

Exodus must answer some serious moral questions to achieve the credibility the group seeks. First, why do different ministries have such vastly different conversion rate numbers? Second, if Wong has a 90 percent success rate, why isn't his program the one that all Exodus affiliates must use? Why should programs with a mere 40 percent success rate still be allowed to participate if a better program exists? Clearly, the national leadership doesn't believe in Wong's numbers, or they are negligently allowing people to take part in inferior programs. If they don't believe Wong is truthful, then why would they keep him on their referral list? And if they do believe him, how can they justify not standardizing their programs to make sure every person who joins Exodus has the best ex-gay curriculum available?

The truth is, Exodus is a fly-by-night organization that haphazardly jerry-rigs a jumble of incoherent and unrelated programs under one brand name. Sadly, the group offers this inconsistent patchwork of deceptions to real people who are putting their lives into the hands of ministries that sell dreams and deliver disasters.

Fake Lesbians and Other Fabrications

A paradox of Exodus is that it is made up primarily of decent people who, in my opinion, are doing indecent work because they are convinced that peddling mistruths is moral if done in the name of what they perceive to be the greater good. They justify their deceit by believing that they are helping people go to heaven. "What's a little fib if it helps people achieve eternity?" they likely reason.

I hesitate to say that Exodus leaders willfully condone "lying." An inarguable fact, however, is that ex-gay leaders have misled on many occasions. For instance, Anne Paulk, an Exodus board member, appeared in a full-page ad in *The New York Times* as part of the religious right's ad campaign attacking homosexuals. In the ad, Paulk described herself as a "wife, mother, and former lesbian" and explained, "By the time I hit my teens . . . I just wasn't attracted to men sexually." Yet, in *Love Won Out,* a book she cowrote with her husband, John, she blatantly contradicted herself. According to her book, shortly after high school she met a man named Mark who "appealed to me sexually. . . . We were drawn together by sheer animal magnetism. . . . I came to see that I could be physically attracted to a male, but I just couldn't surrender my heart to him."[13]

Paulk may have been facing myriad issues relating to men, but sexual attraction clearly wasn't one of them. I think most people would reasonably agree that lesbians don't experience "animal attraction" for men. Many women undoubtedly joined Exodus based on Paulk's testimony, believing she went from absolutely no attraction to men to a robust sex life with her husband. Her book does not support this, and yet this inconvenient truth was nowhere in the ad seen by millions of Americans.

The veracity of her husband's testimony doesn't pass muster either. In an Exodus recruitment ad, John appeared with many other ex-gays under the headline "Can homosexuals change? WE DID!" In his book *Not Afraid to Change,* however, he admitted that when he appeared in this ad, he and others were still in the midst of therapy and continued to struggle with homosexual fantasies.[14]

Anthony Falzarano, another ex-gay leader, postulates that people are gay because they were molested or raped as children. However, the statistics he gives on this vary, depending on to whom he is talking. He told the conservative magazine *American Spectator* that "70 percent of homosexuals are molested as children"; in an interview with News Channel 9 in Washington, Falzarano claimed, "75 percent had been rape or molestation victims"; and in CNN's *Talk Back Live,* the number jumped to 80 percent.[15]

Although the difference between 70 and 80 percent isn't much numerically, it is significant because the numbers he offers have to come from *somewhere.* His random game of musical numbers suggests the lack of a statistical basis for his claims, and that he is pulling these figures out of thin air. Falzarano declined several times to be interviewed for this publication.

Change: A Semantic Game

Exodus justifies its chicanery with word games and political spin, which, as a Christian organization, it is supposed to be above. For instance, Exodus leaders tell people they can "change," but when pressed for a specific meaning of change, with Bill Clinton–like circumlocution, they argue that it depends on what the meaning of "change" is.

After much equivocating, when pushed in our interview, Exodus Executive Director Alan Chambers admitted, "I don't think [change is] going from gay to straight. Just saying that doesn't sound like an accurate representation of what Exodus facilitates or proclaims."[16]

It doesn't? Apparently he hasn't been listening to what other well-known Exodus leaders are saying:

- "I don't think there's anybody who can't change if they just relax and let God do what He wants," said Frank Worthern of New Hope Ministries.[17]
- "If someone as deluded as I was can be brought out of homosexuality then surely anyone can," said Joe Dallas, director of Genesis Counseling in Orange California, and author of *A Strong Delusion*.[18]
- "[T]he bottom line is, you have a choice to overcome it. You can change," said Sy Rogers, who calls himself a former transsexual and is now married with children.[19]

At the Exodus 2001 national conference, clearly, a change to full-fledged heterosexuality was the primary goal. The publications hawked at the conference had unambiguous titles, such as *Coming Out Straight, Homosexual No More*, and *You Don't Have to Be Gay*. Chambers acknowledged in our interview that Exodus was sometimes guilty of overstating what the group can accomplish. "To say that [Exodus] is a great healer or the place for people to become straight, I would think that is not right. . . . If there are Exodus ministries that do that, we need to change that. We need to work on that."

A nice sentiment, but Exodus is *still* peddling the same misleading publications. Natalie Davis, a writer and one of the nation's premier experts on the ex-gay ministries, agreed in our interview that the leaders are not always forthcoming on the definition of change: "When you say to an ex-gay minister now, 'So, you're saying people are going to change,' and they [will] say, 'Well, it depends on what you mean by change.'"[20] Davis, who has gone undercover several times in the ex-gay ministries, continued, "If the change they're talking about is changing one's sexual orientation, . . . then the vast majority of them are going to experience failure before they walk in the door."

These word games nearly destroyed John Napoli, who was involved in efforts to change his sexual orientation for ten years, including seven with Exodus affiliate Regeneration. His experience made him so distraught that he had to take antidepressants, and at several junctures he contemplated suicide. As Napoli explained in our interview, he was told when he began in the ministry that he would get to a point at which he would no longer be tempted by a good-looking man. "They don't tell you that the strong physical response will stay."[21]

Eventually, Napoli confronted group leader Bob Ragan, who did not respond to my repeated requests to interview him. "He [Ragan] said he often has people who got frustrated about it and he challenged me . . . Who am I gonna follow? Am I just gonna follow God or follow my instincts?" said Napoli. "He also challenged me that maybe what I was expecting to happen [i.e., change] was not unrealistic, and that it was very realistic." Napoli continued, "Bob said, 'Expect these feelings to always be there.' . . . He said that [for] some people the feelings would go away but I'd been involved with it long enough that probably they wouldn't. I just need to deal with that fact and consider that is the cross I have to bear in this life." Ragan then tried to justify Napoli's suffering through a biblical story. " 'St. Paul,' he said, 'had a thorn in the flesh.' This would be 'my thorn in the flesh,' " recounted Napoli. When asked whether he felt he had been misled, Napoli replied, "Yes. . . . They need to be honest up-front that change in behavior happens as a result of these ministries, but not change in thought," Napoli continued, "because change in thought hasn't even happened for the leaders."

Even the Leaders Are Still Gay

It became apparent through my research that Napoli was correct in saying most of the major leaders who tout change are still attracted to the same sex. Some examples:

- "I am not totally healed from homosexuality. It is part of my emotional, physical and spiritual history," Love in Action's new leader John Smid wrote on his Web site. "It will not be erased as though it did not exist. I still struggle at times. . . . I still shut down with my wife at times. I periodically have sexual thoughts regarding men."[22]

- "No one has ever left therapy saying, 'Wow, I have absolutely no homosexual thoughts,'" said celebrated ex-gay leader Joe Dallas.[23]

If the ex-gay leaders who are writing books about change are still struggling, what does that mean for their followers? The answer is, most are suffering unbelievably dark, lonely, miserable lives. Brent Almond described his four years in the ex-gay ministries as "dispiriting." "Everyone seemed really unhappy . . . a very somber atmosphere most of the time," said Almond in our inteview.[24] "They didn't ever announce it, but there was always one person I had met who in a couple weeks wouldn't be there. . . . I went back the next summer and most of the people I knew weren't there anymore. . . . 'So-and-so's fallen back into the lifestyle.' . . . It wasn't very encouraging. . . . It was a big downer for the most part."

Scott Melendez also witnessed the many failures of the ex-gay ministries while attending Homosexuals Anonymous (HA) meetings in Tucson, Arizona. "The leader said . . . he was completely heterosexual and hadn't had any homosexual temptations or feelings in years," said Melendez in our interview.[25] "Nobody else really [said they were straight] . . . they were on the path toward heterosexuality. And, of course, I found out later that [the leader] wound up leaving HA and . . . [I] think is still with his partner many years later." Melendez continued, "One thing that really clued me in was [meeting] with my sponsor every week and hearing him talk about his struggles and talking to other people in the group, and there were people in that group who had been going to HA for four, five, six, seven years and they seemed to be at the exact same spot I was. I didn't see any graduates. I saw people that were still there, that hadn't changed. They were still struggling. . . . I don't know anybody from my ex-gay group . . . who claims to be ex-gay now."

A more poignant example comes from "Mike," an ex-ex-gay in Texas who had an unpleasant surprise one Saturday evening while out on the prowl. "I was cruising the bathhouse wearing only my damp towel and out of the thick steam emerges my old reparative therapist who for years tried to cure my homosexuality," said Mike in our phone conversation. "I couldn't get mad because he was just as much a victim of this garbage as I was. Of course, part of me wanted my money back."

Unqualified and Highly Questionable Leaders

Even though the longtime leaders are still "struggling," people who step foot in the door are immediately counted as ex-gay, although they are still homosexual, as I was when I visited the ministry in Southern Virginia. "I think the label in most cases precedes the change," said Davis, recalling her undercover experiences.

Since one is considered ex-gay immediately, Exodus and other groups regularly appoint ministry leaders who are anything but straight. The reasoning? Gay is only an "identity," and if people identify as heterosexual, they are not gay, even if they still have intense homosexual yearnings. For example, Catherine Wulfensmith, now a former ex-gay, said she was recruited to help create a conversion program for America's oldest ex-gay ministry, Love in Action, although she was still a lesbian. According to Wulfensmith, "We tried, but we of course couldn't do it. We, who wanted to change our orientation, were expected on our own to devise a program and then go through it. In retrospect, I don't even know why we attempted it."[26]

Typical of many ex-gay leaders is the testimony of a Chicago ministry leader who told the *Chicago Tribune* that she is still not heterosexual. "Obviously, I have been with women," said Sillman Davis, who runs Chicago's Overcomers. "But that's not the point. My healing process is a journey; it's a walk with Christ."[27]

With only a few more than 100 ministries worldwide, why can't Exodus find at least this many totally cured leaders to run their ministries? If change into heterosexuality is truly possible, one might expect that in Chicago, America's third largest city, Exodus could find at least one "healed" person to run Overcomers, rather than someone who is still on her so-called journey. The reason Exodus can't is because nobody has "changed." A trip through the ex-gay ministries is not a "journey," as they want their recruits to believe, but an endless cul-de-sac, where well-intentioned people eternally circle, heading for a finish line that does not exist.

It is bad enough that Exodus and other ex-gay ministries, such as Homosexuals Anonymous, use leaders who are not "healed." Worse yet, however, is the commonplace use of unlicensed counselors and the intimate involvement in these programs of people who have highly questionable pasts. For example, Bob Van Domelen, director of Broken Yoke Ministries in Pewaukee, Wisconsin, was sentenced to five years in prison for first- and second-degree assault against minors. He perpetrated these acts as a high school teacher.[28]

According to the *Los Angeles Times,* in 1998, one family sued Desert Stream, arguably Exodus's premier ministry, alleging that a minister had sexually abused a teenager while the youth was undergoing therapy to turn him straight. According to the article, the family settled its lawsuit in court for an undisclosed sum. Desert Stream claimed the minister was fired, but it would not discuss the settlement with the *Times,* nor with me.[29] Desert Stream's woes have continued unabated, with a wave of defections that have badly shaken the ministry. According to Desert Stream's leader, Andrew Comiskey:

> At the end of 2000, we faced an unusual number of Desert Stream-related leaders who fell into sexual sin, or who at least demonstrated a colossal lack of wisdom in their social choices. . . . Several were placed on different plans of discipline and restoration.[30]

A Biblical Bathhouse

Athough the vast majority of people involved in these ministries are not sexual predators, a very strong sexual undercurrent runs through these programs. Most Exodus leaders would publicly deny this, but many told me off the record that sex between those in the ministries is rather commonplace. Occasionally, a ministry leader will acknowledge the truth. "There have been instances where there's been a lot of unhealthy bonding," New Hope house leader Howard Hervey told one publication.[31]

Some people even attend these ministries, the leaders complain, not to change, but to meet other gay Christians. That these ministries are filled with people who are repressed creates a volcanic sexual cauldron that can boil over at any moment. "It became remarkably easy. Think of it. All these guys feeling very vulnerable, full of self-loathing, and the only antidote for all that pain was, well, I hate to say it, sex," said Brian who used to attend the ex-gay ministries.[32]

When I went to the Exodus 2001 annual conference in Asheville, I was hit on numerous times. The usual pickup line was, "Do you want to be my prayer partner?" Interestingly, the homely men appeared to have difficulty finding prayer partners.

Like new meat at a singles bar, attractive new participants are often ogled and lavished with attention when they first enter an ex-gay ministry. "My God, a veritable B-Line formed at the conclusion of each meeting. They couldn't wait to meet the new guy," said former Exodus member Karl Gerlott.[33] Napoli, a strapping blond with an attractive swimmer's build, recalled in our interview his not so fond memories of his first ministry meeting: "I remember one guy, he said, 'Hi, nice to meet you. I can't wait to get to know you better.' And he was looking at me in this kind of a funky [sexual] way, . . . [and] to me he was very scary looking."

The Victims

From the previous discussion, it should be clear that, in general, ex-gay groups have a near total failure rate, most of the people are chronically depressed, and the very sex they forbid occurs on a frequent basis. Well, if they are so terrible, how do they stay in business? The answer: they are around because they actually are *helping* a lot of people, but not in ways that one might expect. Generally, four types of people take part in ex-gay ministries for the purpose of being "helped."

The first group, representing a minority of attendees, is young people coerced into going by upset parents. Full of false hope, they tell their children that if they don't "change"—or at least make the attempt—Mom and Dad will no longer pay for college tuition or cough up money for their car loans. So these young people, most of whom know it's baloney, go through the motions to avoid parental retribution. The majority of them tell ministry leaders what they want to hear. In turn, the ministry leaders tell their parents that their children have changed. Exodus counts these individuals as success stories, even as many secretly engage in gay relationships. Often, these young adults go straight from an ex-gay meeting to a gay bar and laugh about it.

Obviously, Exodus is not helping this first group and, at a minimum, is aggravating the coming-out process. Fortunately, most people in this group are not fundamentalist Christians, and they usually leave the ministries within a year with minimal psychological damage.

The second group, representing the largest contingent in the ex-gay ministries, consists of individuals raised in ultrareligious homes who attend ex-gay ministries because they believe if they don't change, they would be better off dead. Most of these people have little exposure to openly gay people, and their church has sheltered them from more secular influences, such as television shows or movies, that portray homosexuality in a positive light. The majority of these folks have very little, if any, sexual experience. This naïveté makes them unusually gullible and susceptible to the misinformation about gay life spread by the ex-gay ministries.

Reverend Jerry Stephenson, a former ex-gay and Southern Baptist minister, was once in this category. He attended an Exodus ministry in Fort Lauderdale, Florida, for several years before he came out. The author of *Out of the Closet and into the Light,*[34] he is now an outspoken critic of Exodus. "These people are in denial—like I was—because they have to be," said Stephenson in our interview.[35] "They think God will hate them, the church will forsake them, and they will rot in hell. That's a pretty big burden to carry and it almost drove me to suicide."

Tracey St. Pierre became involved in an ultrastrict, charismatic, nondenominational church in the 1970s at the age of eighteen. She stayed celibate, fighting her sexual orientation until the age of thirty-two. As with Stephenson, her religion made coming out seem like a pipe dream, though she did everything in her power to change. "I prayed. I fasted. I cried. I begged God to change me. I did whatever I had to do to change," said St. Pierre in our interview.[36]

Another lesbian, who declined to give her name for fear she might lose her job, attended a ministry in the Deep South for six years and had a similar experience to St. Pierre's. "I prayed endlessly," she said in our interview. "I even fasted for days at a time. But this did not make me straight. It just made me a hungry lesbian. But when you are brought up in the church, you believe what you have been taught—no questions asked."

The third group, mostly men, is very similar to the second group and represents about one-third of the people in the ministries. They are extremely religious, they don't see coming out as an option, and they despise being homosexuals. The main difference is that these individuals are sexually active, but their shame and self-loathing usually leads to their sexuality manifesting itself in very unhealthy ways. Instead of normal dating, these folks compulsively seek out anonymous sexual encounters in bathhouses, bookstores, public rest rooms, and parks. Members of this group are often caught in a downward spiral of shame, alternating between "sin" and "repentance"; after each sexual experience, they swear to God that it will never happen again, but when it inevitably does, they feel especially wicked because they believe they once again broke a promise to God. Not surprising is that many of the people in this group are deeply closeted, married men.

The ex-gay ministries can be somewhat helpful to these people, forcing them to address their sexual addictions. In the end, however, the unhealthy patterns reemerge unless the individual finds self-acceptance as an openly gay individual.

The fourth group represents a minority of those in the ex-gay ministries, yet it is the most significant segment because it represents the vast majority of the leadership and nearly all of the spokespeople. This group consists of self-destructive, unstable individuals who lack self-control and have decimated their personal lives. They have been saved from death, jail, or suicide only through religious conversion. I call these people the "formers" because that's how they refer to themselves: former drug addicts, prostitutes, kleptomaniacs, alcoholics, pyromaniacs, sex addicts, porn addicts, chronic masturbators, and so on. A significant number appear to have problems with mental illness. Unfortunately, by focusing on their *perceived* problem of homosexuality, many people do not receive the professional help they need with their genuine problems. However, the short-term cessation of their destructive habits makes some of these people believe they are being helped.

Study of Exodus Testimonies

An analysis of the 40 testimonies (23 men and 17 women) on the Exodus Web site shows that most of the people in the ministries who claim "change" were an astonishing mess, leading volatile, highly ruinous lives. This is especially significant because, rather than a random sample of ex-gays, these are the select few Exodus has specifically chosen to represent the organization.

In all, my calculations reveal that 83 percent of the men and women (33 of 40) who offered testimonies self-reported at least one addiction, and many had multiple addictions. For example, 65 percent of the women (11 of 17) and 30 percent of the men (7 of 23) reported suffering from alcohol abuse before they entered the ministries. Drug abuse was also rampant, with 35 percent of the women (6 of 17) and 48 percent of the men (11 of 23) acknowledging a drug problem.

The ex-lesbians had certain issues more germane to them, such as codependency (29 percent [5 of 17]), and sexual abuse (35 percent [6 of 17]), including 24 percent (4 of 17) who said they had been rape victims. The ex-gay men also had specific problems. For instance, 35 percent of the males (8 of 23) said they suffered from sexual addiction, while 17 percent (4 of 23) were afflicted with habitual masturbation, and 39 percent (9 of 23) were self-admitted porn addicts. Depression was also a major issue for the men (52 percent [12 of 23]).

Both the men and women, before finding the ex-gay ministries, were abnormally suicidal, with 29 percent of the women (5 of 17) and a whopping 48 percent of the men (11 of 23) having seriously contemplated taking their own lives. It is well documented that *all* gay people have a higher suicide rate in their teens because of the difficulty involved with the coming-out process. What makes these suicide statistics remarkable, however, is that the vast majority of "ex-homosexuals" self-reporting suicidal thoughts or actual attempts were well into their adult years. This shows that the natural coming-out process was inhibited and that they had unsuccessfully dealt with the core issues that most lesbians and gay men resolve in their teens and early twenties.

Hallucinogenic Heterosexuals?

Perhaps the most disturbing part of my study was finding that many of the ex-gay leaders appear to have untreated mental disorders. I'll state clearly for the record that I am not a mental health professional and have no credentials to judge any person's mental fitness. Still, an evaluation of the Exodus testimonies reveals an alarmingly high number of ex-gays who report hearing voices and having visions, which very well may be hallucinations. A shocking 41 percent of the women (7 of 17) and 35 percent of the men (8 of 23) self-reported that heavenly or demonic voices and visions played a key role in their becoming ex-gay.

Ex-lesbian guru Leanne Payne, in her book *The Broken Image,* seems to support my observation by proposing the ludicrous idea that insanity is helpful to becoming a devout Christian. According to Payne:

> Many of these persons—having suffered breakdowns and long hospitalizations in the past—end up being the strongest and most effective Christians because, having been under such bondage to the voices of the past and present, they gladly *listen* for the life-giving Word in order to survive as persons.[37]

Many well-respected people in society also report supernatural experiences in their spiritual lives. One should not entirely dismiss these as fanciful hallucinations. They may, in fact, be experiences that are beyond human comprehension. There is no mistaking, however, that the ex-gay leaders have a suspiciously disproportionate number of these supernatural experiences, and anyone with rudimentary knowledge of the Bible realizes that such miracles are the exception rather than the rule; divine acts are not handed out like candy to reward loyal followers. Yet, if you look closely at their literature and read their books, it is clear that a supernatural act from Jesus is almost required to make one straight. In their zeal, they have reduced God to no more than a rabbit's foot, a simple good-luck charm that is used to stop them from masturbating or running to an adult bookstore.

The first time I made the connection between what I perceive to be hallucinations and the ex-gay ministries was when ex-gay leader Anthony Falzarano invited me to his office to chat, and to try to convert me. I was actually there for the Human Rights Campaign to gather intelligence on where the religious right was next going to attack the gay, lesbian, bisexual, and transgendered (GLBT) community. Falzarano, at times a charming and loquacious fellow, engaged me in a jovial discussion. About ten minutes into our pleasant conversation, his visage suddenly became sullen and foreboding. In a serious, matter-of-fact tone, he insisted that God had personally told him that on the millennium He was going to usher in Judgment Day.

"Are you ready for God's wrath?" he asked. "The Lord won't be pleased with your work on the homosexual agenda. And your boss Elizabeth Birch practices witchcraft."

I looked for some sign or expression on his face that would reveal he was only kidding, but none was forthcoming. He continued with his dire, fire-and-brimstone predictions. He said that to save my soul I should join him on a millennium pilgrimage to Jerusalem because the "end is coming very soon and only believers will go to heaven." Of course, he looked slightly embarrassed the next time I saw him in February 2000; clearly, the world had not ended.

Crazy stories are almost as ubiquitous in the ex-gay community as prayer. Anne Paulk is one who seems to receive miracles from God as frequently as most people eat breakfast. No act is too pedestrian for God to tackle when Anne is inconvenienced. One night, for instance, Anne's brand-new contact lens popped out of her eye and God came to the rescue:

> All at once I got down on my knees and prayed, *God, please help me! I've got to find my contact.*
> The next thing I did after giving up, praying, then giving up again, was to put my hand in my pocket. And there, lodged in the corner of my jeans pocket, was my contact. I was stunned! I stared at the contact in disbelief, and for a moment I felt like crying. Could it be that God had actually heard my prayer?
> There was no other explanation—my contact had been found in an impossible location. It never could have gotten there on its own. It had to be God![38]

Also, whereas most women have to rely on sonograms to find out if they are pregnant, Anne—with the help of God—has her own special method of receiving the good news:

> As we stopped beside the road one day, I looked up into the sky and saw an unusual cloud formation. It looked like a baby. *How strange,* I thought, *I've never seen a cloud like that before. I wonder . . .*
> Not long thereafter, I learned that I was pregnant again.[39]

Not to be outdone, her husband, John, had his own miraculous experience on the dance floor of a Columbus, Ohio, gay bar one evening. While dressed in drag and hammered on a combination of alcohol and poppers, God confronted him:

> Then for some reason I glanced upward, and my eyes were suddenly transfixed by a mirror ball that was rotating slowly near the ceiling. I smiled as I watched the intricate patterns of light swirling across the ceilings and walls.

Suddenly, all at once, I seemed to enter another place and time. . . .

"Come back to Me," the voice said, "and I will change your life."

I immediately recognized it as the voice of God. "Come back to Me," He repeated.[40]

Reading the ex-gay testimonies, one might think that it is more likely to hear from God at a gay discotheque than a church. Rebekah Johnston, according to her Exodus testimony, also had a quite extraordinary dance floor vision:

As I looked out onto the dance floor, I saw the most incredible vision: all the smiling faces turned to wax and started to melt. The laughter stopped. The Holy Spirit revealed to me that the broken hearts behind the smiling masks were not really laughing at all.[41]

Darryl L. Foster, Director of WITNESS! Freedom Ministries in Waco, Texas, engaged in orgies, drank, and was hooked on poppers. All that ended one night, however, according to his Exodus testimony, after Jesus appeared on a premium cable channel:

I slumped down in front of the TV and flipped it on. When the screen came into focus, I saw an amazing sight: a badly-beaten man dragging a heavy wooden cross through the streets of a city. Suddenly the man stopped, and looked up at me as blood trickled down his face. Then he said, "I did all this just for you." I began to weep uncontrollably as I realized Jesus had spoken to me.

Sadly, the bizarre stories I presented are the rule, not the exception, for ex-gay leaders. Although most of these self-delusions are harmless, sometimes they cause the leaders to become grossly irresponsible, putting the health of other people at risk.

Michael Lumberger is an Exodus board member and Director of Dunamis Ministries in Pittsburgh, Pennsylvania. Prior to finding the ex-gay ministries, he was a suicidal prostitute with self-admitted pornography, masturbation, alcohol, and drug problems. Despite his homosexuality, he got married but soon tested positive for HIV. In his Exodus testimony he claimed, "Today, with God's abundant grace, and His miraculous power to heal, I walk totally free from the AIDS virus."

Lumberger clearly gives the impression that he was made HIV negative as a reward for pleasing God. This irresponsible testimony contradicts science and is an example of how the religious zeal and delusions of some Exodus leaders can harm others. Lumburger's viral load may be undetectable, but he is not "free from the virus," as he falsely claimed, because at this point in time it is medically impossible. I pressed him on this topic via e-mail, and he explained that the protease inhibitor drug cocktails played a major role in maintaining his health. Nowhere in his testimony did he mention these prescription drugs. Instead, he suggested that it is possible not only to pray away the gay but also to pray away AIDS.

The Personal Owner's Manual from God

Unlike many other communities, the GLBT community is blessed with unparalleled freedoms. One can comfortably choose from a plethora of lifestyles that span the ideological, theological, and fashion continuum with minimal condemnation. The GLBT community encompasses all types of people, from conservative Log Cabin Republicans to flamboyant drag queens. For those who are centered, this unbridled liberty and diversity can make for an incredibly rich and fulfilling life.

However, for those who are weak-minded, mentally unstable, or lacking in self-esteem, the dearth of clearly defined rules in the GLBT community can be a nightmare. Certain people thrive under authoritarian regimentation, and these people have an unusually difficult time succeeding in the open environment offered by the GLBT community. Without unambiguous strictures dictating every detail of their lives, they have to make choices for themselves, and, often, they make terrible choices that lead to addiction, misery, and, in many cases, death.

When these people hit rock bottom, they often mistakenly blame the GLBT community for their own personal failings. When these individuals say they "hate the so-called gay lifestyle," they really mean they disdain a world with limitless options. To thrive these individuals need clear guidance—a roadmap for life—and that is why most Exodus leaders find the ex-gay ministries so appealing.

To join the ex-gay ministries one has to accept a hard-core, right-wing fundamentalism that outlines every minute detail of one's life. This almost always involves joining an authoritarian, right-wing church. The austere strictures such churches offer can help put the brakes on the destructive lifestyles led by these lost souls. Through faith-based programs they can kick their addictions and lead somewhat healthier lives. This quest for a hypercontrolled environment also helps explain why ex-gay leaders were also disproportionately attracted to extreme cults before becoming fundamentalist Christians.

It can be said that most ex-gays are not looking for a religion, but a regimen. They are learning scripture because they seek structure. When they claim they are searching for God, they really mean they are searching for guidance. Jeff Konrad, author of the book *You Don't Have to Be Gay,* explained it this way: "[T]he Bible is also your personal owner's manual from God. . . . The Bible gives us directions for living life properly, abundantly, more fulfillingly."[42]

Furthermore, the mysticism and superstition that are an integral part of evangelical churches appeal to those who are mentally unstable. If one suffers from delusions, the best place to go is a megachurch where thousands of people will reward you as a seer, instead of condemn you as insane.

Ministry Mouse and Deuteronomy Duck

This authoritarian, hocus-pocus worship style was evident when I visited Orlando, Florida, to interview Exodus Executive Director Alan Chambers and his wife, Leslie. Preceding the interview at their immaculate home, I met them at Calvary Assembly of God for Sunday morning services led by the charismatic televangelist Clark Whitten.

The massive, multitier church looked more like a swank Broadway theater than a religious sanctuary. The stage came fully decorated with fifty enormous flags representing different countries. A huge banner hanging in back of the pulpit read "Glory, Praise and Honor," and a humongous television screen suspended from the ceiling provided viewing for those in the nosebleed section. A full choir of at least 150 people dressed in brilliantly colored costumes stood on a three-tiered platform.

I knew I was in Orlando, but I had been expecting to see such a fantastic entertainment extravaganza at Disney, not an evangelical church. The characters Ministry Mouse and Deuteronomy Duck would have been right at home on this gargantuan stage.

When the preaching started, however, you knew you were in a Southern right-wing church, not the Magic Kingdom. The sermon focused on a laundry list of rules the congregants were supposed to follow to avoid hell. The sermon, full of strictures, was perfect for a person trying to maintain the ex-gay facade. It was thoroughly legalistic and dictated every aspect of one's life. The preacher began with warning the flock not to worship false Gods, fake religions, heresy, witchcraft, and the occult. Reverend Whitten then embarked on a bizarre tangent about the dangers of sorcery. I couldn't help thinking, When is the last time this preacher actually met a sorcerer? Was sorcery a real problem in society or was he watching too many Saturday morning cartoons?

In the middle of the sermon, several people spoke in tongues, flailing their hands in the air. One lady with "big" hair and layers of thick makeup rushed the stage and, like a slam dancer in a mosh pit, rolled on the floor as if having a seizure, speaking in tongues and yelling "Hallelujah!"

The final part of the sermon was revealing, focusing on "rebellion and authority." Congregants learned they should obey their leaders because they are ordained by God. This was, in my opinion, an authoritarian interpretation of scripture designed to limit dissent within the church. Lack of disagreement is another hallmark of the ex-gay ministries. "I never witnessed dissent," said Natalie Davis. "Before walking into those doors, there is kind of a given. If you are not a conservative Christian person, chances are you are not going to walk through those doors. If you are walking through those doors, then chances are you already believe in biblical inerrancy."

Nonfundamentalist Christians Keep Out!

Indeed, the vast majority of ex-gay ministries are for only born-again Christians. A Jewish friend of mine, Richard Davis, went undercover in the Fort Lauderdale–based ministry Worthy Creations. He asked the leader if he would have to convert to become straight. "No, you don't have to convert," she slyly told him. "You can become a Jew for Jesus," she said, while slipping him Jews for Jesus program materials.

Most ex-gay programs are dismissive of any religion or belief system that is not fundamentalist Christianity. For instance, Portland Fellowship, Oregon's leading ex-gay ministry, hands out a questionnaire that lumps many legitimate religions with a series of bizarre practices or behaviors. Their survey asks ministry participants if they are involved with a list of taboo behaviors, including bestiality, Satanism, molestation, black magic, and witchcraft. Included in this list, however, are religions such as Mormonism, Scientology, the Unification Church, Jehovah's Witnesses, Christian Science, and Zen Buddhism. In other words, if it isn't fundamentalism, it is a product of Satan, and if one communes with the devil, he or she cannot be cured of homosexuality.

In my interview with Alan Chambers and his wife, Leslie, they artfully danced around my question about whether one must embrace fundamentalist Christianity to become an ex-gay. Finally, they became exasperated with my inquiry and blurted out the truth. "Without Jesus Christ, I don't know what the purpose is," said Alan Chambers. "I don't think that change would be as significant without Jesus Christ." Added Leslie, "You probably wouldn't want then to stay at Exodus . . . because Exodus-based groups are based on help through Jesus Christ."

Nonfundamentalist Christian Ex-Gay Ministries

A few ex-gay fledgling ministries target people who are not fundamentalist Christians. One such group is Jews Offering New Alternatives to Homosexuality (JONAH), but this group is no more than a front organization for Christian political groups in their dubious efforts to add the veneer of diversity to the ex-gay cause. JONAH's role is usually to refer Jews to "reparative therapists." The group, however, offends many Jews because it encourages them to read books that tell them they must become Christian to change, offering this disclaimer: "Many of these books are Christian, but offer plenty of helpful ideas for nonbelievers, too." Still, anyone who is familiar with the content in these books knows that they are about Christian conversion. Jewish parents who contact this group won't get ex-gays as children, but they do run the risk of getting "ex-Jews."

Another nonfundamentalist ex-gay group is Evergreen, a Utah-based group for Mormons. Although not formally associated with the Mormon Church, this organization often receives referrals from it.[43] The Mormon Church's particularly intolerant stance on homosexuality ensures that Evergreen will remain a busy ministry, as conflicted Mormons search for a cure that will never come. One Mormon from San Francisco, Stuart Matis, committed suicide because he was unable to change his sexual orientation. Mathis wrote the following suicide note:

> The church has no idea that as I type this letter, there are surely boys and girls on their callused hands and knees imploring God to free them from their pain. They hate themselves. They retire to bed with their fingers pointed to their heads in the form of a gun. I am now free. I am no longer in pain and I no longer hate myself. As it turns out, God never intended for me to be straight. Hopefully, my death might be a catalyst for some good.[44]

The Catholic ex-gay group Courage was founded in 1980 by the Reverend John Harvey to "establish a spiritual support system for men and women with homosexual inclinations." According to the group's literature, it is "the only such organization in the Catholic Church approved by the Vatican," and the group fervently backs the Catholic Church's view that "homosexuality is objectively disordered." What separates Courage from Exodus and other ex-gay groups is that it doesn't promote a "cure," but "the gift of chastity." This stance has been controversial in ex-gay circles and Exodus's Chambers derided their program as "limiting" during our interview. Today, Courage has chapters throughout the United States and in eight other nations. However, the group has a very limited appeal because most people do not want to be sentenced to a lifetime of celibacy. Despite the power and reach of the Catholic Church, Courage will remain a bit player until the day they start promising miracles and divine intervention, as does Exodus.

The Devil Made Me Gay

Some ex-gay leaders claim they are much happier now, and I believe they are sincere. They have left behind colorful, three-dimensional lives of uncertainty and despair for monochrome, one-dimensional lives of relative stability and security. To reach this place of equilibrium, all these people had to do was give up their natural sexuality. To the vast majority of people, this would be an unacceptable compromise, but to many ex-gay leaders, it makes all the sense in the world.

These individuals cannot handle freedom. The only way they can avoid the affliction of excess is by eliminating temptation altogether. Whereas most people enjoy sex in its proper place, these individuals become sexual compulsives. Instead of enjoying a drink at the bar, they don't stop until they pass out. Whereas some people occasionally experiment with illegal drugs, these folks turn their bodies into full-fledged chemistry labs. With most ex-gay leaders, it is a black-and-white world of all or nothing. Who can blame these folks for choosing nothing, when all means almost certain death?

Most of the ex-gay leaders have channeled all of their addictive, self-destructive behavior and pent-up sexual energy into a form of religious fanaticism—nothing more than an addiction of a different kind. This misplaced religious fervor can be witnessed in the ex-gay community in the way they embrace "spiritual warfare."

Satan and his dastardly band of demons are a central part of ex-gay culture. Nearly all ex-gay leaders fight against the devil, but the lead general in this spiritual jihad is Andrew Comiskey, founder of Desert Stream in Anaheim, California. Comiskey, arguably one of the five most influential ex-gay leaders, got involved with Exodus after a wild ride in the gay community that included drugs, wild sex, and a ghastly battle against anal warts. Today, his main battle is against Satan.

His book *Pursuing Sexual Wholeness* is filled with hateful examples of how homosexuality and the devil go together like rice and soy sauce. The following illustrates Comiskey's linking homosexuality—which he lovingly calls "spiritual disfigurement"—with Satan:

Satan delights in homosexual perversion because it not only exists outside of marriage, but it also defiles God's very image reflected as male and female. . . . Another related source of
demonization is the homosexual relationship itself. . . . That attachment and communion are indeed inspired, but their source
is demonic.[45]

Ex-lesbian Jeanette Howard, author of *Out of Egypt: One Woman's
Journey Out of Lesbianism,* is also one of the lead holy warriors in
battling against Satan. According to Howard:

Choosing to leave the lesbian life brings us into direct conflict
with the satanic realm. . . . Only when we understand and imple-
ment spiritual warfare can our walk into wholeness be successful.[46]

This emphasis on spiritual warfare pushed by ex-gay luminaries
can lead to psychologically unhealthy, obsessive battles against imag-
ined evil forces. *"All I know is that God and Satan are fighting in me.
My body is the battleground and I don't know who is going to win,"*
Patricia Allan Lawrence wrote in her Exodus testimony.

As a lesbian, Sunny Jenkins had started drinking at age thirteen
and had taken the street drug crank each day for five years. However,
one day after having corrective heart surgery she woke up in the hospital to find that she had miraculously lost all attraction to women and
kicked her crank habit without a single withdrawal symptom, according to her Exodus testimony. Unfortunately, apparently Satan was so
ticked off that she had beat crank and quit lesbianism that he attacked
her with pestilence. "God showed me that since [S]atan could not
reach me in the same way he used to, sickness was a new weapon he
was aiming at me," declared Jenkins.

The biggest weapon the ex-gay ministries have against Satan is exorcism. An ex-gay with whom I was not familiar once enthusiastically offered to cast the demon of homosexuality from me while I was
attending a conference. I told him that I would allow him to do it if he
would capture the demon in a jar so I could keep him as a pet. What a
great "conversation piece at a party a jarred demon would be," I excit-
edly told him. Apparently he didn't like my suggestion and lumbered
away to find another possessed someone who was lower maintenance
than I.

Not everyone is lucky enough to escape these deliverance—and I stress *Deliverance* (cue the music)—ministers, however. In our interview, Tracey St. Pierre recounted the story of her failed deliverance from lesbianism. The church group she attended believed "that demons can influence and actually . . . have power in humans' lives, and that humans allow these demons to influence by engaging in certain activities or behaviors and that you create a weakness where you allow the devil to control your life," said St. Pierre. "And so they told me I had a demon and that I needed to have it cast out of me. . . . So [my counselor] laid hands on me and prayed for me and rebuked the devil and prayed in tongues."

Karen B. Hindman was a deliverance minister for sixteen years, casting demons out of people for all kinds of sins. With one particular sin, however, the demon seemed illusive. "It was exceptionally difficult for me when a woman came to the altar requesting that I cast away her homosexual demons, because I could not cast this demon from myself," wrote Hindman in the Human Rights Campaign's landmark publication, *Finally Free—Personal Stories: How Love and Self-Acceptance Saved Us from the Ex-Gay Ministries.*[47]

Hindman now rebukes deliverance ministries, saying they are harmful to the mental health of lesbians and gay men. "Efforts to deliver people from homosexuality involve taking Scripture out of context and misusing it as a tool to make gay people feel terrible about themselves," wrote Hindman. "[I]n the end, this grueling exercise ultimately leaves people mentally suicidal and yes, still homosexual."[48]

The most evil part of using spiritual warfare is that when a miracle does not occur, it is easy to blame the victim. The ex-gay ministries have perfected the art of deflecting blame onto members of their flock. They often tell these struggling people that supernatural acts are commonplace and will certainly happen if they say the right prayers. This creates a dynamic for those involved in the ministries whereby they spend every spare moment of their lives currying favor with God so He will reward them with heterosexuality.

Using miracles as a carrot to attract new recruits is incredibly cruel and psychologically abusive. In the end, the carrot is a stick to torment mentally those who have not changed. When you have a system based on rewards for those who please God, then those who are not rewarded clearly have run afoul of Him. Thus, the ex-gay ministries, in aggregate, are people who feel they have let down God and are desperately trying any combination of prayers or wacky ideas to appease Him. This spiritual warfare that the ex-gay ministries have waged on Satan is actually psychological warfare on those who are struggling mightily to become heterosexual because of religious and societal pressures.

The Ex-Gay Lifestyle

The perverse paradox of the ex-gay ministries is that they give stability to the insane while making the sane unstable. While the ex-gay ministries help the irresponsible, self-deluded, and self-destructive rebuild their lives, they wreak havoc on normal gay people who get sucked into these dangerous programs. The "formers," full of bravado and religious fervor, having kicked their addictions, lure religious people with few homosexual experiences into their web of lies. Having no knowledge of or familiarity with gay life, these innocent gay Christians believe much of the antigay propaganda directed at them.

"The stories are that all there is in the gay community is this hedonistic lifestyle of drugs and sex," said former ex-gay Clint Trout in our interview,[49] "but there is no commitment, there is no depth, no love. It is a really bleak picture. So . . . I have these desires and they are never going to get met anyway. It is a really hopeless feeling. It is a really dead feeling."

Thus, the group dynamic of almost every ex-gay ministry is one involving a charismatic leader who claims to have become straight and is leading a group in which *all* the people are still gay and "struggling." It is extraordinarily difficult to find people who are not in paid leadership positions to say they have sustained change for more than five years. Also, those in leadership have had to make extraordinary sacrifices to *believe* they are now heterosexual. First and foremost, they have to quit their normal jobs and become full-time ministers. My experience has shown me that almost no ministers who claim heterosexuality have real jobs; they are almost always full-time professional heterosexuals.

This hypothesis was confirmed through my study of the forty Exodus testimonies on their Web page. Of the success stories offered, 68 percent (30 of 44) are full-time ministry leaders, with 59 percent of the women (10 of 17) and 86 percent of the men (20 of 23) running an ex-gay program in some capacity.

Interestingly, Exodus did not post testimonies of even one ex-gay success story by a person who lives a normal life, someone, for instance, who has a regular nine-to-five job, a happy family, and no history of extreme behavior. The sober accountant with a spouse, three kids, and a house with a white picket fence does not seem to exist in the ex-gay world. I'm sure if they looked hard enough they could trot out a couple to disprove my theory, but they certainly are not advertising these people, and I have yet to meet any.

The ex-gay ministries will downplay this, calling it no big deal when, in fact, it is. Imagine for a second that the only openly gay people in America worked as paid, political lobbyists for gay organizations. If this were the case, one would seriously have to wonder whether there were actually more than a hundred or so gay people in the country. This, however, is the reality inside the ex-gay ministries. They present the same few spokespeople over and over, and outside of these paid ministry leaders, little evidence supports the existence of "normal" ex-gays. Sure, thousands of people attend these ministries—the vast majority for less than a year—but only an infinitesimally small number of these people claim the programs actually work, and those who do claim success are usually spokespeople on the dole.

"Their leaders have turned it into an occupation," said Mel White, an ex-ex-gay and the founder of the spiritual activist group Soulforce. "If they change they not only lose their income, but they lose their credibility. So they can't change and they go on and on."[50]

Honeymoon Horror

The overwhelming majority of ex-gays, having no attraction to the opposite sex and being forbidden from same-sex relations, are stuck in a celibate hell. Although opposite-sex attraction will rarely, if ever, develop, some ex-gays pursue marriage because they want to start a family or simply because, for years, they have been starved for human intimacy. Others marry because that is what their family, society, and their church expect them to do. Still, some ex-gays want to marry so they can ascend to the top of the Exodus leadership, which is nearly impossible if one is single.

Many of those who marry are to some degree bisexual. They are able to sublimate their homosexuality and have normal heterosexual relations. For those who are truly gay, however, marriage can be a tricky thing. Ex-gays have all kinds of bizarre issues to deal with that most heterosexual or homosexual relationships never have to face. For instance, a premarital tiff that almost caused Anne and John Paulk to cancel their wedding started after John complained to Anne that she should wear more makeup, similar to Candi, his drag queen alter ego from his homosexual club days. "[H]e was comparing me to Candi and to his mom," wrote Anne. "I was deeply hurt by his words."[51]

John recognized his boorishness and made amends for his loutish behavior. "I had projected Candi on to her," explained a remorseful John. "I was no longer dressing in drag, but I was still trying to create the ideal woman through makeup, hair, and clothing. . . . Real love is what I had with Anne, and I didn't want to lose it."[52]

For other ex-gays, the main fear is sexual performance. After all, they are not really attracted to their spouses, and they technically aren't allowed to fantasize about the same sex to help maintain arousal. This can lead to disastrous honeymoons, such as that of Alan and Leslie Chambers. In our interview, they described their nightmare scenario on what was supposed to be a night to remember.

"I was just scared to death," said Alan. "The actual act [was] difficult. It was like, 'How do you get that there and how does that all work?' And it was like, . . . 'Why didn't this work?' and immediately just dealing with 'I'm not a man.' "

The initial disappointments only increased Alan's anxiety and the failures became a way of life. "We would get back to the same place night after night and it wouldn't work, and we went on like that," Alan explained. "I was very discouraged and we cried."

Finally, however, Alan ended the river of tears with a memorable performance so exciting that it was recorded for posterity. "I remember the night when it finally happened the way they say it should happen. It's like, 'Wow!' When it was over we bawled," explained Alan. . . . "It was this amazing experience. In the middle of the night . . . I was like, 'Get out your journal. Let's write about this. Let's talk about what happened.' . . . Since then it's not a problem at all."

I asked Alan if he was still attracted to men and he denied that he was. However, probing a little deeper, I saw that his dreaded homosexual feelings continuously lurked below the surface. "Put me in a bathhouse. . . . Would I find people attractive or would that stir me? It probably would," said Chambers. "I'm not a raging heterosexual . . . where I have to worry about if [a] lady walks in the room and I have to turn my head, where some guys are like that." Still, Chambers claimed, "I do feel heterosexual. I do believe I'm heterosexual."

But how heterosexual is he? Many ex-gays, when pinned down, will admit that, although able to perform periodically, their attraction to the opposite sex is extremely limited. Instead of acknowledging their shortcomings, however, they try to make it seem as if regular heterosexuals are dysfunctional because they happen to have normal libidos. "I don't think that as unhealthy as I was homosexually, I [would] want that heterosexually," continued Alan. "I wouldn't want to be attracted to every woman who walked up to me, or to have this overwhelming desire to have sex with numerous women or numerous people. I find that very unhealthy."

In ex-gay Jeff Konrad's book *You Don't Have to Be Gay,* he also refers to normal heterosexual attraction as unhealthy. "Now don't get me wrong," wrote Konrad. "I don't lust for women as some men do; that is not healthy behavior either."[53]

What is unhealthy is that when many ex-gays get married, they are actually creating divorces and estranged families. The ex-gay ministries love to show wedding photos, but they never show the divorce papers and shattered lives they have helped create.

"There were a couple of married guys [in the ex-gay group] whose wives didn't know about their problem," said Clint Trout. "They would go cruise the bathrooms or bookstores and then come home and lie to their wives. That was their way of life. It was a circle of shame."

Scott Melendez said in our interview that many ex-gays get married for selfish reasons at the expense of their husbands and wives. The stress on the heterosexual spouses trying to cope with the problem can often be too much and lead to painful divorces. "Some of the men that were married would bring their wives and . . . [these women] loved their husbands so much," said Melendez. "Yet, they were devastated inside because they didn't know what they were doing wrong. Why weren't they enough for their husband[s]? It helped me realize that . . . denying myself as a gay person is one thing, but to then get married and drag another person into that just seemed appalling."

As I have demonstrated, the leading ex-gay ministries are a disorganized, shockingly unprofessional collection of unqualified counselors and fundamentalist shamans who cause untold damage to the very people they are supposed to be helping. These groups, although often run by well-intentioned people, have an astronomical failure rate. They lure vulnerable and desperate people by twisting the facts and manipulating the truth. The bizarre methods they use are arbitrary, capricious, and often comical, making a mockery of religion, science, and psychology.

The only people who on rare occasion seem to benefit somewhat, if at all, are those suffering from hard-core addictions, mental illness, or sundry other problems that have nothing to do with being gay. These individuals would be better off in programs run by credentialed professionals. To get any of the supposed benefits, it seems one must quit his or her job and become a full-time ministry leader. For normal, well-adjusted lesbians and gay men, the ex-gay ministries can be a soul-shattering experience that leads to low self-esteem, depression, and sometimes suicide.

These programs can best be described as peddling false hope to the feckless. It is no wonder, then, as we shall explore in the ensuing chapters, that the ex-gay ministries are littered with a disquieting history of follies and failures.

A Trilogy of Tragedy

Scene I: The Original Cast of Characters

The 1969 Stonewall riots in Greenwich Village and the American Psychiatric Association's (APA) 1973 decision to remove homosexuality from the list of mental disorders were revolutionary changes that paved the way for a major shift in public opinion on homosexuality. While millions of gay people participated in or watched these events unfold with jubilation, another group of homosexuals believed these happenings were relatively inconsequential to their lives. These individuals were lesbians and gay men who grew up in hard-core fundamentalist households and believed their sexual orientation was a God-given curse. In their minds, gay activists and the APA could not change the fact that sexually active homosexuals were destined for hell. If laws were passed that protected openly gay people from job discrimination, it simply meant that gays could hold jobs before they roasted for eternity. If the APA said gays were not sick, it proved only that they would be sane when they came face-to-face with Lucifer. For these folks, the rapid changes taking place around them were "of this world," while they had their eyes on the magic kingdom in the sky. Life was about, not earthly pleasures, but cutting a deal with God, whereby they pledged to endure a celibate or married hell on earth in exchange for an eternity in heaven.

The societal changes fostered by the gay liberation movement gave these individuals, on occasion, the option to verbally affirm their sexual orientation, but their religion still prohibited them from acting on these professed feelings. This created a nascent subculture of lesbians and gay men who were out in word but could not be in deed. This, in a bizarre sense, was very liberating because in some instances their friends, families, and churches would still support them, but the support came with very cruel strings attached: "Jesus loves you and so do we," they would say, "as long as you don't love." Some sufficiently repressed gays were able to make this demented deal and sell their hearts so Jesus would save their souls—according to their beliefs. Increasingly, however, many of these people were unable to live joyless lives and sought to reconcile their sexuality and spirituality in healthier ways.

The bright lights and freedom of emerging gay Meccas such as San Francisco, Los Angeles, and New York suddenly beckoned with irresistible magnetism. It became clear that if fundamentalist gays were to be able to adhere to their religion's authoritarian version of scripture, then they would need support groups to help them weather the crippling desolation and crushing loneliness. Enter the birth of Love in Action (LIA), the world's first official ex-gay ministry.

In the early 1970s, John Evans and his life partner, Ron Morano, owned an art gallery in Sausalito, directly across the bay from San Francisco, where they lived. It was an exceedingly happy time for the couple of ten years. Business was booming, they had a number of close friends, and they were both active Christians who attended church together. This picture of bliss and domestic tranquility soon met a tragic fate.

One day, Evans met Reverend Kent Philpott, owner of a nearby bookstore and pastor of the Church of the Open Door. Joined by their strong faith, they quickly became friends and frequently had lunch together. About six months into their friendship, Philpott went to the art gallery one day and asked, out of the blue, "John, are you gay?"[1]

Shocked by the frankness of the question, Evans hesitated, paused, caught his breath, and finally asked, "How do you know?"

"The Holy Spirit showed me," Philpott responded.

This conversation led to Evans conveying to Philpott that there was a real need for the church to start ministering to gays. Having grown up in the unsupportive environment of the Assembly of God Church,

Evans thought churches should not drive away homosexuals, and, to his surprise, Philpott wholeheartedly agreed.

The next morning, Philpott called Evans with miraculous news. "John, you won't believe this but two people just came in and admitted to me they were gay. They had never done that. You know I would love to get a ministry started to gay people."[2]

Through this historic exchange, Love in Action was born in 1973. Philpott and Evans, however, had radically different ideas of what this new ministry should seek to accomplish. Evans had pictured a program that ministered to openly gay people and nurtured their spirituality. Philpott, on the other hand, had envisioned a ministry that saved homosexuals from hell by helping them go straight.

In the author's exclusive interview with Philpott, he denied that the intention of LIA was ever to make gay people heterosexual. "The idea of making somebody straight was never in our minds," Philpott told me. However, during our conversation the reverend offered statements that were incongruous with his contention that LIA was not out to "change" homosexuals. "People would come to us and say, 'I'm a homosexual, I'm a Christian, there is an enormous conflict here, and I need some support and help,'" said the LIA cofounder. "It was like a twelve-step group, but no formal [program]."

If it were similar to a twelve-step program, then clearly the agenda *was* to change a certain type of behavior, in this case homosexuality. So, the ministry was, in fact, about conversion.

In any case, through Philpott's charismatic personality, his vision of the nascent group eventually prevailed. Evans was a quiet, reserved guy, while Philpott was a gregarious, natural leader who could manipulate the malleable to conform to his stringent point of view. Evans was mesmerized by Philpott and succumbed to his every wish as though he were a messianic prophet showing him to the holy land of heterosexuality. As Evans further surrendered to Philpott's powerful spell, the reverend ordered Evans to leave his life partner, Ron, a commandment that would forever change his life.

"Kent told me I had to break up with my lover," Evans wistfully told me over the phone from his Sonoma, California, home. "It broke my heart and Ron's. We were really happy together. The breakup eventually drove Ron to drugs and despair. He died a broken man. It still hurts me to this day."

Shortly after the founding of the ministry, a few gay people trickled in to check out what it had to offer, but they soon found that LIA was open only to lesbians and gay men who were "not open." The ministry considered homosexuality evil and unnatural, and all participants were forced to adhere to this view if they wanted to stay in the group. "Homosexuality is a sin against God, a sin against the Creator," Philpott told me.

I asked Philpott if it were possible that people were joining his ministry to escape an oppressive society that discriminated against homosexuals.

"That's a pretty lame argument," he said. "People just didn't like it. . . . The drugs, the alcohol, the relationships that didn't last, and the constant disappointment . . . are why they wanted out. . . . That's an absurdity! There is an internal kind of conflict that is set up that is cross-cultural. . . . It has always been there and it always will be. . . . People are deeply conflicted and looking for hope."

Within a month of Love in Action's birth, Philpott wrote a wildly influential book titled *The Third Sex?,* which was the first ever ex-gay book touting conversions to heterosexuality through prayer.[3] "After about a month there were six people," said Evans. "That's when he said, 'Well, I'm gonna write a book on homosexuality,' but he knew nothing of gay life."

Using pseudonyms, Philpott wrote that these six people had changed, when, in fact, none of them actually had. Moreover, he had known most of these people for only less than one month. "He just went ahead and wrote the book without even letting us look through it," Evans revealed to me. "We all [confronted him], . . . but he said, 'This is God's will.'"

Despite the blatant inaccuracies, in 1975 the book was shipped throughout the country and became the impetus for individual ex-gay start-up ministries. From day one, the foundation for the ex-gay ministries was built on a myth. "Once that book [*The Third Sex?*] hit . . . Wow! The dam burst open," Philpott exclaimed. "We had so many people showing up. They showed up in the middle of the night with a suitcase . . . from the Midwest someplace. It just expanded."

As the ministry grew, Evans plunged deeper and deeper into the group he had cofounded. Eventually he moved into Love in Action's group home, Glory House, where people who were recovering from assorted addictions lived. He stayed in this oppressive setting for two months before he knew he had to get out. "I couldn't handle it. . . . Philpott really chewed me out and told me, 'The devil is going to get you if you move away from us.' It was like a prison camp . . . that's all it was," Evans told Sylvia Pennington.[4]

Evans's best friend, Jack McIntyre, was also part of the ministry. He, along with the rest of the participants, struggled mightily with temptations and did everything in his power to change his sexual orientation. As with nearly everyone else in the original ex-gay cast of characters, however, he could not change and remained as gay as the day he walked through the door.[5] For McIntyre, the ministry led to feelings of inadequacy and intensified his belief that he had failed God.

Eventually, the strain became too great and he attempted suicide, overdosing on pills in a motel room. McIntyre survived this suicide attempt, but to protect his friend from further harming himself, Evans committed him to a mental hospital in Marin County, outside of San Francisco. The institution's constant surveillance was not enough to keep McIntyre from carrying out his wish to die in order to please God. "He said, 'John, I'm gonna do it,' " said Evans. "He saved up pills . . . and he had enough medication to kill himself." With a handful of toxic meds, McIntyre finally became the ex-gay that Love in Action promised he could be.[6]

After two years, the ministry Evans had helped found seemed more like Death in Action. Evans and others in the group blamed Philpott and ministry participant Frank Worthen for McIntyre's suicide, and these two men blamed Evans, saying the cofounder was a subversive force.[7] "It devastated the group," admitted Philpott. "It was like we failed. Here was a guy, we were meeting at his house, and now he's dead."

To this day, Philpott adamantly denies any connection to McIntyre's death. Instead, he claims that his suicide was a result of mental health deficiencies and drug abuse. "I think Jack had difficulty with prescription drugs," said Philpott. "He had enormous mood swings, probably [what] we would call bipolar." Philpott described Evans as happy one day and depressed the next.

I asked Philpott if McIntyre's suicide could have been caused by his disappointment with LIA's futile attempts to help him change, as suggested in his suicide note. He admitted that this was how others viewed it, but, when asked how he felt about this characterization, as do most ex-gay apologists, Philpott used the "free will" argument to justify this tragedy. "How can that possibly be true? He contacted us. He wanted to be a part of the group," insisted Philpott.

What Philpott overlooks, however, is the pain and mental anguish McIntyre must have been in to *want* to join a group that attempted to change his sexual orientation.

The fissure over McIntyre's suicide grew into an irreconcilable chasm. Philpott eventually kicked Evans out of the ministry and replaced him with Worthen, who would go on to become the group's perennial leader. As for Philpott, he ultimately left the Church of the Open Door. "I went through a divorce, and I know they pretty well wrote me out of the history of it [LIA]," explained Philpott.

The irreverent reverend is now the pastor of the Miller Avenue Baptist Church in Mill Valley, California, and, not surprising, a televangelist on a local cable channel. "I'm an old-time gospel preacher," he said with pride as we ended our interview.

In the years since he left LIA, Evans has taken an active role in warning people about the dangers of the Frankenstein monster he played a key role in creating. The following are excerpts from an interview he had with this author about his LIA experience and the modern ex-gay ministries:

- When asked how the ministries affected his life, Evans replied, "I lost my lover. He went insane, . . . and my best friend went insane and killed himself. I've seen the broken lives and . . . pick[ed] up the pieces. I see what a catastrophe it is when they see that the 'cure' is not possible, and that means they're going to hell. People have actually gone crazy [over this]."
- Asked what happens to those who become disappointed by the ministries, Evans explained, "When they are asked to leave [LIA] they are literally just kicked out on the street. I know many people that were just devastated. We have a group in San Rafael that just collects the Love in Action dropouts."
- When questioned whether he ever publicly takes on the ministries, Evans described how he confronted ex-gay leaders at a conference: "One time I did and the hate was unbelievable. They finally were going to call the police and told me to get off the campus. They are so angry and then they claim you are 'of the devil.' They're terrible people. It's so sad what they're doing,

but I thank God that there are groups out there like . . . Evangelicals Concerned . . . that the message [that one can be Christian and gay] is getting out."

- In response to the question of how the ministries react to his exposing them publicly, he said, "My life has been threatened. . . . I was on *60 Minutes, 48 Hours,* and all the talk shows. I finally had to change my phone number. . . . I'd get calls two or three in the morning, 'You're going to hell,' or 'You are going to cause my children to turn gay.'"

- Asked whether Worthen's misrepresentations of gay life anger him, Evans replied, "Frank's description of gay life was hitting the bathhouses, the glory holes, . . . that's not real gay life. I had a lover for twenty years [who] passed away, and my lover now, we have been together for nearly eleven years, and we're monogamous."

- When prodded for his views on why the ministries regularly misrepresent gay life to attract people to their programs, Evans explained, "They are making so much money that if they did tell the truth, their whole pyramid would collapse. . . . People make a good living off of it."

- Asked what he thought about John Paulk being caught in a gay bar, Evans said, "In a way it makes me mad . . . but down inside, I know how he feels, and I actually feel sorry for him."

- When questioned about his feelings regarding *The Third Sex?* and the people who had not changed sexual orientation as suggested in the book, Evans explained, "A few years later [after publication of *The Third Sex?*], four of us that were in the book, we filed a lawsuit against him [Philpott] and the local publisher. We said, 'This is damaging to us. We're still gay. We're not changed.' So that was when the book *The Third Sex?* was taken off the market."

- Asked how he feels about Philpott today, Evans said, "One day we had lunch and I said, 'I . . . disapprove of what you did, but being a Christian I will forgive you.' His reply to me was, 'John, I will never say anything bad about homosexuality again.' But, knowing Kent, it's hard to trust him."

Evans's admonition about not trusting Philpott is solid advice that should be heeded. When I first began my interview with the reverend,

I was startled when he pretended not to know Evans's name, feigning only vague familiarity with the LIA cofounder whom he had intimately known for nearly three decades. "What was his name?" Philpott asked, as if perplexed and searching to remember an obscure person from high school whom he hadn't thought of in years. "John . . . I'm looking at a painting of his now. John was a Sausalito artist."

"John Evans," I replied. After I had offered the last name, Philpott no longer feigned not remembering Evans. In fact, he vividly recalled conversations they had had and intimate details about Evans's life. Still, it was chilling that this man who had helped ruin Evans's life was completely at ease with his deceit. The more I thought about it, however, the more I realized, What else should I have expected? From day one, Love in Action has stood on a false foundation and today continues as a mirage, offering false hope to desperate and lonely people.

Scene II: Just Jack's Undercover Adventure

Jack Pantaleo looked across the cavernous church and saw a man so distraught and utterly downtrodden that he worried the man might commit suicide on the spot. This individual looked as though a steamroller had crushed his spirit and his soul had been thrown into a Cuisinart.[8]

"Let me guess, you're a Love in Action dropout," Pantaleo gently prodded.

The humiliated, trembling figure was unable to speak and simply nodded affirmatively at his inquisitor.

As the founder of Evangelicals Concerned, San Francisco, a national fellowship of gay evangelical Christians, Pantaleo had seen an increasing number of men and women similar to this individual. They came seeking spiritual guidance after LIA had devastated their lives. Some of these folks had been unceremoniously thrown out of LIA and into the street for falling off the "hetero wagon." Other LIA refugees had voluntarily left the program midstream because they realized it was a fraud. Still others had graduated from the group's multiyear, live-in program and believed they had been "healed," only to come to the bleak realization that, once out of the close confines of LIA, they were still homosexuals. No matter a person's unique situation, what they all had in common was they equated failing in Love in Action with failing God.

"I was really frightened by what I had heard," said Pantaleo. "People were telling me that they were being confined to the houses in San Rafael where Love in Action was stationed at the time. I had heard some people were very suicidal . . . and it hit home then that this was serious and dangerous."

It was 1980 and a lot had changed in LIA since the early days. After Reverend Kent Philpott's moral mudslide, the well-organized and hyperambitious Frank Worthen took over. Worthen transformed the group into a full-time, live-in program, but the constant surveillance and surrender of personal possessions to LIA's leaders led to charges by some people that it was a cult. Even Philpott was somewhat troubled by what had become of his organization. "I've had people say there are cultic aspects of it," said Philpott. "I wish them well . . . but maybe [they should be] recapturing a little bit of the old vision of being a [Christian] support group."

Pantaleo, convinced it was a cult, had seen enough of the human wreckage and decided he would check out the ministry. Although the idea of going undercover frightened him, he thought infiltrating the group would help him minister to the LIA refugees who came to him in despair. Pantaleo entered LIA by attending their twice-monthly recruiting meetings at the Nineteenth Avenue Baptist Church in San Francisco.

At the first meeting, the stealthy activist was pulled aside by Worthen and given the two basic ground rules a person had to accept before being allowed to take part in LIA meetings: a person had to acknowledge verbally that homosexuality was sinful behavior, and all remnants of gay life had to be purged immediately. This included giving up sex, dumping a life partner, abandoning gay friendships, and disposing of all gay paraphernalia. Worthen pushed hard in this initial meeting for Pantaleo to say homosexuality was a sin, but the undercover advocate found a way to get around this requirement. "I'm here to find the truth. Is it OK if I stay under those conditions?" Grimacing at Pantaleo, Worthen reluctantly agreed but warned him that he would soon have to play by the rules.

The first meeting began very much like any other church group service. The participants read Bible verses and sang uplifting hymns. Soon, however, it became clear that this was not your typical church social, when the people gathered in a large circle to talk about temptation and the difficulty they were having with same-sex fantasies. What initially struck Pantaleo was that no one seemed to be "healed" from homosexuality. For some, these daily battles were painful, yet manageable. For others in the group of roughly thirty-five, the experience was crushing.

"At one point, a man named Dan fell on his knees with tears streaming down his face," recounted Pantaleo in our interview. "He confessed being attracted to another man in the room and begged the man for forgiveness. Finally, he lay prone on the floor, begging God for forgiveness for having sexual feelings for the man, and I was shocked by the true horror of where I was and it really hit me," he continued. "It was just a devastating feeling, how I hurt for this man." Later in that meeting, the focus became teaching the group how to cross their legs. As Pantaleo explained, "They said, 'Real men cross ankle over ankle or on the opposite knee. But only the effeminate cross knee over knee.' I really thought it was a joke at first, but they were very serious."

At the next meeting, each person prayed to find the root cause of his or her sexual orientation. The program was a strange brew of old-time fundamentalism and New Age psychology. To find the root, the participants desperately scoured their pasts for hints of trauma that might have triggered their homosexuality. Many of the people pointed fingers at their parents, while others blamed sexual abuse.

By the third month, LIA's leaders grew wary of Pantaleo's refusal to submit to their rules. Worthen, in front of the group, demanded Pantaleo say homosexuality is a sin, but the headstrong activist would say only that he was still "searching for the truth." This infuriated Worthen and he called in the group's "hatchet man" to interrogate Pantaleo and break down his resistance.

"He began to quote scripture . . . in Leviticus [where] it says, 'A man shall not lie with a male as with a female; if he does he shall be put to death.' And he kept repeating that and repeating that, and he says, 'Don't you know what it says in Leviticus?' . . . I was quite stunned that he was giving me the third degree like this," Pantaleo continued. "He began to yell, and then he would shift to different scriptural passages. . . . After about an hour and a half, he gave up and he said, 'There is nothing more I can do for you.' "

Pantaleo suspects that LIA's leaders became suspicious after the failed cross-examination and had him followed. The alleged sleuthing led to a climactic confrontation one evening at San Francisco's primarily gay Metropolitan Community Church where Pantaleo was slated to give a speech on the ex-gay ministries. "When I walked out to speak, I was stunned that a good half of the audience was people from Love in Action," said Pantaleo. "There were two people at each door . . . and they stood there saying 'We place the blood of the lamb over this sanctuary. May the people in here die, so they cannot spread anything evil.' "

Once he began speaking, the angry ex-gays became unruly, interrupting his speech and verbally abusing him. "Dan, the man who was so guilt-ridden [during the first meeting] stood up and began yelling at me that I was a traitor, a murderer, and that I had deceived them all," said Pantaleo. "So I said, 'I understand you feel betrayed, . . . and I consider some of you friends, but I want you to know this is the true story of who I am and what I believe.' "

Pantaleo's undercover journey gave him firsthand experience and a rare window into the ex-gay world. Still, even armed with his new knowledge, the process of healing those harmed by the ex-gay ministries is an onerous task. "I don't know of one person at any period of time in an ex-gay group who has come out unscathed. The scars are so deeply ingrained in people, [and] the guilt is so deeply ingrained."

Still, Pantaleo remains sanguine and believes groups such as Evangelicals Concerned and the Metropolitan Community Church can offer hope to victims of the ex-gay ministries. "What really changed people, what really got them to begin to accept that maybe they could be loved as they are, is by being with other like-minded people, . . . by seeing the gift of the Spirit manifest in others."

Scene III: From Marquee to Marked Man, the Wade Richards Story

On an unseasonably cool March 2000 evening, I lay in bed in my Washington condo with my eyes half closed, tightly cradling the phone to my ear. I suddenly heard an audible click, reminding me that I had absentmindedly forgotten to turn off the call-waiting feature before the radio show. I cringed as I pictured the many thousands of drivers and people at work and at home laughing at my faux pas as they listened to the heated conversation.

"It's written in the Bible," admonished a Brooklyn caller with a thick Jamaican accent. "Homosexuality is a curse and lesbianism too! Wade needs some help because the devil is busy out there."

The caller on Alan Colmes's nationally syndicated radio show was referring to Wade Richards, an ex-gay spokesman representing the Saviors Alliance for Lifting the Truth (SALT), a struggling right-wing start-up based in Los Angeles. The SALT had just moved into new digs near the gay Mecca of West Hollywood. From inside a dusty, barren office, Richards, twenty-one, maneuvered his way around stacks of unpacked boxes to argue that gays could change "through the power of Jesus Christ"—as he brashly proclaimed he had done three years earlier.

"The caller is right," replied Richards. "If we let history take its place, we'll see it to be true. In prefallen Rome, when the homosexual agenda and community became very much an acceptable lifestyle, Rome fell."

I briefly pressed the mute button to let out an uproarious laugh. The very thought of a "gay agenda" in ancient Rome was just too funny for words. I was picturing the Roman Senate debating a domestic partners bill, and Caesar weighing the political implications of allowing gays to serve openly in the military. Richards may have needed a history lesson, but he was a worthy opponent who had the gift of sounding extraordinarily sincere when delivering his testimony. He had perhaps the most earnest voice I had ever heard on radio.

As the hour-long show progressed, the debate intensified. "Why would you want to change [sexual orientation]?" asked Colmes, the liberal talk show host.

"The lifestyle was so unfulfilling," Richards solemnly declared. "The sex acts were so unfulfilling. It was deceptive. The relationships I was in were emotionally abusive."

Adequately worked up, I rose out of bed and stalked around the darkened bedroom as I tersely replied, "You're saying that people should change because you had bad sex and [made] bad choices in your relationships? Can the reverse work for straights?

"If you choose to change, you can, and it is possible. There is a way out. . . . I know that I can change this through the power of Jesus Christ."

A caller broke in: "Isn't it ridiculous for you who is supposedly still struggling with your homosexuality to go out across the country and preach? Who are you?"

The battle raged on, reaching its crescendo when Richards delivered an impassioned plea for gays to turn to Jesus to become straight. "God's plan is for us to be men of God, not men of homosexuality. . . . But yes, I am free from the bondage of my homosexual mind-set. I no longer deal with sexual issues, no longer deal with masturbation issues. I have joy. I have peace that surpasses all understanding."

"Alan, never trust a person who says he never masturbates." Click.

"Well, that's all folks," said Colmes. "I'd like to thank our guests Wade Richards from the SALT and Wayne Besen from the Human Rights Campaign."

Despite Richards's obvious passion and persuasive storytelling abilities, I knew a little secret. As with nearly all ex-gays, he was fighting an internal war; he desperately wanted to come out but did not know how. I sensed that he was frantically searching for help, and so as the show-ending music was cued I offered it. "Wade, one day, you, like all people trapped in the ex-gay lifestyle, will come out. And when you are ready, contact me. I'll be here to support you." The piped-in music finally overshadowed my voice and the gig was over.

After the show, Richards left his West Coast office feeling dejected and a bit shaken. Although he had sounded supremely confident on the air, only weeks before he had met a young man in a West Hollywood coffee shop who had set his head to spinning and made Wade question whether he had actually changed, as he believed he had. Even after years of working tirelessly to become straight, just one smile from the right boy cracked the facade of his ex-gay identity. Although he had abstained from having an intimate relationship with this young man, he knew it was what he wanted more than anything else in the world, but Wade felt he had to try to continue to fight his feelings because he had invested so much of his life in changing.[9]

Wade Richards was born into a Wisconsin family that was in absolute disarray. His mother and father were married to other people, each with a separate family, but they both dumped their spouses and married each other. However, the union was short-lived, as his parents divorced before Wade was a year old. As a result, he claims his mother became emotionally unstable, leaving no one to adequately care for him.

As early as elementary school Wade became aware that he might be gay. To rid himself of these feelings, he tried to do "guy stuff," such as play sports and chase girls. Instead of finding a refuge in sports, however, he found rejection. He became the subject of endless taunts and harassment because of his effeminate behavior. Richards described himself as starving for male affirmation and attention.

A few years later, a man in Wade's neighborhood sexually abused him. The experience, which lasted five years, made him feel "dirty," "used," and "broken." Still, he continued to return time and again because he enjoyed receiving the attention that he so desperately craved from another man.

Shortly after his twelfth birthday, he attended a church youth group at the invitation of a girl with whom he was friends, and that night he asked to receive Jesus as his Lord and savior. He thought that after he became a Christian his homosexual feelings would end and he would feel like a "normal" guy.

After three years, however, Wade was distraught because he was unable to pray away the gay, so he explored his homosexuality primarily through short-term relationships and anonymous sexual encounters with older men. During this period he would go to gay bars and stay out all night using drugs.

Unable to fully express himself as an openly gay man at home, Wade left rural Wisconsin and moved to New York City where he ended up prostituting himself for an older gay couple. After two weeks they fired him, making him feel even more like a failure. Desperate and hungry, Wade moved into a youth shelter where he was led to a nearby church and met a group of men who befriended him. For the first time in his life he felt secure and safe. He joined Bible studies with them and learned homosexuality was a sin. Then he decided he would leave his sexual orientation behind and become straight. A pastor suggested that he join Love in Action, a live-in ex-gay group in Memphis, and he did.[10]

Wade got off the plane in Memphis and was greeted at the airport by Love in Action's leaders Frank and Anita Worthen. The Worthens drove to a large house located in an ordinary leafy suburban neighborhood. Inside the house, Wade's luggage was crudely dumped out,

as a team of nosy queens rummaged through his most personal possessions, picking out items they deemed inappropriate. "I was in shock,"
confessed Richards. "They took away my Calvin Klein underwear . . .
because they believed it's an FI, [which stands for] false image. It
seemed to be more of a sex appeal [issue] for men to wear Calvin
Klein than it would if they wore Fruit of the Loom. But anything like
that—old pictures, even of my friends, because they believed [they
were] FI."

LIA housed ten homosexual "strugglers" in four large rooms, as
well as staff who were hired for twenty-four-hour penis patrol. This
surveillance wasn't cheap: $950 per month, plus a $2,000 initiation
fee. For this charge, one was assigned a personal staff member, received room and board, given ex-gay reading material, referred to an
on-site Christian psychologist, and assigned a temporary job, though
most of the money earned went to pay for the exorbitant program fee.

It took between one and a half to three years to graduate, depending on how quickly one completed the five-phase curriculum. "There's
people who are very friendly from day one," explained Richards,
"and then there's people who had been there for a while who . . . were
pretty harsh."

Several times a week the "clients" were taken to LIA's offices for
sessions of group prayer and behavior modification classes, which included lipstick application seminars for women and touch football
games for men. Of course, these activities did not make anyone
straight. They just created lipstick lesbians and gay men who could
tell the difference between a first down and a touchdown.

Following their "makeovers," the group of men and women would
separate into small units to explore the "roots" of their homosexuality. Using the work of Christian psychologist Elizabeth Moberly,[11]
Love in Action counselors explained to Wade that he was homosexual because while growing up his father had been distant and aloof.
This supposedly traumatized Wade and made him ultimately reject
his father, as well as his male peers. The way to become straight, according to Moberly's theory, was for Wade to form nonsexual same-
sex friendships, which would eventually allow him to see men in a
nonsexual way. Once members of the same sex are "demystified," the
homosexual loses interest, according to Moberly, and begins to fancy
the opposite sex. However, at LIA, the same-sex friendships they en-

couraged sometimes became a little too buddy-buddy, leaving those in the know to call the place "Love the Action."

"Did people do it [have sex]? Did it happen? It did," said Richards. He explained that it didn't happen all the time because most people were highly motivated to change and subject to constant surveillance. People who were caught got thrown out of the program if they didn't shape up. These people often left feeling confused, guilty, and more ashamed than ever. Once gone, they were considered FI, so other group members were allowed no further contact with them. "The treatment of those who were dismissed or chose to leave the program was hard and inhumane, in my view," said Richards.

Although Moberly's theory lacked solid scientific basis, Wade eagerly embraced it because her causation model mirrored his own life: he was not close to his father and had been rejected by his male peers. Wade finally felt he had all of the answers to why his life was so screwed up for the short duration he was an openly gay teenager, and he truly did believe he was changing because his life was improving so drastically in nearly every area. He had a group of people who cared for him, he was working full-time, and gone were the days of mindless promiscuity and mind-numbing drug abuse. These tangible developments combined with the ubiquitous man monitors diverting his libido made him feel as if he were in the fast lane to heterosexuality. In fact, he was so confident that "change" was at hand, he was prominently featured in a segment about LIA on the ABC newsmagazine *20/20*.

Even in the zenith of his "transformation," however, he faced disquieting hints that he was still gay. For example, on one of his temp jobs, an attractive openly gay man shared the same lunch hour as Wade. After it became impossible to shut out completely all sexual thoughts of his co-worker, Wade asked his superiors if he could eat lunch at a later time. Through deceptive maneuvers such as this, he was able to repress his sexual orientation and successfully buy into the illusion that he was no longer gay. After persevering for a year and a half, Wade became the youngest "graduate" in the group's history, and the only client in his class to make it through the entire program.

The ink was hardly dry on Wade's LIA diploma when the SALT's ambitious young leader Christine O'Donnell hired him to speak out against gay issues. "Here I am, literally overnight, an 'ex-gay' poster child," exclaimed Richards. "It was amazing. . . . For the first time I thought I was being heard. It was definitely exhilarating!" The SALT paraded Wade around as "living proof" that homosexuals could change. They shined a spotlight on him, giving him numerous speaking engagements and media appearances.

The highlight of his ex-gay career came when he was a featured speaker at an Americans for Truth press conference at the celebrated National Press Club in Washington, DC. The group's founder, Peter LaBarbera, is notorious for donning leather garb and sneaking into sundry gay S&M bars to take supposedly incriminating pictures of naughty gays. LaBarbera is obsessive with following the seamier side of gay life, even frequenting establishments where gay sex occurs. For him, no bathhouses are too remote to discover, and no dark, grimy dungeons not worthy of exploration. It is no exaggeration to say that the man has probably frequented more gay venues than RuPaul and Mr. Leather USA combined.[12]

"[Peter] was very intense," said Richards. "The office freaked me out. I had never seen so much gay pornography in my whole life. . . . It was crazy. . . . [There were] thousands [of gay magazines]—all kinds. . . . [He said they were] for research. . . . I had no clue what fisting was until I met Peter LaBarbera. . . . It was a crazy experience."

Despite his very public statements of "change," reality was beginning to surface. He was out of the group, with no man monitors, and the real world was full of earthly temptations. Richards explained, "I now lived and breathed this program and I had hardly [any] contact with homosexual people. . . . I move out on my own . . . and now what do I do? How do I live my life and . . . what happens when I have a same-sex attraction? You think you are trained to deal with these issues and you are not. . . . Why was it so much easier for me to deal with it in the program? Well, it was because you were on twenty-four-hour surveillance."

Four months later, I was in my office with my head draped over the air conditioner to cool off from the scorching DC summer heat. I sat down in my oversized burgundy chair and peered up at my computer screen to read my e-mail:

Dear Wayne,

It is Wade Richards from the Alan Colmes radio show. You said to call when I was ready to come out. Well, I'm taking you up on your offer. Please keep this confidential.

Wade Richards

Within a week of sending the e-mail, Wade came to the Human Rights Campaign's office and we went to lunch. Over plates of pad thai and crisp spring rolls at Café Asia, we discussed his desire to flee the ex-gay movement. He knew he had had enough, but he was scared of reprisals from the far right. He was well aware that, to avoid a PR nightmare, they would do everything in their power to keep him, and if he did defect successfully, the far right would work to undermine his credibility. Wade, believe it or not, also felt guilty because the right had invested so much in him, and now he felt he was letting them down.

As the news of Richards's possible defection reached fundamentalist and ex-gay circles, Wade was frantically contacted by all of the major ex-gay and antigay organizations: the Family Research Council, Focus on the Family, Love in Action, Exodus, and, of course, the SALT, where he had taken a "leave of absence." They desperately tried to woo him back. However, the one thing they could not offer him was the option to be himself—an out and proud gay man.

Wade agreed to tell his story to *The Advocate*'s Chris Bull, and, shortly thereafter, it hit newsstands, sending shudders down the spines of the ex-gay ministries and the religious right. Predictably, the people who once had celebrated Wade now dismissed him with scorn. At a Family Research Council press conference, LaBarbera told me that Wade was just "a confused little boy." Before a television show debate, the SALT's O'Donnell described Wade to me as a lost kid who had absolutely no credibility.

It is amazing that as long as he was toeing the religious right's party line, his age was irrelevant and his credibility was beyond reproach, but now that he had defected, he was an inexperienced, untrustworthy pariah who lacked integrity. Despite the unrelenting fire from his former "moral" allies, Wade was happy he had elected to come out. "The experience was liberating," said Richards, who has started a successful gay activist youth group called StandOut in Huntsville, Alabama. For his efforts, *The Advocate* magazine named him one of America's most innovative activists in July 2001.

"I know if someone had said to me . . . it's OK that you're gay, . . . [I wouldn't have had] to explore my homosexuality in ways that would be destructive." Richards wants to work as a mentor to gay youth to keep them from making the same mistakes he did.

Richards also recently came out to his mother and father. "My dad's cool. . . . He's a big, burly, Harley-Davidson mechanic, and he had said, 'Son, some people are born left-handed and some people right-handed. Some people are gay and some people aren't. I love you.' . . . [My mother] was pretty horrified at first. But . . . she asked me today, 'Wade, are you really happy? All I want to know is are you really happy and I'll be happy for you. I will support you.' I said, 'Mom, I've never been happier.'" Following in the footsteps of LIA cofounder John Evans, former ex-gay poster boy Wade Richards has found his voice and now warns people about the dangers of conversion ministries.

Founding Follies

The Ex-Gay Movement Goes Worldwide

The success of Reverend Kent Philpott's book, *The Third Sex,* spread false hope to small pockets of tormented homosexuals throughout the fundamentalist world. Although no one in his book actually had changed, the people reading it had no idea the stories were fallacious. As far as they knew, a magical place offered the secret for making gays into straights. Inspired by his book, a few enthusiastic individuals spontaneously began their own ex-gay ministries.

Within three years, more than a dozen such ministries organically sprang up in such places as Los Angeles, Minneapolis, Montreal, and Tulsa. As these ministries serendipitously became aware of one another, two leading ex-gay counselors at Melodyland Christian Center in Anaheim, California, Gary Cooper and Michael Bussee, decided to organize a conference where the ex-gays could meet one another and network. In September 1976, Cooper and Bussee's vision was realized, as sixty-two ex-gays journeyed to Melodyland for the world's first ex-gay conference. The outcome of the retreat was the formation of Exodus International, an umbrella organization for ex-gay groups worldwide. The new group would serve as a way to promote ex-gay theories and as a referral service to help people find an ex-gay ministry near their homes.[1]

A Tale of Two Founders

Learning Shame at the Liebrary

Michael Bussee was a twelve-year-old with a big secret. While other boys in his class were awkwardly discovering a newfound attraction to girls, Bussee found himself coming to the horrifying realization that he liked boys. It was the mid-1960s in suburban Riverside, California, and there seemed nowhere that a struggling lad could turn for information on homosexuality. At the time, gay people in Riverside were invisible, either blending into society by living a lie or surviving on society's margins, furtively meeting in dark, clandestine places. Bussee truly felt as if he were the only person in the world who had these feelings. Desperate for answers, the confused young man ventured into the Riverside Public Library and anxiously searched the dusty card catalog for books on the topic. "They listed, oh, ten or fifteen books on homosexuality; of course, all of them were negative," said Bussee in our interview. "The books that I found, I had to ask the librarian to see them because they were all marked 'locked case.' So, they were naughty books, and it was very distressing, very disturbing."

Once Bussee began looking through the books, he only felt worse. All of them listed homosexuality as either a perversion or a psychosexual abnormality, but one of the books held out a sliver of hope: if a person is bisexual, highly intelligent, motivated, and young, it might be possible to change his or her orientation. Although Bussee felt no attraction to the opposite sex, he desperately grasped this information, hoping he was still young enough to change.

Fishing for Answers

In high school, Bussee considered himself an atheist, although he had grown up in a moderately religious household, with his family frequently attending the Reorganized Church of Jesus Christ of Latter-Day Saints, a Mormon Church breakaway group. One afternoon in his senior year, Bussee read a flyer advertising a meeting of the Fish Club, the school's Christian group. Bussee thought it would be fun to go to a meeting and razz the members. "I'm gonna go, and I'm gonna talk these people out of their faith," Bussee said of his intentions. "And the opposite happened . . . the idea that there was a God who created everything and that loved me was a very attractive idea. . . . But I didn't tell anyone I had gay feelings then. I was searching."

The Hotline at Biblical Broadway

Bussee's burgeoning faith continued to grow in college at California State University, Fullerton, where he was pursuing a master's degree in psychology. While at Cal State in 1974 he met a volunteer for the Melodyland Christian Center who asked him to use his knowledge in psychology to help at the megachurch's crisis hotline.

The church, located across the street from Disneyland, was a former theater-in-the-round seating 3,000 people. Bussee described it as sort of a biblical Broadway. "It was one of these huge neocharismatic circuses. It was a huge production every Sunday, with lighting and sound and an orchestra and choir. Lots of gays were attracted to it."

Bussee agreed to volunteer at the superchurch, but on the volunteer application one of the questions was, "Is there anything else in your background, for example, former drug user, former homosexual, etc., that might influence your ability to be a counselor?" The question shook Bussee but also intrigued him. "My eyes just glued on that 'former homosexual' and I thought, 'Former homosexual? Is that possible?' "

Bussee did not answer the question but eventually went to the head of the hotline service to discuss his problem. "You know, when I filled out that application, I left it blank that I'm Christian and homosexual," Bussee nervously confessed. According to Bussee, the hotline leader replied, "No, you're not. If you're a Christian, you're no longer homosexual. That's gone." The leader opened the Bible to I Corinthians 6:11 and pointed to the words "And such were some of you," which was interpreted to mean that a number of sinners, including homosexuals, had changed their wicked ways.

"They believe in what came to be known as a kind of 'name and claim theology,' " said Bussee, "that you may not be completely healed now, but by claiming that you're healed and continuing to claim that you're healed, God will eventually reward that faithfulness and cause the actual healing."

Bussee was perplexed, if not more than a little skeptical. He knew that in the Bible when Jesus healed a blind man, for instance, he could see—immediately. This slow, faith-based healing process seemed somewhat unbiblical to Bussee, but he so much wanted to be heterosexual that he began to rationalize the hotline leader's words. "What he told me is that I needed to start considering myself a former homosexual," Bussee continued, "even if I didn't feel that way. . . . And I said, 'But I'm not heterosexual, and I don't have any feelings toward women.'" To which the man replied, "That doesn't matter. The Bible says you are a former homosexual; therefore, you are."

"It was the early seventies and the height of the Jesus movement," Bussee said. "There were all sorts of people coming forward and telling all sorts of testimonies about how they used to be a heroin addict or they used to be a prostitute, . . . there were exes everywhere . . . so I thought, 'Well, maybe the same kind of thing would be possible when it comes to your orientation.'"

Reflecting on his past, Bussee now sees some of the mental techniques and semantic tricks he used to fool himself as a form of mind control. "I guess the more you say something, the more you believe it. And the more it's reinforced to you, the more you believe it."

A Good Woman Is the Cure

Around the same time, Bussee started dating a wonderful woman named Anne, an attractive anthropology major from the university. As the couple grew closer, he eventually told Anne about his struggles with homosexuality. To his great delight, she was supportive and vowed to help him overcome his problem. As the relationship flourished emotionally and spiritually, the couple finally decided to have sex. To Bussee's amazement, he was able to remain sexually aroused, although he said he "didn't enjoy it terrifically." His ability to perform, however, allowed him to convince himself that he was on the right path to heterosexuality. "Because God has brought this woman into my life," explained Bussee. "And I had read something when I was younger that said if you were really a homosexual it would be impossible for you to have a relationship with a woman. I thought, 'Well, here I am having a relationship with a woman.'"

Even after their relationship was consummated, the struggles continued. Michael would often confess his homosexual fantasies to Anne, and the couple would pray for God's mercy and forgiveness. Through it all, Anne and Michael stayed together and eventually decided to get married. "I would tell . . . leaders at Melodyland that I was still having a struggle. They said, 'Every Christian still struggles, so don't worry about that.' Nobody said, 'Well, hey, maybe you shouldn't get married then.'" As a result of the recurring fantasies, they did postpone their wedding on several occasions, but they eventually tied the knot in a wedding that never should have taken place.

Love at Hot*line*

Bussee increased the time he spent at the church crisis hotline and worked with another "former homosexual" taking calls from people deeply troubled by their own homosexuality or that of a family member. One day a young man named Gary Cooper, who was also fighting his homosexuality, came in to volunteer. The young blond, a married man with two children, was studying at Melodyland School of Theology to become a minister. Although Bussee and Cooper could not admit it then, they felt an instant, overwhelming chemistry between them. "I just thought he was the cutest thing," admitted Bussee. "It was immediate attraction. He was a father; I was about to become a father. He was my age, similar kind of struggle. . . . He was deeply Christian, deeply religious, and just on a physical and emotional level there was a definite attraction."

The hotline proved to be a challenge for the three "former homosexual" volunteers. Mirroring the ignorance of society, many of the phone counselors were deep and endless reservoirs of prejudice and misinformation. They regularly counseled gays by repeating hateful myths and propagating ugly stereotypes. "They thought all homosexuals were child molesters," explained Bussee. "They thought all homosexuals had been beaten or molested by their fathers, and we heard them saying these things to callers on the telephone. So we both thought we needed to educate our own counselors so they didn't say stupid things on the phone."

To combat this ignorance, the "former homosexuals" created a monthly workshop to train counselors at Melodyland. It was so successful that word spread quickly to other churches and the men were suddenly in demand to speak on this issue. They also started a support group and prayer meeting at Melodyland that was designed to cure homosexuals. While forming this group, Bussee coined the term *ex-gay*. "We were struggling with what to call ourselves," said Bussee.

"We thought, 'Let's call it EXIT,' and it stood for Ex-Gay Intervention Team. Who you gonna call, you know? We're gay busters. It was that kind of feeling."

Word of this ministry soon filtered through the fundamentalist grapevine, and EXIT began receiving letters requesting help from people throughout the country. As the ministry grew, the leaders of EXIT began to come into contact with leaders from other fledgling groups. One afternoon, Michael and Gary decided they should bring these diverse ministry groups together to meet. "It would be cool to get all these people together and share our experiences and find out if they are on the same wavelength as we are," Bussee said. "So, we decided to host a conference, and it was quite a collection of individuals!"

The Big Coming-Out Party

In September 1976, Melodyland hosted an eclectic group of characters that had one thing in common: they hated their homosexuality and desperately wanted to be heterosexual. The atmosphere in the mammoth Anaheim cathedral was festive, though, with Bussee describing it as a "big coming-out party." "Most of these people have been so closeted and so isolated and never told anybody within the church that they were gay," Bussee said. "Finally, here is a place where they could say, 'You too? Ah, me too.'"

Despite the fantastic sense of relief felt by many of the participants, a profound sense of shame permeated the gathering. Many people went to bizarre lengths to hide their true selves. "There was one transsexual who went through the operation and then became a Christian and now was living as a man again. So he had deliberately put on an extra one hundred pounds so that you couldn't notice his breasts as much. He was a hoot. He was so fun and so sincere and so screwed up."

Even at the first conference there was disagreement over whether using the term *ex-gay* was dishonest. One group of conference participants believed that using the controversial term was appropriate because it was an expression of faith and they believed healing was possible. A competing bloc of participants thought that true heterosexuality was unattainable and promoted the use of the term *homosexual celibacy.* In other words, they believed that Exodus should be honest about its limitations.

Cooper and Bussee were in favor of the term *ex-gay,* with their lives ostensibly reflecting the absolute change they fanatically preached. Bussee was married and had one child, while Cooper was married with three children. The two Exodus cofounders were, it appeared, living proof of God's ability to transform homosexuals into heterosexuals.

Apostles of Change

The founding of Exodus created numerous speaking opportunities for Bussee and Cooper, who were now inseparable friends. They were apostles of change dedicated to spreading the "good news" of their conversions across the nation. The two men traveled extensively together, visiting churches and conferences to give their captivating testimonies. As charismatic spokespeople, they were extraordinarily convincing, and their "performances" were applauded by enthusiastic Christian audiences. Part of their success on the speaking circuit came from their natural chemistry together; they liked each other immensely. This enthusiasm came out in their presentations, and audiences picked up on that.

In fact, their lives had become increasingly intertwined. Their wives were best friends, and so were two of their daughters, born a week apart. Gary's sons called Bussee "Uncle Mike." The two families took day trips together, went camping, and barbequed at each other's houses. Cooper's family eventually moved into the same apartment complex as Bussee's.

This unusually close bonding might have raised alarm in some people, but Bussee said his wife embraced the situation. "My wife was relieved that I had somebody who understood, to talk to, because she was, quite frankly, puzzled by me. Here I was calling myself an ex-gay and yet she's crying herself to sleep almost every night because I would never initiate sex with her. So when Gary came along and we became friends, she finally met a friend, Gary's wife, and they had so much in common. They both had husbands who were struggling with the gay issue, they both had kids, and they both were Christians."

Over time, the two men grew progressively closer through their extensive time on the road. Bussee and Cooper had a vibrant personal connection; they would complete each other's sentences and could talk to each other for hours. Clearly, Bussee and Cooper were in love, but this truth remained unspoken, while the lies resounded within churches across America. As the wives stayed behind to care for their families, the two ex-gays often traveled to far-away churches to give their riveting testimonies.

The Plane-*Spoken Truth*

One day, the two men were on an airplane headed to Indianapolis to speak in front of the United Church of Christ General Senate. Bussee was reading a book, *Bless the Beast and the Children,* about a group of boys who never felt that they fit in with other boys. Finally, they realized they were not misfits and decided to release a herd of captive buffalo that were scheduled for slaughter. Moved by the book, about halfway through the trip, Bussee began quietly reading the ending to Cooper.

"There was something about the theme of the book, about breaking out of those constraints and not allowing people to think you're defective and showing what you're really capable of," Bussee explained. "By the end of it, he was crying and I was crying. . . . I said, 'Gary, I can't do this.' And he said, 'What?' 'I can't go there and pretend to be and feel something I don't feel.' . . . And just about that time the stewardess came and saw us both crying, and she saw the book and said, 'Must be a pretty good book.' I said, 'Gary, I have very strong feelings toward you. You know that. I love you as one man to another. I love you as a gay man.' He said that he felt the same way."

After they had acknowledged their feelings toward each other, they discussed how their work was hurting people. "We're damaging people, Gary. I don't believe in what we're doing anymore," said Bussee on the airplane. "I just pray to God that none of these people we counseled committed suicide because of something that we said."[2]

Indeed, there was good reason to worry that people had been hurt by their efforts. The two men claim they counseled "hundreds" of people, many of whom "became suicidal" or "actually attempted suicide." Some of their clients became despondent, while others resorted to self-mutilation when Exodus could not help them. "I had a gentlemen whom I counseled who deliberately slashed his genitals repeatedly with a straight-edged razor and poured Dranó on the wounds because he wasn't able to change his feelings," said Bussee.[3] He also described how another prominent ex-gay leader told him about going to gay bars and even straight bars to try to find people to beat him up because the leader felt so bad about being a failure in the ex-gay ministries.

Interestingly, when the two men arrived in Indianapolis, the hotel accidentally placed them in the same room with one king-size bed— the first time that had ever happened. "We jokingly said that we took that as a sign from God," said Bussee.

With their feelings for each other out in the open, the two lovers could no longer promote the ex-gay illusion. The night before their presentation, they scrapped their old speeches and prepared remarks that reflected their new reality.

The auditorium was packed and conference attendees anxiously awaited what they thought were going to be inspirational stories of "change." That was exactly what they got, but not the type of change they had expected.

In the back of the room angry protesters were prepared to denounce the ex-gays with signs that read "Love Not Cure," but as Bussee and Cooper delivered their remarks, something unexpected occurred. "[The protesters] in the back actually started clapping and the people who had asked us to come there started giving us scowls."

Leaving One Family and Starting Another

Although abandoning Exodus was difficult, it was not nearly as painful as having to break apart their families. Both men were afraid that if they told their wives the truth they would lose custody of their children, so for nearly a year they furtively carried on their relationship while remaining married to their wives. Eventually, however, their double lives took their toll. "The masquerade was over and we had to tell everyone," said Bussee. "It was not a deliberate deception. It was a self-deception. We had fooled ourselves. . . . It's brainwashing. It's the repetitive message that being gay is something you shouldn't be. Being gay is bad."[4]

One night, Bussee's wife brought up the subject of having a second child. The conversation agitated Bussee, who couldn't tell his wife,

Anne, why he didn't want more children. When asked why he didn't want a second child, he replied, " 'Anne, I thought we weren't going to talk about this.' . . . 'Why won't you talk about this?' 'Anne, I'm gay. I'm not ex-gay. My feelings have not changed.' . . . And so she said, 'What are we going to do?' and I said, 'Well, I think we are going to have to divorce. And she and I sat on the living room floor, holding each other and rocking each other and crying. Because neither one of us wanted to have that happen, but we knew that it had to happen."

Within minutes of this event, Bussee received a call from Cooper, who said he had also told his wife that he was gay and wanted a divorce. "We hadn't talked about that," said Bussee. "We hadn't planned that. . . . The timing was striking."

When their wives found out about the affair, they were enraged and threatened to sue for sole custody of the children and deny visitation rights. Eventually they came around, however, and allowed the men to play an active part in the upbringing of their children.

Free at last to be who God intended them to be, their relationship flourished, as the two men got an apartment together in Anaheim. They were such a model couple that friends suggested, half jokingly, that they get married. At first they didn't take the notion too seriously, but the more they thought about it, the more they liked the idea of formalizing their lifelong commitment.

Wearing matching baby blue tuxedos and exchanging vows and wedding bands, the two cofounders of Exodus International married each other on May 9, 1982. Friends and relatives celebrated the commitment ceremony with music, dancing, and a large wedding cake topped with two plastic grooms.

Sadly, in 1991, at the age of thirty-nine, Cooper succumbed to AIDS-related complications. Before he passed away, he and Bussee delivered an inspiring message in a documentary about the ex-gay ministries titled *One Nation Under God.* "People need to learn that being different isn't being bad," they said in the documentary as they were shown walking hand in hand on the beach. "There are a lot of differences within the human population and these are differences that can be appreciated."

Today Bussee lives in Riverside, California, with his significant other of one year, who also happens to be an ex-ex-gay. Bussee is an elder in his Presbyterian church and the director of a counseling program at a psychiatric hospital in Riverside. Nearly three decades after cofounding Exodus International, Bussee still sees the destruction caused by the ex-gay ministries. "I have a guy in my group right now that is an ex-gay fallout. He got married in September and he's saying, 'Oh, God, what have I done?' He's suicidal. He's depressed. He says, 'Oh my God, what a mess.' "

Looking back, Bussee sorrowfully reflected on his key contributions to the formation of Exodus International. "I never expected that it would become that big a deal. . . . . I just kind of wish it would go away. I feel that I'm not proud of the part I played in the formation of it."

Real Courage

Similar to the Bussee and Cooper episode is the story of a pioneer of the ex-gay movement in Great Britain, Jeremy Marks, who renounced Exodus's claims to "heal" gay people in 2001. His revelations rocked the ex-gay movement in England and had transatlantic reverberations when I helped break the story in America.[5]

Marks, forty-eight, grew up in a religious home and did everything in his power to fight his sexual orientation once he discovered he was gay. On his zealous quest for heterosexuality he flew to America in 1987 to meet Love in Action's Frank Worthen. Inspired by the Exodus live-in program, Marks returned to the San Rafael compound, where he spent four months training to start his own Exodus ministry, Courage, in London.

During this time period he married a longtime friend, with whom he remains today. "When I got married in 1991, . . . I said, 'Well, I haven't really changed, but I don't want to spend the rest of my life living a celibate life," Marks said in our interview. "We thought it would be a lot more fun to spend our lives together than on our own. But we didn't go into it with great hopes of having a wild heterosexual life."

As the ministry grew, Marks received media attention from both the secular and the Christian press. One headline in London's *Guardian* newspaper blared, "This Man Wants to Change Britain's Gays and Make Them Straight!"

However, after fourteen years of running London's oldest and largest ex-gay ministry, it was not gays who were changing, but Marks's mind about Exodus's ability to "heal" homosexuals. "It [change in opinion] has been very gradual," explained Marks. "I would share my concerns [with my wife] that many of these things that we had been doing were not truthful. The people hadn't changed their orientation. . . . Some of the ways we minister [are] a dead end."

Marks, a popular member of Exodus Europe's Board of Directors, eventually went public with his new views in his Courage newsletter. Several board members and a few members of his own ministry were infuriated by his candor, but Marks was well liked, so instead of firing him, Exodus allowed him to take an indefinite hiatus. Marks still thinks Exodus can help people, but he now believes that the group should exist to support gay Christians, not condemn them. That means, according to Marks, helping some people remain celibate if that's what they believe God calls on them to do, while for others it means helping them accept themselves as openly gay Christians. Marks no longer believes in the Exodus approach of offering fanciful and phony notions of healing.

"When you look back several years later, you think, . . . '[These people] may have grown in confidence, but they haven't become heterosexual,'" said Marks. "I tracked what was happening to them and . . . some of them had begun to meet [gay people] and explore that, and found it really helpful. And I could see what a difference it had made. They were much more at peace with themselves."

Exodus is not enamored with his new techniques, but Marks's honest approach has attracted new Christian converts. "Because of the change a lot of people started coming who would never come anywhere near us before because they couldn't stand the whole ex-gay thing."

Marks intends to stay married to his wife because he loves her and does not want to break apart his family, but the man who once wanted to "change Britain's gays" is a changed man himself. "I would not treat it as a sin if they [a gay couple] are genuinely gay and love each other and want to share their lives together," explained Marks. "I think their desire to live a life of companionship should be respected and I wouldn't call that a sin."

Lifting the Fraud

> It's like your Alcoholics Anonymous sponsor giving you a drink.
>
> > Former Colin Cook client,
> > after Cook made a pass at him[6]

He was the Bill Clinton of the ex-gay ministries, a Teflon man who brushed off scandals like lint from a sweater. No matter how many times Colin Cook, the charismatic founder of Homosexuals Anonymous, ransacked his personal life and professional reputation, he would rise from the wreckage to lead once again.

Cook was born the son of a fisherman in England and gravitated toward religion at a young age. He became a popular Seventh-Day Adventist pastor, using his supreme intellect and magnetic personality to attract followers, but the preacher had a secret that threatened his career: He was a closeted homosexual who habitually trolled parks and rest rooms for anonymous erotic encounters, racking up more than 1,000 sexual partners in his lifetime.[7]

Cook even once admitted on tape that he had sexually abused teenage boys in England, saying, "I could have been in prison today—a molester."[8] Afraid his illicit sexual misadventures in the United Kingdom might catch up with him, Cook migrated to the United States more than twenty-five years ago. Once in the United States, he took up ministry but was defrocked in 1974 for having sex with a man in his church.[9]

The only thing that surpassed Cook's insatiable sexual appetite was his burning desire to minister, but he knew an openly gay man would have no chance to stand at the pulpit. Thus, he decided to undergo a radical reinvention into a heterosexual using a fourteen-step program he created that was modeled after Alcoholics Anonymous. To complete his transformation he married Sharon, who also was involved in ministry.

Unusually intelligent and a gifted orator, in 1979, Cook convinced church officials that he had been rehabilitated through therapy and was completely healed of his homosexuality. Backed by a $47,000 grant from the Adventists, that year he started an ex-gay ministry, the Quest Learning Center, in Reading, Pennsylvania, and also founded Homosexuals Anonymous (HA), a national ex-gay group.

Through Cook's captivating personality and mesmeric leadership, HA quickly grew to sixty chapters nationwide and threatened Exodus's supremacy as the lead ex-gay organization. Appearing twice on *The Phil Donahue Show,* in the early 1980s, Cook solidified his reputation as the nation's premier ex-gay spokesperson. His media exposure made him a minicelebrity and led self-loathing gay people from across the nation to move to Reading to take part in the Quest live-in program. It seemed, however, that the only "change" Cook wanted people to make was into something a little more comfortable. Rumors began to circulate that Cook was a sexual predator who molested men and even teenage boys.[10]

This led Ron Lawson, an openly gay Adventist and sociology professor at Queens University, to conduct a series of in-depth interviews with disillusioned Cook clients. Eleven of the fourteen erstwhile Quest members Lawson questioned said Cook had hit on them.[11] They claimed that Cook would greet them with hugs—lasting as long as ten minutes—during which he would grind his erect member against their bodies. They also said Cook would lead mutual masturbation sessions, talk dirty to Quest members, and give them nude massages.[12]

"There was never any feeling Colin wanted me to change [orientation], but only that he wanted to have sex with me," said one disheartened former client.[13]

Cook's ex-gay empire ostensibly collapsed in 1986 after Lawson sent a thirteen-page letter to church officials meticulously outlining Cook's indiscretions. The Adventists withdrew their financial support, and the shamed ex-gay closed down Quest and resigned from HA.

Cook told the *Los Angeles Times* that he "fell into the delusion" that nude massage and other questionable activities were a normal and healthy part of counseling to "desensitize" clients to the plea-sures of male flesh. "I allowed myself to hug and hold my counselees thinking I was helping them," Cook told the *Times*. "But I needed it more than they did."[14]

Cook's behavior almost cost him his family as well. "I did not fully realize how difficult it was going to be," said Sharon Cook. "I thought it was in the past. Certainly, I should have asked a lot more ques-tions."[15]

Cook's ex-gay obituary was premature, however, as the protean Cook amazingly reinvented himself again, claiming that he was cured after undergoing rigorous counseling. Gullible church leaders once more bought his act, and he was open for business, as Quest leader, six months after his apparent downfall. HA, too, endured after it was taken over by "John J," a man who once served jail time for mo-lesting boys.[16]

The Adventists' unconcern for Cook's victims infuriated one for-mer Quest member who wrote a letter to the *Adventist Review*, the church's newsletter, that stated, "Church monies were used for the rape of individuals."[17]

Six of Cook's angry clients filed a lawsuit against him in June 1988 in Berks County, Pennsylvania, but they abandoned it because of lack of financial resources. According to court records, the case was ter-minated in 1991 because of inactivity.[18]

Looking to restart his life, Cook moved with his wife and two chil-dren to Arvada, Colorado, in 1993. Once there, he started a new ex-gay business, FaithQuest Counseling Center, Inc.

Cook had impeccable timing with his move to the Rockies. Colo-rado for Family Values (CFV), a statewide antigay group, was gear-ing up to try to pass Amendment 2, a referendum on a state constitu-tional amendment prohibiting antidiscrimination laws for gays and lesbians. CFV's executive director, Kevin Tebedo, saw Cook as use-ful in their propaganda war. He enlisted the controversial ex-gay leader and featured him at "Time to Stand" seminars in support of Amendment 2. Cook was also enthusiastically embraced by Colo-rado Springs–based, right-wing powerhouse Focus on the Family. With Cook's help, Amendment 2 passed on November 3, 1992, a cat-astrophic defeat for Colorado's gay and lesbian community. The im-pact of Cook's message that gays don't need job protection because they can "change" cannot be underestimated in this right-wing victory.[19]

After the vote, with the continued support of CFV, Cook traveled throughout the state putting on "Lifting the Fog" seminars. "I don't like going to gay bars and bathhouses . . . but I must go there [to evangelize]," said Cook at one seminar. "When you're open to God you're heterosexual. When you suppress God you're homosexual."[20]

It was soon clear that, if his theory were true, the Bible-toting Cook had suppressed God in a major way. *The Denver Post* broke a devastating story, supplied once again by Lawson, on October 27, 1995, in which several of Cook's clients accused him of lurid behavior, including phone sex, mutual masturbation, and inappropriate hugs. One client made tape recordings of his "counseling" sessions with Cook, "sessions filled with discussions of sex."[21]

"Think of Jesus being 'in the room with you giving you his love as he gives you an erection,' Cook told Eddy over the phone," according to tape transcripts. Eddy was also urged "to tell Jesus exactly what you sexually desire. Get by your bedside, naked, maybe with a hard-on. And say, 'Jesus, I would like to suck a penis right now . . .'" Also, according to *Denver Westword,* Cook prodded a client named "David" (pseudonym) into revealing his penis size. Cook, impressed by the ample measurement, replied, "Wow, you should thank God for it."[22]

These tapes have enough incriminating material to last for dozens of pages. Instead of slinking away in shame when confronted with it, however, Cook adamantly defended his therapy as legitimate. "The term 'phone sex' wickedly misrepresents the purpose and intent of my phone conversations," he said. "When someone says I'm unorthodox, I put my flag up and say, 'Amen.'"[23]

Surprisingly, a confrontational Tebedo passionately defended Cook. "Colin's message is valuable and the response to Colin has been tremendous. All the people [at the seminars] thought he was top-notch."[24] The fallout from Tebedo's ill-conceived defense was so intense that it reportedly cost him his job at CFV.

With nothing left to lose, the two beleaguered men held a surreal press conference where they combatively defended the indefensible. "I'm not a lustful monster trying to get his own jollies satisfied," said Cook at the press conference.[25] While Cook claimed he wasn't a sex-crazed beast, Tebedo blamed *The Denver Post* and gay activists of a vast left-wing conspiracy to bring down the two men. Following the press conference, Tebedo verbally abused Boulder gay activist Rick Cendo with false allegations, according to *Denver Westword,* yelling, "You're sick and perverted! You want to have sex with children!"[26]

In the aftermath of Cook's shenanigans, HA has struggled to survive, having been whittled down to the near irrelevancy of a mere twenty-five chapters, and has clearly been eclipsed by Exodus as the premier ex-gay group. Currently, most of HA's chapters are in Podunk towns such as Winona, Minnesota, and Azusa, California.

Cook is now a diminished force in the ex-gay movement, but he is still influential. In fact, Dr. Joe Nicolosi, the nation's lead reparative therapist, frequently uses Cook as a resource in his work.

Cook is a man of great perseverance who cannot easily be dismissed. He has risen from the political grave before to overcome scandals and resuscitate his career. After this lifetime of spectacular catastrophes, would it not be a pleasant surprise if Cook finally rejected the ex-gay myth? Although he failed to "lift the fog," there is still time for him to begin anew and "lift the fraud."

The Invisible Men

It is said that people study history to prevent repeating the same mistakes in the future, but Exodus and Homosexuals Anonymous, the two largest ex-gay groups, avoid introspection by omitting or rewriting these crucial parts of their histories. Cooper's and Bussee's names are nowhere to be found in Exodus's literature and there is only one arcane reference to them deeply entombed on its Web site. HA has only one mention of Cook on its Web site, and this reference is a sanitized version that omits his history of seedy behavior. HA refers to him as "founder," but never as "failure." By reading the group's Web page, one would think that Cook was a smashing success and paragon of heterosexuality.

By purging these embarrassments while promulgating airbrushed histories, these groups are cheating prospective clients. Bussee's and Cooper's defections are the equivalent of Fidel Castro rejecting Communism. Describing Colin Cook as simply the "founder" of HA is an understatement as absurd as describing O. J. Simpson as no more than a former Heisman Trophy winner from the University of Southern California.

Ex-gay groups will argue that these defections and scandals simply mean that these men have "fallen off the wagon" like alcoholics reverting back to drinking. But let's face it, these men built the wagon, and they say it has always been a faulty model that never worked. If the men who invented these programs now denounce them or show they have failed to heal through them, how are they going to work for those who blindly follow in their footsteps?

This unwillingness of the ex-gay ministries to confront their true history is the reason why history keeps unpleasantly repeating itself. If the unvarnished facts had been presented to Paulk from day one, maybe he wouldn't have gotten himself ensnared in the ex-gay trap. Recently I got an e-mail from a major ex-lesbian author who now rejects the notion that a "cure" is possible, saying, "In my case, the hope for 'healing' has worn pretty thin after sixteen years." She requested anonymity because she is not quite ready to go public, and her "coming out" would be another devastating blow to the ex-gay ministries.

Clients have a right to know the truth about these organizations from the beginning. Each new client should at the very least be informed about Cook, Marks, Bussee, and Cooper. Until Exodus and Homosexuals Anonymous end their historical revisionism, their claims of being moral groups will "wear as thin" as their notions of so-called healing.

The Propagandists

A Plague from Biblical Times

By the early 1980s, the many high-profile failures of the ex-gay ministries were beginning to take their toll. Bussee's and Cooper's defections were especially damaging to Exodus's credibility and threatened its very existence. At the same time, society had become increasingly tolerant of gay men and lesbians. The visibility and success of the gay liberation movement gave hope to millions of people and made the ex-gay ministries and reparative therapy a less attractive option.

Then came AIDS.

The acceptance that gay and lesbian Americans had fought so hard for was threatened by a plague that seemed, to many fundamentalists, to jump straight off the pages of the Old Testament. Gay people were confused and terrified as they watched their friends and life partners waste away and perish. This mysterious disease created a climate of fear, which proved to be a fertile recruitment ground for Exodus and Homosexuals Anonymous. "The impact of AIDS on the work of Exodus has been profound," bragged former Exodus President Sy Rogers.[1]

The AIDS epidemic seemingly validated the ex-gay lifestyle choice while supposedly proving that God was against homosexuality. It was nothing short of a boon for the ailing movement, and ex-gay groups grew exponentially by promising prospective members that the ministries could keep them from becoming infected with HIV. "Ex-gay groups function as the big condom to prevent people from getting AIDS," said Jack Pantaleo. "If I run to an ex-gay group I won't have to worry about unsafe sex. It's sinful and evil and you won't ever have to do that again."[2]

Into this pestilent cyclone of chaos and mayhem stepped two therapists who grotesquely exploited AIDS hysteria for their own benefit: English psychologist Elizabeth Moberly and American psychologist Paul Cameron. The work of the exploitative pair resuscitated the ex-gay ministries and almost surely saved the ex-gay movement from impending collapse.

The Matronly Matchmaker

Moberly entered the ex-gay scene with the release of her 1983 book, *Homosexuality: A New Christian Ethic*.[3] Although she fancies herself a "pioneer," little of Moberly's work is original. "Moberly's ideas are really just a rehash of some dated psychoanalytic ideas that people are homosexual because of the relationship with their parents," said Christian psychologist and Evangelicals Concerned founder Ralph Blair.[4]

Nevertheless, her book provided the ex-gay ministries with the psychological underpinnings they desperately needed to attract new members. Up until her arrival, the leading ex-gay ministry, Exodus International, relied almost exclusively on prayer to rid clients of homosexuality. After one or two years, most clients realized that they had not changed and usually abandoned the programs in frustration. With the advent of Moberly's book, however, Exodus now had a tangible plan to embrace that combined pseudopsychology with divine intervention. This broadened the group's appeal, empowering clients to explore their childhoods rather than just passively waiting for God to heal them.

Moberly championed the following four main ideas that, to this day, are central to ex-gay theory.

Defensive Detachment

According to this theory, a person becomes homosexual because a disruption during adolescence creates an emotional detachment from the same-sex parent. The child perceives this distance as rejection and, in turn, as a defensive mechanism rejects the same-sex parent, including his or her gender identity.

One might think Moberly would have overwhelming evidence on which to base a theory that stereotypes millions of people and subjects them to everything from expensive therapy to shock treatment. It turns out, however, that Moberly's entire theory is based on nothing more than a hunch. According to a book written by reparative therapist Joe Nicolosi:

> Moberly discovered her first clue to the dynamic of defensive detachment while in conversation with a gay-activist friend. He said he sometimes suspected their meetings were "jinxed," since divisive arguments would almost always break out among members. It was from this, that she first began to suspect an unconscious negative dynamic.[5]

In other words, because a few gay activists bickered, Moberly surmised all gay people were mentally ill. One could easily apply this reasoning to any group of activists, especially the Christian right. Lately, groups such as the Christian Coalition and Family Research Council have been plagued by fratricidal power struggles that have been anything but Christian. During this same time period, national gay groups, such as the Human Rights Campaign and the Gay and Lesbian Alliance Against Defamation, have been stable and growing at a fantastic rate. Based on these facts, Moberly could reasonably argue—according to her theory—that right-wing political activists, herself included, suffer from an "unconscious negative dynamic."

Gender Rejection

A boy suffering from defensive detachment, Moberly explained, will avoid sports, while a girl will shun her femininity and embrace more masculine endeavors, such as fixing cars. This causes the individual to become further isolated from his or her gender group and to gravitate toward homosexuality.

This conclusion, of course, ignores the fact that many lesbians participate in stereotypically feminine activities and many gay men excel in sports. "The idea that playing a sport will affect your sexuality . . . must have been thought of by someone who has never had the courage to participate in a sporting event, has a tremendously narrow mindset, and refuses to accept that all people are not the same," wrote openly gay, former major-league baseball player Billy Bean. "In my opinion, using something as pure and healthy as sport as a cover for an absurd, unfounded form of emotional abuse is unconscionable," continued Bean. "I feel sorry for the people who are really just exploring the truth about themselves, and are in an environment that will only make them feel worse about themselves instead of reinforcing their individuality and uniqueness."[6]

At the onset of puberty, according to Moberly, a child suffering from defensive detachment may seek to undo his or her respective masculinity or femininity deficit through homosexual encounters. The "defective" person, unbeknownst to him or her, is not really looking for sex, however, but instead seeking to heal the wounds caused by the aloof parent. "In this sense, the homosexual love-need is essentially a search for parenting," wrote Moberly.[7]

Same-Sex Ambivalence

Without offering supporting data, Moberly further speculated that gay and lesbian relationships are doomed to failure because of a psychological phenomenon she called "same-sex ambivalence." This theory claims gay relationships will almost always implode because both partners are really looking for parenting through each other, yet they can't provide parenting to each other because they are both damaged individuals. Eventually, each partner will project unconscious hatred toward the same-sex parent onto the other partner. This, of course, leaves lesbian and gay people to the gloomy fate of roaming hopelessly from partner to partner, only to break up in the end.

Of interest is that the never-married Moberly did not adequately address the countless lesbian and gay relationships that have lasted decades, nor did she attempt to explain the 50 percent divorce rate among heterosexual couples.

Same-Sex Friendships

Moberly's cure for homosexuality is for gays to form close, nonerotic, same-sex friendships. She postulated that these relationships would eventually allow a homosexual to identify with his or her peers in a nonsexual way. Once members of the same sex are "demystified," a homosexual loses interest, according to Moberly, and begins to fancy the opposite sex. "Such friendships are central, and indeed essential, to the solution of the problem of homosexuality," explained Moberly.[8]

First, it escaped Moberly that there are literally hundreds of thousands of examples of platonic friendships between gay and straight individuals of the same gender. Although these friendships may be strong, they do not change the sexual orientation of either person involved.

Second, the vast majority of relationships within the lesbian and gay community consist of platonic same-sex friendships. For some reason, Moberly wrongly assumed that the only contact homosexuals have with one another is in bed. This conclusion lacks even a rudimentary knowledge of gay life.

Finally, my experience has shown that Moberly's theory of same-sex bonding is probably the number one reason why ex-gay men and women end up having sex with each other. These "platonic" friendships more often than not provide an excuse for sexual intimacy for these intimacy-starved individuals. Her theory on curing homosexuality has actually ended up bringing many gays and lesbians out of the closet. If you count the number of couples her theory has brought together, she is an extraordinary matchmaker.

Dangerous Rhetoric

Moberly's pedestrian book came out right as the AIDS epidemic was on the verge of exploding, giving her a platform to discuss why gay men should change their "sinful" ways. She was also greatly helped by the emerging culture of celebrity that blossomed in the 1980s. Moberly, the quintessential ham, trenchant hawker of her wares on talk shows—including *Donahue*—emerged as an "expert" on homosexuality. By astutely exploiting the media, Moberly went from a "nobody" to a "notable" without having produced a single memorable contribution to the field of psychology.

When not downright dangerous, Moberly's ideas can border on surreal. In her book, she applies her defensive detachment theories to Jesus Christ, arguing that her work *proves* that Jesus could not have been gay:

> The scriptures testify to Jesus' close and deep communion with his heavenly father—a relationship such that there could be no possible basis for speaking of a deficit and a drive to make good this deficit, i.e., the homosexual urge.[9]

As if her Jesus analogy weren't bizarre enough, Moberly sends the quack-o-meter off the charts with her comparison of homosexuals to orphans, claiming *both* are against God's design:

> The perfect will of God for human growth is checked whenever a child is orphaned. However, although being an orphan is in this sense, 'against the will of God,' one does not therefore seek to punish an orphan for being an orphan. . . . To thwart the resolution [in gays] of these deficits . . . is comparable to oppressing the orphan. To facilitate the needed fulfillment is as acceptable as are other forms of helping orphans.[10]

As crazy or dangerous as Moberly's rhetoric might be, the general frenzy surrounding the AIDS crisis made many people listen to her. For those who did not want to be gay and feared contracting AIDS, she provided the answers they wanted to hear.

As opportunistic as Moberly is in the promotion of her theories, her response to people living with AIDS is angelic compared to Paul Cameron's, whose extreme rhetoric and infamous scare tactics led people to the ex-gay ministries in record numbers.

Propaganda Paul

My first exposure to a "former homosexual" came in 1992, my senior year at the University of Florida, during an on-campus debate between a local activist and arch-right psychologist Paul Cameron. During the forum, Cameron painted gays as sex-addicted monsters, responsible for everything from spreading disease to causing increases in crime. In the crowd that day was a small group of ex-gays unctuously applauding Cameron's every word and volubly declaring they had changed their sexual orientation.

As Cameron recited his statistics on lower life expectancy for gays, I overheard a Campus Crusade for Christ leader comforting an attractive ex-gay sophomore. "I know you have struggled to find Christ and become straight," said the well-meaning, but misguided leader. "But, thank God, you escaped this destructive lifestyle. Just listen to the disgusting things homosexuals do to each other." The ex-gay earnestly bobbed his head in agreement.

Fascinated by this encounter, not to mention attracted to the ex-gay, I approached him after the seminar while he was loudly preaching the joys of sexual conversion to anyone who would listen.

"I have changed through Jesus Christ and I have never been happier," he exclaimed. "The Bible says the truth will set you free. And I am free from attraction to men!"

Not intending to be cruel, I asked him, "If you have changed, then how come you still look gay?" I had barely finished my, I thought, innocuous comment when tears began streaming down his anguished face.

"I don't look like a fag. I'm not homosexual," he shrieked through his cascading tears. My words had clearly upset him because he thought he was successfully butching up through Moberly's model of touch football and platonic same-sex friendships. When my comment highlighted that the ex-gay ministries were not changing how he was perceived, his entire self-image was shattered and his self-worth plummeted.

This student clearly would have benefited from the thriving gay group on campus—not to mention a date with me. Thanks to Moberly's theories as well as Cameron and his parade of antigay statistics, however, this conflicted young man did not see self-acceptance as an option. After all, the images Cameron regularly fostered of gays ingesting feces and drinking urine are hardly an inducement to coming out for most people.[11] Though he did not practice reparative therapy himself, Cameron's statistics painted such a vile portrait of homosexuality that, for many gays, such as this student, the ex-gay ministries seemed the only viable alternative.

Cameron's Coming-Out Party

Dr. Paul Cameron was like no one the gay and lesbian community had ever seen before. Whereas Moberly attained notoriety for evangelizing about the *causation* of homosexuality, Cameron came out of the woodwork to publicize the *consequences* of same-gender sex.

Similar to Moberly, Cameron is a fundamentalist Christian who cloaks his antigay religious beliefs in the guise of science. His specialty is conducting "studies" for the religious right to show that lesbians and gay men are depraved, diseased individuals who are a menace to themselves and society. He once wrote that homosexuality was an addiction that causes an "octopus of infection stretching across the world."[12]

Cameron was also instrumental in the growth of the ex-gay ministries, and his influence in the ex-gay sphere can't be overstated. Armed with his studies, ex-gay leaders could make the case that change was not only *possible* but *essential* for anyone who didn't want to suffer the terminal consequences that came with the "lifestyle." To this day, almost every leading ex-gay ministry leader or reparative therapist cites Cameron's work either directly or indirectly. He did nothing less than provide the pseudointellectual underpinnings for the key question of *why* a gay person should attempt to change.

Throughout the 1980s and 1990s, Cameron's work caused so much damage to gay rights causes that *The Advocate* magazine called him "The most dangerous antigay zealot in the United States today."[13]

Cameron attended the University of Louisville in Kentucky and received his PhD in psychology in 1966 from the University of Colorado at Boulder. After graduation Cameron became an associate professor of human development and the family at the University of Nebraska, but he was canned in 1980.

As he descended into the professional wilderness, Cameron desperately groped for a new start. To find his niche he focused on controversial political/social issues and opportunistically weighed each one to see which offered the most potential for career advancement. "I looked at the panoply of things happening to our society—abortion, homosexuality, suicide, euthanasia," said Cameron. "I had dabbled in each of these areas."[14]

With the AIDS epidemic in its embryonic stages and gay rights battles flaring up from coast to coast, Cameron correctly speculated that the antigay movement was uncharted territory where he could prosper. The right-wing political groups needed statistics to show why people should vote against lesbian and gay equality, and as a psychologist and former associate professor at University of Nebraska, Cameron had the credentials to provide exactly what these right-wing groups needed in their antigay crusades.

Cameron made his splashing debut on the antigay political scene in 1982 as the chairman of the Committee to Oppose Special Rights for Homosexuals. His group's goal was to defeat a Lincoln, Nebraska, gay rights amendment that supported banning discrimination based on sexual orientation in housing, employment, and public accommodations. During this campaign Cameron pulled out all the stops, unleashing for the first time his barrage of frighteningly dehumanizing statistics. He spoke liberally about gays recruiting children and spreading disease and even said they were more likely to commit "sexual mass murder."[15]

This campaign also marked for Cameron the first of many ethical lapses that would come to define his career. In a speech on May 3, 1982, at the University of Nebraska Lutheran Chapel, Cameron announced to the crowd, "Right now, here in Lincoln, there is a four-year-old boy who has had his genitals almost severed from his body at Gateway mall in a restroom with a homosexual act."[16] The townsfolk went apoplectic over this disclosure and demanded justice for this poor young man. When police said no such record of this event existed, now backed into a corner over his twisted tale, Cameron admitted that it was only a rumor but still persisted with his innuendos, saying that it "could have happened."

University of Nebraska psychology professor James K. Cole told Ward Harkavy, a reporter with *Denver Westword:*

> It's fascinating that someone with his capacity, a trained scientist, would do these things. He was willing to take any outlandish statement and use it to his purpose. . . . The guy has no moral inhibitions. I find it surprising that the Christian right would follow someone who has no moral inhibitions.[17]

The local newspaper, the *Lincoln Star,* hammered Cameron for his fabrication but rightfully predicted that the damage to the gay rights movement was permanent. The measure for lesbian and gay equal rights was easily defeated by a four-to-one margin.[18]

Emboldened by the victorious campaign, Cameron opened a pseudo–think tank, the Institute for the Scientific Investigation of Sexuality (ISIS). Here, Cameron transformed himself into a national "expert" on homosexuality and cranked out volumes of "statistics" that portrayed homosexuality as destructive. Even to this day, a large portion of the most virulent antigay and ex-gay literature can be traced back directly or indirectly to the word processor of Paul Cameron.

One Cameron pamphlet, *Child Molestation and Homosexuality,* has on its cover a creepy picture of a man pulling a child by the arm into a rest room for sex. The bottom of the pamphlet cover reads, "Homosexuality Is a Crime Against Humanity."

Another Cameron pamphlet, *Murder, Violence and Homosexuality*, features this tag line: "What Homosexuals Do in Public Is Offensive; What They Do in Private Is Deadly!" According to his skewed data, "You are 15 times more apt to be killed by a gay than a heterosexual during a sexual murder spree," and "most victims of sex murderers died at the hands of gays."

In yet another Cameron brochure, *Medical Consequences of What Homosexuals Do (It's More Than Merely Disgusting)*, the doctor claims gay men are fourteen times more apt to have syphilis than heterosexual men and three times more likely to have lice. The brochure also notes that lesbians are nineteen times more likely to have syphilis than straight women and four times more likely to have scabies.

Cameron's studies are incredibly skewed, according to writer Mark Pietrzyk, in *The New Republic* magazine: "Several studies Cameron cites to support his conclusions rely on the responses of gay men who were recruited entirely from V.D. [veneral disease] clinics."[19] Now, let's stop for a moment to think about how Cameron deduces venereal disease statistics for *all* gay men based on *random* samples from VD clinics. Obviously, taking samples of homosexuals from these treatment centers will show a disproportionate number of gay men with VD. This is the equivalent of deducing that "90 percent of gay men like hamburgers" through exclusive sampling of gay men eating at Burger King, or finding that "95 percent of lesbians enjoy auto racing" from a sample of lesbians at the Indy 500. Clearly, Cameron's work is hardly reliable, nothing more than extremism disguised as science.

The peddling of old stereotypes, such as pedophilia, in new scientific packages may have been vintage hate mongering, but Cameron saved most of his invective for gay people living with AIDS.

Cameron's Crusade

Cameron appeared at a time when much of America was ignorant of the nature of this deadly disease. People were still debating whether HIV-positive children should be allowed to attend school or whether HIV could be transmitted through the sharing of eating utensils. As the disease's incidence mushroomed, Cameron became America's leading apostle of misinformation. He seemed to take perverse pleasure in generating community-wide AIDS hysteria. "The ominous specter now is that it looks as if mosquitoes may be able to transmit AIDS," Cameron said. "Normal people probably could take a hit or two from a mosquito carrying AIDS but a small child couldn't. If children start dying of AIDS, I don't think a homosexual's life will be worth a damn."[20]

Cameron's fusillades against people living with AIDS are characterized by a heartlessness and detestation that lack even a hint of decency and humanity. There are seemingly no boundaries this man has not crossed in his mission to rid the world of homosexuals—under the guise of combating AIDS.

At a militant antiabortion group Human Life International conference, Cameron called for the government to brand HIV-positive people with an "A" on their foreheads.[21] In 1985 at a symposium in Washington sponsored by the Conservative Political Action Conference, Cameron made headlines by calling for the quarantine of homosexuals as a way to stop the spread of AIDS.[22] "Gays posture as victims but they earn their AIDS," said Cameron. To protect the rest of society, all of them should be "confined to quarters."[23] If these measures failed to work, Cameron predicted a "final solution" at the right-wing conference: "Unless we get medically lucky," Cameron proclaimed, "in three or four years, one of the options discussed will be the extermination of homosexuals."[24]

Cameron's depravity and utterly empty soul were best captured on an episode of Geraldo Rivera's tabloid-style television talk show.[25] During one segment, Cameron shared the stage with Jeanne Manford, who had just lost her son Morty to AIDS. As the conversation heated up, Cameron took part in what may be one of the lowest moments in the history of television (any episode of *Jerry Springer* notwithstanding). Without a hint of remorse, he cold-heartedly turned toward the grieving mother and attacked: "Let me tell you a little story, . . . because this is the first time this has happened to me," said Cameron. "I was on the plane and there, sitting up, was a *New York Times,* which I ordinarily never read because I'm from DC. . . . So what do I turn—right there it's at the obituary page, and just as a coincidence, I pick it up, and I say, 'Who's there and who isn't?' It's Morty Manford. And I look at that, and what a coincidence." Most of the studio audience groaned at Cameron's contemptible remarks. This act of cruelty was even too much for Geraldo: "I let free speech—but this is a woman who lost her son two weeks ago," scolded Geraldo. "I beg you to have some—some sensitivity, please. Enough."

Aside from his breathtaking cruelty, Cameron may best be remembered for his notorious "study" that found the average life span for gay men to be forty-three years of age. To arrive at this chilling number, Cameron took the back issues of urban gay papers, read the obituaries, and averaged the ages of those who had passed away. An American Enterprise Institute demographer described this method as "just ridiculous."[26] Centers for Disease Control and Prevention statistician John Karon called Cameron's number unquestionably skewed because "you're only getting the ages of those who die."[27] As Walter Olsen of *Slate Magazine* noted:

> The actual average age of AIDS patients at death has been about 40. . . . For the number 43 to be the true average death age for the entire population of gay males, HIV-negative gay men would, on average, have to keel into their graves at 46. Looked at another way, if even half the gay male population stays HIV-negative and lives to an average age of 75, an average overall life span of 43 implies that gay males with AIDS die at an implausibly early average age (11, actually).[28]

The scientific bankruptcy of this particular "study" has not stopped the religious right from citing it with reckless abandon, most notably by former Education Secretary William Bennett during an antigay jeremiad on ABC's *This Week*.[29] After writer Andrew Sullivan took him to task in *The New Republic* for using Cameron's statistics, however, he was forced to distance himself from the "scientist": "Given what I now know, I believe there are flaws with Paul Cameron's study. One cannot extrapolate from his methodology and say that the average male homosexual life span is forty-three years," said Bennett.[30]

Cameron Gets Caught

Cameron's bad science and calumnious antigay rhetoric eventually caught up with him. Several psychologists whose work Cameron had cited accused him of manipulating their data. The American Psychological Association (APA) began an investigation and found that

Cameron had, in addition to misrepresenting the work of others, used unsound methodology in his own studies.

"He was misrepresenting and distorting other peoples' psychological research and using it to sensationalize his point of view on homosexuals," said Dr. Natalie Porter, assistant professor of psychology at the University of Nebraska and one of six Nebraska psychologists who requested the APA start an investigation. "He talks about homosexuals being mass murderers and child molesters and credits other people for those findings. If you read their research, they have in no way made such claims. We have letters from those researchers saying his [work] has distorted their research."[31]

In December 1983, Cameron was branded with the "Scarlet Q" (as in quack) and booted out of the APA. According to *Denver Westword*, "Complaints from other scientists about Cameron's ethics prompted his ouster from the American Psychological Association."[32] Cameron, of course, insists that he resigned.

The rebukes from his peers continued unabated, with scientific authorities doing virtually everything but banishing him to Siberia. Cameron's credentials were sinking like the *Titanic* and it appeared he had no future. For example:

- In 1984, the Nebraska Psychological Association adopted a resolution stating that it "formally disassociates itself from the representations and interpretations of scientific literature offered by Dr. Paul Cameron in his writings and public statements on sexuality."[33]
- The American Sociological Association, in 1985, adopted a resolution that stated, "Dr. Paul Cameron has consistently misinterpreted and misrepresented sociological research on sexuality, homosexuality and lesbianism."[34]
- In 1985, a U.S. District Court judge in Dallas called Cameron's sworn statement "fraud." In this case *(Baker v. Wade)*, Cameron claimed, "Homosexuals abuse children at a proportionately greater incident [sic] than do heterosexuals." After looking at Cameron's sloppy work, the judge said, "There has been no fraud and misrepresentations except by Dr. Cameron."[35]

Under normal circumstances, these humiliating reprimands would have ended the discredited psychologist's career, but Cameron wasn't an ordinary doctor and the religious right was no ordinary client. The right still needed antigay statistics and was not about to let Cameron's lack of credibility stand in the way of obtaining the precious gems of misinformation he produced. Apparently, scientific veracity was a mere inconvenience in their quest to win the "culture wars" in the name of morality.

Right-Wing Rebirth

To more efficiently serve his right-wing political masters, Cameron moved to Washington in 1987 and renamed his pseudo–think tank the Family Research Institute (FRI). During the period from 1985 to 1998, Cameron traversed the nation on behalf of the religious right, giving "expert" testimony wherever gay rights battles raged. Cameron's road show appeared in dozens of states. Whether it was Arkansas or Maine, California or Colorado, Cameron was a staple of the antigay industry and their campaigns to limit equal rights for homosexuals.

In the aftermath of a Cameron visit, outbreaks of ignorance and intolerance were usually not far behind. For example, after Cameron visited Bangor, Maine, a fundamentalist Baptist church refused to hold Sunday services in a college building that was used on Saturday nights as a gay dance hall. The Reverend Harold Blackorby cited fear of catching AIDS and pointed to a Cameron booklet as proof that his congregation was in danger of infection.[36]

Judging by the effect he was having in his travels, the religious right knew they possessed a potent weapon, so they invested heavily in Cameron, using his "studies" in almost all of their antigay literature. The Traditional Values Coalition, the Rutherford Institute, Focus on the Family, the American Family Association, and especially the Family Research Council disseminated Cameron's faulty work to millions of Americans.

What the Cameron phenomenon revealed was that most people at the time did not know someone who was openly gay or lesbian. This allowed antigay forces largely to shape people's perceptions of homosexuals. Remember, Cameron's rise to power began when media coverage of the AIDS crisis was sparse at best, and he catapulted himself to prominence more than a decade before the closet doors were blown off their hinges through the exhaustive media coverage of then-President Bill Clinton's efforts to lift the ban on openly gay military service members. At the time, there was no *Ellen,* no *Will &*

Grace, and no *Queer As Folk.* Gay and lesbian visibility was usually confined to daytime talk shows such as *Donahue* or *Geraldo.* This created a dangerous climate that the religious right could exploit with Cameron.

One individual who sought Cameron's "expertise" to boost his political fortunes was Representative William Dannemeyer (R-California). In 1985, the Orange County Congressman hired the "doctor" to advise him on gay and AIDS issues. Dannemeyer once suggested that people with AIDS "emit spores that have been known to cause birth defects" and should "take a glass of water upon arising with seven or eight squirts of liquid garlic" as a palliative.[37]

Cameron's statistics even oozed their way into the bitterly divisive "gays in the military" debate in 1993. At the height of the controversy, a twenty-minute video, *The Gay Agenda,* was circulated by the religious right to allies in Congress and key members of the military establishment who opposed then-President Clinton's efforts to lift the ban on gays. The video was produced by Spring Life Ministries, an infamous church in the Mojave Desert that first made national news in 1987 by reordaining shamed televangelist Jim Bakker. The exploitative video featured a slew of "experts" discussing the horrors of homosexuality, and their testimonials were interspersed with lurid scenes surreptitiously filmed at a gay pride parade.

One of the "authorities" featured prominently in *The Gay Agenda* was Stanley Monteith, a physician and former head of the Santa Cruz chapter of the John Birch Society.[38] In the video, he recited a plethora of Cameron statistics, including the claim that "average homosexuals had between 300 and 500 lovers in a lifetime," and "28 percent engaged in sodomy with more than 1,000 men."[39] This all could have been laughed away as ridiculous nonsense, except that it had a major impact at the Pentagon and in the halls of Congress. According to one report:

> General Carl Mundy, chief of the U.S. Marine Corps, showed his copy around the Pentagon including the Joint Chiefs of Staff, as well as Sen. Sam Nunn, chairman of the Armed Services Committee. "It warrants a factual assessment," wrote Gen. Mundy in a letter to key members of Congress.[40]

So, in essence, our nation's public policy on gay service members was partly determined by a fringe church that produced a video showcasing a John Birch leader who used statistics by a psychologist who was kicked out of the APA. With such informed opinions, is it any surprise we ended up with the hapless "Don't ask, Don't tell" policy?

Burned by His Fire and Brimstone

For more than a decade, Cameron had provided the ammunition for the far right's fearsome jihad against lesbians and gay men and indirectly helped the ex-gay movement expand. As time wore on, though, Cameron became sloppy and started to contradict his own supple words in public forums. For instance, in one of his five appearances on *Geraldo,* Cameron tried to show that gays needed no legal protection from discrimination because they were more successful than straights. "Some repression," spewed Cameron. "A repressed minority that makes more money on average than most people in general."[41]

In other venues, when his objective was to prove that gays were inferior, however, he would reverse course and suggest lesbians and gays were economic failures. "Most people who engage in homosexuality are of the lower strata," spouted Cameron. "These are people who are waiters and busboys and bums and hobos and jailbirds and so forth."[42]

The glaring inconsistencies in his statistical carpet-bombing campaigns began to erode further his credibility. By the mid-1990s, Cameron was becoming a liability for the extreme right, especially since new polls showed that the years of acrimonious attacks on gay and lesbian Americans were backfiring. The right started to realize that they must move away from overt hostility and find new ways to assault gay and lesbian equality. This evolving strategic shift meant Cameron's role would have to be greatly diminished, since his excesses were largely to blame for the growing perception that right-wing Christian groups were intolerant.

Another change that greatly affected Cameron's declining influence was growing AIDS awareness. With notable heterosexuals such as basketball hero Magic Johnson announcing they were HIV positive, Americans finally realized that anyone was susceptible to contracting HIV. Cameron's mosquito scare tactics now seemed anachronistic and made his religious right backers look like carnivorous dinosaurs rumbling through the Stone Age, mindlessly destroying everything in their path.

As criticism of their antigay slash-and-burn techniques mounted, influential religious right leaders convoked in 1994 with leading antigay activists, including Paul Cameron, to ask them to tone down their rhetoric. At the conference in Glen Eyrie Resort in Colorado Springs,[44] Focus on the Family officials laid the groundwork for a more warm and fuzzy brand of homophobia. Focus official John Eldredge implored the activists to avoid the appearance of bigotry and said, "To the extent we can control our public image, we must never appear to be bigoted or mean-spirited."[45]

Eventually, this softening of rhetoric would lead to the rise of reparative therapists, such as Joe Nicolosi, and to the religious right's embracing the ex-gay ministries in a 1998 ad campaign. "Ex-gays" were the perfect antidote to the poison that dripped from Cameron's fangs. By touting these therapies and ministries, the right could claim to "love the sinner" by helping the person to change and still "hate the sin" by fighting against legal equality for gay people. None other than John Paulk marked the shift in strategy when he rebuked Cameron on behalf of Focus on the Family, saying, "I don't adhere, and Focus doesn't adhere, to Cameron's statistics."[46]

Getting High on Homosexuality

Cameron's fall from favor with the far right does not mean that he is not still a menace. The colossal amount of work he disseminated over the years has ensured his bilious statistics will linger on and continue to resurface in gay rights battles across the land long after he is no more than a distant bad memory.

People often wonder what drives a zealot such as Paul Cameron in his all-consuming obsession with homosexuality. Perhaps it was the fact that when he was four years old a man in an apple orchard molested him. "I must have been a beautiful and charming little boy," said Cameron. "But I didn't like it much. . . . I remember that he was kind of dirty, and that bothered me."[47] Later, a woman also sexually abused Cameron, but he viewed this experience as more enticing.

Cameron's fixation on gay sex might be attributed to the doctor's struggle with his own personal demons. According to Cameron:

If you isolate sexuality as something solely for one's own personal amusement, and all you want is the most satisfying orgasm you can get—and that is what homosexuality seems to be—then homosexuality seems too powerful to resist. The evidence is that men do a better job on men, and women on women, if all you are looking for is orgasm. . . . It's pure sexuality. It's almost like pure heroin. It's such a rush.[48]

No study in existence shows that gay sex is more satisfying than heterosexual sex or gives a rush similar to heroin. One can only speculate as to how Cameron reached these conclusions.

ACT II

REPARATIVE THERAPY

Massaging in the Manliness

It was a brisk autumn day, only one month after I had uncovered Paulk, when I entered the opulent Mayflower Hotel in downtown Washington, DC. Elegant chandeliers gracefully hung from the immense lobby's artistically sculpted ceiling above the long marble floor. The lavish surroundings could not, however, lend even a shard of respectability to the travesty of the conference that was taking place inside the hotel's bowels.

Hoping not to be spotted by conference leaders, I quickly entered the basement ballroom, completed a sign-up sheet, and handed it to a bubbly volunteer who had no idea that I was working undercover for a gay advocacy organization. "Thank you for your commitment to healing the homosexual," she said with a broad grin as she waved me through.

Now that I had overcome my first hurdle—penetrating the annual conference of the National Association for Research and Therapy of Homosexuality (NARTH)[1]—I was fairly certain that I would not be stopped. Once firmly behind enemy lines, I slipped into the bathroom and admired my intricate disguise. The darkened, slicked-back hair and the new glasses were a great touch, I thought, in a moment of self-congratulatory hubris. I took one more look in the mirror and thought, "I'll never be caught!"

I furtively snaked my way to the back of the ballroom and inconspicuously positioned myself in the center of the room to hear the upcoming presentation on "touch therapy," the basis of which was a theory postulating that people are gay partly because they have been deprived of nonsexual touch by members of the same sex. As I settled in for the illuminating presentation, I felt a firm tap on my shoulder.

"Hi, Wayne," said Bob Knight of the antigay political group the Family Research Council.[2] "Did you get a new hairdo?" "Busted," I thought, as I sheepishly grinned at him with my hand-in-the-cookie-jar look and shuffled my papers in anticipation of getting the heave-ho. To my great surprise, though, he let me stay and moved on.

I moved to my right and almost bumped into the Reverend Lou Sheldon, founder of the antigay Traditional Values Coalition. He recognized me as well, but he just gave me a nasty look and grunted something about Sodom, and, I think, Green Bay, but it might have been Gomorrah. It was amazing how NARTH, a group that claims to be about science, not politics, had so few scientists and so many politicians at the conference. You could watch *The McLaughlin Group* and not see this many political operatives.

Richard Cohen, psychotherapist and ex-gay author of *Coming Out Straight: Understanding and Healing Homosexuality,* pranced up to the podium and began telling his life story to the estimated 125 people in attendance. The audience was an eclectic mix of extraordinarily old psychoanalysts, distraught parents of gay kids, a handful of younger psychotherapists, and a peppering of desperate ex-gay men and women who were hoping to find a panacea to end their same-gender attraction.

It was easy to spot the ex-gays. They were the ones who hung on every one of Cohen's words and gazed at him with looks of tremendous expectation, as if Cohen were the Florida explorer Ponce de León about to unveil the elusive Fountain of Youth or, in this case, the Fountain of Heterosexuality.

Cohen was talking about the importance of gay men who are "transitioning into heterosexuality," finding straight male mentors to help them discover the "man within." The largely middle-aged crowd was with him, nodding their heads in approval, when he broadsided them with this little personal nugget from his past: "I solicited all three of my straight male mentors," Cohen recalled. " 'Would you like me to service you? I'm really good at it,' I told each one of them. When they rejected me, I knew they loved me for who I am, not just for the sex, like so many other men who had left me before."

With this revelation, the elderly and middle-aged men and women—and, not incidentally, a smattering of teenagers—suddenly looked as if they had just downed bad fish, an apparent case of "mass nausea." Seemingly oblivious to the inappropriateness of Cohen's remarks—not to mention the audience's reaction—Joe Nicolosi, NARTH's executive director, looked on, snickering with noticeable delight.

Following his riveting autobiography, Cohen had the crowd stand up and split into groups of seven so he could demonstrate "touch therapy." After his previous comments, likely a few of the straight parents were more than a little apprehensive about what "touch therapy" might entail. Suddenly, the lights dimmed and New Age music played from a portable sound system. Cohen ordered each group to stand in single-file lines so that each person could begin massaging the person directly in front of him or her. "Relax, relax," Cohen whispered into the microphone in a soothing baritone. "I almost forgot, take off your shoes. This is what we call nonsexual touch. We are getting in touch, through touch, but remember it is nonsexual. No sex involved here. Touch *yes!* Sex *no!*" he bellowed.

One of the ex-gays, who quickly untucked his shirt, was clearly failing miserably in this exercise. "Now breathe in," Cohen hypnotically sighed. "Breathe out. We are getting in touch with our inner masculinity. We are becoming men among men. Do you feel more manly?" The lesbian-wannabe-straights in the massage lines looked perplexed about whether they should nod agreement.

I have to give Cohen credit. Here we were in the middle of Washington, with more than 100 shoeless archconservatives massaging heterosexuality into one another, while humming to what they would have considered pagan music only moments earlier. On top of this, he got to tell these folks from the heartland lewd tales about his past sexual trysts. If I had tried to get away with this, I would have been tarred and feathered. No doubt about it, this guy was smooth.

"Now that you have seen how I help people transition from homosexual to straight, you can buy my new book, or you can purchase my therapeutic tapes, and don't forget my hope and healing videos. I'm also available for speaking engagements. And, of course, I take credit cards. God Bless. Amen. Be straight."

Desperate parents and hopeful ex-gays rushed the stage and threw money at the avaricious Cohen, as if he were a holy guru offering sublime truth. (The chapter "Radical Richard" further examines Cohen's surreal methods.) Two things were clear from this particular session: (1) desperate people can easily be inveigled out of hard-earned money, and (2) none of the ex-gays left the seminar saying they were straight. I exited the conference both disgusted by the way people had been bilked and thankful that reparative therapy was considered outside the mainstream. It wasn't always this way; as late as 1973 the viewpoints and bizarre therapy NARTH now advocates represented the prevailing opinion of the mental health establishment.

A History of Hurt and Horror

To fully understand today's ex-gay ministries and modern reparative therapy it is essential to first become acquainted with the mental health establishment's ominous history of systematic discrimination, marginalization, and abuse against gay and lesbian people. For most of this century, gay men and lesbians have served as unwitting guinea pigs for narrow-minded psychiatrists who labeled gays sick for no other reason than that homosexuals didn't meet, in their view, cultural and societal norms.

An outstanding book by Kenneth Lewes, *Psychoanalysis and Male Homosexuality*, offers a complex history of the origins of psychoanalytic treatment toward gay men from the time the word *homosexuality* was first used by German doctors in 1869 to the present day. Lewes shows how Freud, the founder of psychoanalysis, was open-minded to differences in sexual orientation. Freud reasoned that many homosexuals could lead normal, healthy lives and contribute greatly to society, pointing to the accomplishments of the ancient Greeks, Michelangelo, and Leonardo da Vinci. Freud was very clear on whether he considered gay people sick. On October 27, 1903, in *Die Zeit*, a Viennese newspaper, Freud addressed this question unequivocally:

> I am . . . of the firm conviction that homosexuals must not be treated as sick people, for a perverse orientation is far from being a sickness. Would that not oblige us to characterize as sick many great thinkers and scholars of all times, whose perverse orientation we know for a fact and whom we admire precisely because of their mental health? Homosexual persons are not sick.[3]

Freud was also dubious of so-called cures for homosexuality, believing that they were likely to fail:

> "in actual numbers the successes achieved by psychoanalytic treatment of . . . homosexuality . . . are not very striking," and "in general to undertake to convert a fully developed homosexual into a heterosexual is no much more promising than to do the reverse." . . . Most homosexuals appear for treatment because of "external motives, such as social disadvantages and danger attaching to his choice of object."[4]

Although Freud was relatively open-minded, the prejudices of the time began to seep slowly into the burgeoning field of psychology. The science was supposed to be based on objectivity, but subjective biases were used early on to label gay people sick, without credible supporting evidence. Jack Drescher, author of *Psychoanalytic Therapy and the Gay Man* and the chair of the American Psychiatric Association's committee on gay, lesbian, and bisexual issues, described how homosexuality came to be labeled a mental illness: "In the nineteenth century . . . a whole range of behaviors that were socially unacceptable were moved from the realm of sin to the realm of illness," explained Drescher in our interview.[5] "So drunkenness became alcoholism, and . . . possession became insanity, and sodomy became homosexuality."

The move toward labeling gay people sick was greatly exacerbated during World War II when the Nazis relentlessly persecuted psychoanalysis. The Nazis forced the center of psychoanalysis to move from Freud's more liberal Vienna to London and eventually to New York City, which was firmly established as the epicenter for the discipline by the early 1950s. As a result, psychoanalysis no longer reflected the tolerant worldview of Vienna, but the conservative values of 1950s' *Leave It to Beaver* America.

Heavily influenced by the conservative cold war era, psychoanalysis slowly became the defender of the political and cultural status quo. This led to a plethora of bizarre "scientific" theories about homosexuality that were almost never challenged because gays were explicitly barred from practicing psychoanalysis.

What played perhaps the most significant role in the evolution of the mental health profession's view of gays was the use of unrepresentative samples of homosexuals in studies. Almost without exception, theorists would extrapolate "professional" opinions on *all* gay people based on their limited exposure to a small number who were committed to mental institutions or who visited their offices looking for help. The behavior of a *single* gay person observed in a study—no matter how disturbed—came to represent the behavior of *all* gays and was universally labeled as typifying *the homosexual*. Of course, this is just as absurd as taking the behavior of a singular straight person and assigning his or her actions to *the heterosexual*.

In all fairness, it was extraordinarily difficult for researchers in that era to find samples of openly gay people, since homosexuality was illegal and there was virtually no gay social or political movement. Nevertheless, this abdication of professional standards and relinquishment of moral authority are wholly inexcusable. Difficulty in obtaining samples of "normal" gay people is no excuse for defaming an entire class of human beings and ultimately using the results of these defective studies to label this group sick and dysfunctional.

Gay Guinea Pig Era

With gay and lesbian people virtually invisible, and biased psychiatrists with flawed samples operating unhindered in the McCarthy era, it was literally open season on gays. This period saw a wretched excess of eccentric doctors offering peculiar, if not intentionally cruel, theories on homosexuality. It sometimes seemed as if psychoanalysts were vigorously competing for the title "Most Wacky Quack." For instance:

- Psychoanalyst Hermann Nunberg had a theory on how circumcision supposedly led to less homosexuality among Jews: " 'Man had always rebelled against this attachment' to the father. By giving up part of the genital to him, Jews were able to 'renounc[e] instinct gratification and at the same time initiat[e]' sublimation of their homosexuality."[6]
- Another gem of scientific inquiry comes from researcher C. Allen: "the homosexual 'is ill in much the same way as a dwarf is ill—because he has never developed.' "[7]
- Psychoanalyst W. Silverberg speculated that passive gay men were a threat to society because of their amazing ability to lure straight men away from women: "the passive homosexual is try-

ing to extinguish the race [so] society is justified in its violent feeling towards him and . . . in taking steps against him."[8]

- Therapist F. Regardie claimed that he could cure homosexuality in forty sessions through hypnosis.[9]
- Analyst H. Lewinsky said people became gay because of a severe childhood prohibition against masturbation, which the patient understood as permitting him to touch the penis of another man.[10]
- Abram Kardiner's research offered cruel stereotypes of homosexuals based on his limited exposure to gay people: "In many there is in addition a compensatory vindictiveness and a hatred of all people. The common judgment that homosexuality is a form of anti-social activity is not altogether unwarranted."[11]
- Based on the testimony of a patient who feared having injured his mother at birth, psychiatrist I. Berent hypothesized that men and women could be made straight by watching childbirth in hospitals.[12]

In modern reparative therapy, homosexuality is not seen as a sexual issue, but as a symptom of a larger trauma caused by environmental factors. Much of this theory came from psychiatrist Lionel Ovesey in the 1960s, who proposed the theory of "pseudohomosexuality": homosexuals are just confused straight people who have been deceived into thinking they are gay. Ovesey believed that "the wish to incorporate the therapist's penis orally is really a wish to appropriate his omnipotence and not so much a desire to indulge in homosexual gratification."[13]

The indisputable psychoanalytic king of gay bashing was Edmund Bergler, who was enormously influential in producing reams of antigay data. He should be considered the grandfather of today's reparative therapy movement because of this obsession with homosexuality and his willingness to say and do anything to belittle gays. Bergler, who claimed that 99.9 percent of all cases of homosexuality could be cured, frequently wrote diatribes against his gay patients. He passed off stereotype for science and offered judgmental opinions, such as homosexuals tend toward "megalomaniacal superciliousness" and have an "amazing degree of unreliability."

The appalling thing about this man was that for decades he was a public spokesman and considered one of the leading "experts" on homosexuality. Many of the horrible views about gays that people still hold today can be traced back to Bergler, whose statements on homosexuality created the blueprint for today's religious right in their war against gays. Here are some of his "scientific" statements:

> "There are no happy homosexuals," he claimed. . . . "The amount of conflicts, of jealousy, for instance, between homosexuals surpasses everything known in bad heterosexual relationships."[14]

> I have no bias against homosexuality . . . [but] homosexuals are essentially disagreeable people, regardless of their pleasant or unpleasant manner . . . [which contains] a mixture of superciliousness, false aggression, and whimpering. . . . [They are] subservient when confronted with a stronger person, merciless when in power, unscrupulous about trampling on the weaker person.[15]

> [I]f new recruits are not warned by dissemination of the fact that homosexuality is but a disease, the confirmed homosexual is presented with a clear field of operations—and your teen-age children may be the victims.[16]

The nadir in this shameful period came in 1962 when Dr. Irving Bieber published his study *Homosexuality: A Psychoanalytic Study of Male Homosexuals*. At the time, his ten-year study on the causes of homosexuality was considered landmark because it employed a copious sample of patients in analytic treatment—106 male homosexuals, compared with 100 heterosexual males. Bieber and his team of nine mental health workers compiled data from a 450-item questionnaire. Bieber's study had three major findings:

1. Most of his gay patients had overbearing mothers who encouraged alienation between father and son and also in peer relations.
2. In all 106 cases, the gay men experienced "profound interpersonal disturbance" in their relations with their fathers.
3. Gay men fit the sissy stereotype while growing up and shunned conflict with more masculine men by avoiding aggressive activity.[17]

When his study first came out it received high praise, but over the long haul it was severely discredited. Time and again, his findings could not be replicated and were disproved by more diligent researchers. Most egregious of all, the sample he used to represent all gay people included twenty-eight schizophrenics, thirty-one neurotics, and forty-two patients with character disorders.

I have heard Bieber's study mentioned by contemporary reparative therapists such as Nicolosi, but I have yet to witness one honest enough to discuss the problems caused by his flawed sample. This suggests that either these modern-day cure warriors are deliberately concealing the facts, or they are ignorant of the very work they trumpet. At the NARTH conference I attended, the organization dedicated their new library to the late Bieber. His wife, Toby, an antigay psychologist herself, tearfully accepted the "honor."

Social Ramifications of Psychiatric Abuse

The bad science had tangible effects that extended beyond the shrink's couch and played a major role in the way gays were treated—and are still viewed—by society. For instance, the Pentagon denied gays security clearances because they were viewed as sick. Thousands of gays were fired from the federal government, particularly during the McCarthy era. The New York Taxi Commission required homosexual drivers to undergo psychiatric examinations twice a year to see if they were fit to drive. In some instances gay attorneys were denied licenses to practice.[18]

It was in the arena of shaping public opinion where these witch doctors had their most deleterious effects. A vivid example of this came during the first ever network television special featuring gay people. In 1967, the newsmagazine *CBS Reports* aired an hour-long segment, "The Homosexuals," that gave America its first glimpse of gay and lesbian Americans.[19] Thanks to the efforts of antigay psychiatrists, gays were vilified in front of 40 million people, solidifying despicable stereotypes that would last for more than a generation.

The landmark broadcast included an interview with a closeted homosexual whose face was concealed by dark shadows cast by a large office plant. "I know that inside now I'm sick," he told reporter Mike Wallace.[20] "I'm not sick just sexually. I'm sick in a lot of ways, immature, childlike, and sex is a symptom, like a toothache is a symptom of who knows what."

This memorable image of disease, timidity, and shame was juxtaposed with the confident, self-assured doctors Irving Bieber and Charles Socarides, who offered lurid illustrations of gay life. In one segment, Socarides appeared to be answering unprompted questions during a symposium at the Albert Einstein School of Medicine, where he taught. "I was wondering if you think there are any 'happy homosexuals' for whom homosexuality would be in a way their best adjustment to life," a female student said. Socarides replied, "The fact that somebody's homosexual—a true obligatory homosexual—automatically rules out the possibility that he will remain happy for long, in my opinion." Socarides went on to say that the notion of a happy gay or lesbian person is a "mythology."

In the next segment, Bieber followed with his own devastating display of misinformation. "I do not believe it is possible to produce a homosexual if the father is a warm, good, supportive, constructive father to his son."

The most damaging part of the broadcast came when the respected Mike Wallace offered his calumnious assault on what he thought, at the time, was an objective view of gay life:

> The average homosexual, if there be such, is promiscuous. He is not interested in nor capable of a lasting relationship like that of heterosexual marriage. His sex life—his "love life"—consists of chance encounters at the clubs and bars he inhabits, and even on the streets of the city. The pickup—the one night stand— these are characteristics of the homosexual relationship. And the homosexual prostitute has become a fixture on the downtown streets at night.

Nearly one out of every five Americans witnessed this incomparable catastrophe. With the ubiquity of this show, it is no exaggeration to say that this broadcast can easily be viewed as the single most destructive hour of antigay propaganda in our nation's history. To get a handle on the enormity of this PR nightmare, one has to consider the time period in which it took place. There were no cable stations, satellite dishes, Internet Web sites, or countless special-interest magazines in which dissenting views could be aired. There were no obnoxious television shows where talking heads endlessly bloviated on divisive issues. There were simply newspapers—most of which would not publish gay-related stories unless they were about a homosexual getting arrested for public sex—or the omnipresent networks, where the point of view presented was often considered gospel. The lack of venues to disseminate messages was compounded by the general absence of openly gay people in society. With few avenues to counter the destructive message of *The Homosexuals,* the show not only had a devastating effect on public opinion but also was a psychological nuclear bomb dropped on the psyches of gay and lesbian Americans, who, prior to this show, had never been represented as a group on national television.

Imagine being a gay person from a small town who has never met another homosexual. This show sent the message that one had either to live miserably in the closet or to accept an underground gay life of crushing loneliness and breathtaking instability. We will never know how many lives were ruined as a result of this broadcast, but there can be no doubt that multitudes of people were driven to despair. Worse yet, they went to doctors such as Bieber and Socarides to help them overcome the despondency that these very doctors worked to create.

Mike Wallace has since come to regret his participation in this broadcast, blaming the antigay therapists for spreading misinformation about gay people. Wallace repented in an interview many years later:

> Well, I said it. That is—God help us—what our understanding was of the homosexual lifestyle a mere twenty-five years ago because nobody was out of the closet and because that's what we heard from doctors—that's what Socarides told us, it was a matter of shame.[21]

The Inside Story Behind the Insanity

Society changed rapidly in the years following this broadcast. The nation convulsed in violent seizures of cultural upheaval that included Vietnam War protests, the civil rights movement, the women's movement, and the incipient modern gay rights movement that began at the Stonewall Inn in June 1969. During this period, conventional wisdom was often challenged and prevailing viewpoints were disputed. No longer were gays—and many enlightened doctors—allowing homosexuals to be called sick without proof, and when the established beliefs on homosexuality were put to the test, time and again they were shown to have no merit.

The scientific community was beginning to prove that homosexuals were not different from other people, with the exception of their sexual orientation. However, it was left to gay activists of the early 1970s to pressure the medical and mental health establishments to brush aside decades of bias and review the actual evidence. "We had to get rid of the sickness label," said legendary gay activist Barbara Gittings. "But it was hard, because everything you said could be attributed to your sickness."[22]

The goal of the activists was to remove homosexuality from being listed as a mental illness in the APA's *Diagnostic and Statistical Manual of Mental Disorders.* The evidence certainly existed to overturn its inclusion, but the prejudice of activist doctors such as Bieber and Socarides prevented an honest dialogue from taking place. So gay advocates forced the issue, beginning in 1968, with the Gay Liberation Front (GLF) storming the American Medical Association's annual meeting in San Francisco. In 1970, again in San Francisco, gay activists barreled into the APA's annual meeting during a session on "aversion therapy."[23] Advocates from the Society for Individual Rights (SIR) and Daughters of Bilitis interrupted the meeting, calling aversion therapy a form of "torture." *The Washington Post* ran a story on the incident headlined "Gays and Dolls Battle Shrinks."[24]

Three years of these theatric protests were beginning to have a measurable effect. In May 1971 gay and lesbian advocates were asked to participate in an official APA panel in Washington. During the panel, the advocates, who were scattered throughout the convention hall, stormed the meeting and took it over. Activist Frank Kameny seized the microphone and bellowed into it what most lesbian and gay people thought of the APA: "Psychiatry is the enemy incarnate. Psychiatry has waged a relentless war of extermination against us. You may take this as a declaration of war against you."[25]

While the activists continued to pressure the APA, several studies came out that bolstered the claim that homosexuality was not a sickness. Dr. Charles Silverstein released an exhaustive survey that showed that previous work labeling homosexuality a mental illness was either skewed or biased. Dr. Evelyn Hooker, using a grant from the National Institute of Mental Health, proved that homosexuals were psychologically no different from heterosexuals. Hooker compared thirty heterosexual men with thirty homosexual men in terms of intelligence, educational level, and age. She then subjected them to identical inkblot and other psychological tests and presented the unidentified results of all test participants to two psychoanalysts for their opinions. The doctors could not identify the gay men from the heterosexual men. Hooker concluded that homosexual individuals may be as ordinary as heterosexual ones, and therefore indistinguishable.

By 1973, the psychiatric community was considering taking homosexuality off the list of mental disorders. At the annual convention in Honolulu in May, the APA heard arguments on both sides of the issue. Dr. Judd Marmor led the fight for the change, while Bieber and Socarides volubly led the opposition. After presenting his case, Marmor called the work of Bieber and Socarides "essentially meaningless" and chastised them and their cohorts for the bias that was so evident in their work: "The cruelty, the thoughtlessness, the lack of common humanity in the attitudes reflected by many conservative psychiatrists is, I think, a disgrace to our profession," Marmor scolded.[26] By the time Socarides and Bieber took the stage, the tide had clearly turned. The once acclaimed doctors were ridiculed and heckled by their own colleagues, with boos and jeers filling the auditorium as they presented their anachronistic data.

Six months after the meeting in Honolulu, the board of trustees, led by Dr. Robert Spitzer (see the chapter "*Political* Science" for more on Spitzer), voted for the landmark change to the *Diagnostic and Statistical Manual.* The new language read that homosexuality "does not necessarily constitute a psychiatric disorder," with the word *necessarily* added to placate conservatives who were bitterly protesting the change. To further appease conservatives, a new category was created—sexual orientation disturbance—for gay people who were troubled by and deeply conflicted about their sexual orientation.

Bitter Shrinks Retreat and Regroup
As Reparative Therapists

This new category was just the loophole needed to keep unethical therapists such as Socarides and Bieber in business and was also key in the establishment of modern reparative therapy. Now these doctors could claim they were just "helping" people who were unhappy and suffering from "unwanted homosexuality." The tragic part is that the people most in need of gay affirmative therapy were the ones most likely to visit the very doctors who were responsible for creating negative attitudes toward gay people in the first place. This further lowered these patients' self-esteem and reinforced feelings of inadequacy.

Still resentful of the change, Socarides used parliamentary maneuvers to send the board's resolution back to the whole membership of the APA.[27] In April 1974, more than 10,000 ballots came back by mail and the rank and file upheld the decision by a nearly three-to-two margin. To date, this is probably the biggest victory in the history of the GLBT movement. After the vote, the National Gay and Lesbian Task Force's headline in their newsletter summed it up best: "The Earth Is Round."[28]

The debate had ended for most psychiatrists, but still a cabal of indignant conservatives were embittered because their peers resoundingly rejected the work to which they had dedicated their lives. They had wrapped their careers and self-worth around outdated notions and now they were left with nothing to show for their efforts. One can only imagine the trauma Bieber faced when his study went from laudable to laughable in slightly more than a decade: "If you had devoted your whole life to a particular view of the world and then the world changed around you, it might be very difficult to give up that view," said Jack Drescher, author of *Psychoanalytic Therapy and the Gay Man*.

Much like the humiliated fundamentalists after the Scopes Monkey Trial in the 1920s, scientists such as Bieber and Socarides retreated in shame. Embattled and increasingly marginalized, they withdrew further and further from mainstream psychiatry. In their isolation, however, they found new allies with both political and moral stakes in keeping their disgraced work alive and well. The unholy alliances forged between embittered psychiatrists, the religious right, self-loathing gays, and culturally conservative politicians eventually formed the base of what is now known as the reparative therapy movement, led by Joseph Nicolosi.

Nicolosi's Nonsense

A kid gets killed in Wyoming, and we can't even have a scientific meeting.

> Dr. Joseph Nicolosi
> on the death of Matthew Shepard

Dueling in the Desert

To escape the blistering Las Vegas heat, I stood hunched over a slot machine at the Egyptian-themed Luxor hotel. With gigantic plaster pharaohs hovering above my head, I energetically yanked the lever to try to win back the money I had lost throughout the afternoon. I was just beginning to get lucky when my pager beeped. The call was from a producer from the *Hannity & Colmes* show on the Fox News Channel who wanted me to square off against Joseph Nicolosi, the premier reparative therapist in America and Executive Director of NARTH.[1] I was on vacation and hardly wanted to get in a suit and head to a studio in the middle of the desert, but I couldn't pass up the opportunity to debate Nicolosi, the undisputed ringmaster of the reparative therapy circus.

On this particular day, I was uncharacteristically blunt on TV and my temper was as hot as the Las Vegas sun. Generally I try to keep cool in even the most challenging and confrontational situations, but it was unusually difficult to keep composed when up against a man responsible for much of the modern antigay propaganda in circulation today.

"[P]eople go to Dr. Nicolosi . . . because their self-esteem is destroyed," I caustically bellowed on the show. "They're made to hate themsel[ves[for who they are because of programs such as his. [T]hey [patients] go there, he bilks them for money for years. They never change."

"Well, first of all," responded Nicolosi, "I want to know why my opponent is so angry. . . . This is a therapy for people who want to change, . . . [b]ut the point is that people can change. . . . That is a direct threat to gay activists like my opponent."

"Are you angry, Doctor? You're screaming. Doctor Nicolosi, first of all—"

"I'm not screaming," he screamed, as he cut me off. ". . . Listen, I've been doing this work for twenty years."

"You've been a quack for twenty years. . . . Let me explain why your work is a fraud, Doctor Nicolosi."

"You're calling me a fraud. You're calling me a quack."

"You are a fraud. Yes and yes."

"I thought this was going to be a discussion of the facts," shrieked Nicolosi.

"You've never had a fact in your life," I responded.

My delivery on the television show may have been a bit confrontational, but my observations were certainly on the mark. By manipulating people into buying an expensive, flawed product, Nicolosi was able to become the reigning king of reparative therapy.

An Underachiever Finds His Niche

Propaganda Paul Cameron's reputation had made him such a liability that the religious right was no longer able credibly to use his work. Yet, the right still needed antigay medical and mental health statistics to supplement their religious condemnation of gays. Into this vacuum created by Cameron's demise stepped Joe Nicolosi, a California psychologist who shrewdly recognized his opportunity and lunged at it.

By all indications, Nicolosi's prospects of contributing to the field of psychology seemed bleak. In 1977, he graduated from the California School of Psychology near downtown Los Angeles. In a 1996 study published by the American Psychological Society, the school was ranked 176th out of 185 graduate psychology programs.[2] Strangely, during the time Nicolosi attended the school, it was no more than a storefront.[3] The place was so obscure that Nicolosi told one publication that he "doesn't remember" where it used to be located while he was a pupil.[4]

Nicolosi's matriculation suggested that he was headed toward a nondescript career of inconsequentiality and moderate wages. The doctor realized, however, that if he took over Cameron's role as the religious right's chief propagandist, the future held no limits. He could gain notoriety in his field, achieve fame through television appearances, and earn a substantial sum of money.

Nicolosi was cunning enough to know that the days of espousing raw antigay hatred had passed. The doctor introduced the novel idea of preaching love for gays, all the while flooding the nation with antigay medical statistics and propaganda. He would fashion himself as Cameron Lite. Instead of trying to save America from homosexuals—as Cameron had—his message was that he was trying to save homosexuals from themselves. Through reparative therapy, he claimed that he helps his clients to avoid contracting HIV and to escape the supposedly unhappy "gay lifestyle."

Unlike Cameron, who openly mused of exterminating gays, Nicolosi posed as an impartial, secular psychologist simply trying to "help" those who wanted to change. Nicolosi was neither secular nor impartial, however, but, in fact, a deeply religious political operative with strong ties to the religious right. His strategy was subtler than Cameron's, but it was just as mean-spirited. Similar to Cameron, Nicolosi adamantly opposed gay and lesbian equality, and his goal was to portray all gay people as sick degenerates who needed psychiatric treatment.

Nicolosi's religious beliefs were the primary reason for his claim that gay and lesbian people can change. When confronted by reporters, however, Nicolosi would tell them he was not religious and refer them to ex-gay groups, such as Exodus, for the religious angle. "Religion has nothing to do with it," Nicolosi once said on the CNBC television show *Equal Time*.[5]

A closer look at Nicolosi's career path shows that religion was more than a peripheral subject that happened conveniently to mesh with his therapy. A hard-core conservative Catholic, in 1980, Nicolosi started his Thomas Aquinas Psychological Clinic to "offer therapy in harmony with Catholic teaching." According to one news report, his office was filled with publications from infamous religious right leader James Dobson.[6] The doctor also surrounded himself at conferences with known religious extremists, such as the Traditional Values Co-alition's Lou Sheldon and Bob Knight, formerly of the Family Research Council and now with Concerned Women of America.

Many of Nicolosi's original patients were gay Catholic priests struggling to reconcile their faith and sexual orientation. His work with priests led to a consulting job with the Catholic Archdiocese of Los Angeles, but his relationship with the Archdiocese soured as they became more aware of his offbeat therapy methods. They began to view him as a brazen, arrogant know-it-all. "Suddenly to say, 'I know what the truth about this is, and I know what the solution is,' I find frightening," Father Peter Liuzzi told the *New Times Los Angeles*, explaining the reason the Catholic Church severed ties with Nicolosi.[7]

The Quacks Organize

Nicolosi's early influences included Moberly, Bergler, Bieber, and, especially, Socarides, whom he saw as a role model. It was through Nicolosi's association with Charles Socarides and Sacramento psychiatrist Ben Kaufman that NARTH was founded in 1992. The trade group was formed to coincide with the twenty-year anniversary of the American Psychiatric Association removing homosexuality from the DSM.

The founding of NARTH was monumental to the survival of reparative therapy. Before the group was founded, the practice was in decline and consisted primarily of controversial lone rangers such as Moberly and washed-up psychiatrists such as Socarides, who were still embittered by the American Psychiatric Association's 1973 decision. Thanks to NARTH, the quacks were able to organize into a cohesive unit behind their aggressive, brash new leader. Nicolosi's efforts resuscitated this lucrative industry and offered a national platform from which to administer their psychological poison. "He opened reparative therapy up to the masses," said ex-gay leader John Paulk,[8] explaining Nicolosi's importance in saving the discredited practice.

NARTH served to empower these malcontents and emboldened them to repackage their old, outdated ideas as new. With membership dues, an annual meeting, and access to the media, NARTH offered a veneer of respectability and a safe place where these "doctors" could validate one another's work. The group also solicited for antigay psychiatrists to appear as expert witnesses in court cases that involved gay parenting and child custody as well as same-sex partnerships and marriage legislation.[9]

The fringe organization gave a home to twisted antigay doctors such as Jeffrey Satinover of Connecticut, who proposed that antidepressants my be a cure for homosexuality. According to Satinover in his book *Homosexuality and the Politics of Truth:*

> When we consider that there is no objective distinction between homosexuality and the other perversions, we can easily see how the development of the homosexual "habit" fits into this framework [of cures through medication]. In fact, some paraphelias are being successfully treated with fluoxetine (Prozac). Here, too, sexual reorientation is reported to have occurred incidentally.[10]

I asked one gay friend on an antidepressant if the drug had made him think of becoming heterosexual. "No," he replied. "Now, I'm just gay in every way. I'm gay as in my sexual orientation and also gay as in happy. No pun intended, but the whole theory that Prozac can make · you straight seems a bit queer."

Another major NARTH contributor is Holocaust revisionist Scott Lively, co-author of *The Pink Swastika.* Lively, in an act of astonishing bigotry, wrote a 200-page book partially blaming gays for the Holocaust, even though it is historical fact that homosexuals were victimized in Adolf Hitler's Nazi regime. "The Pink Swastika will show that there was far more brutality, torture and murder committed against innocent people *by* Nazi deviants and homosexuals than there ever was *against* homosexuals," wrote Kevin E. Abrams in the preface describing Lively's book.[11]

NARTH may have saved reparative therapy, but it is still a cottage industry, with the organization claiming no more than 1,000 members. Compare this to the American Psychological Association, which has 151,000 members. A large membership or even credibility doesn't seem necessary, though, to spread an incalculable amount of misinformation—just a fax machine and a Web site (www.NARTH.com).

Ultimately, NARTH's long-term goal is to work toward having gays once again labeled sick. This is made very clear in numerous public statements offered by NARTH officials: "Homosexuality is a psychological and psychiatric disorder, there is no question about it," said former NARTH President Charles Socarides. "It is a purple menace that is threatening the proper design of gender distinctions in society."[12]

Without an unforeseen dramatic shift in public opinion and political circumstances, NARTH will most likely not reach their goal of having homosexuals reclassified as mentally ill. In fact, the only way NARTH could accomplish their goal of reclassification would be to stage a monumental stealth campaign to take over the American Psychiatric Association, surreptitiously placing conservative psychiatrists in leadership positions. Fortunately, the mental health professionals I spoke with believe such an occurrence is highly unlikely, and if it did occur, mainstream psychiatrists would probably regain control of the group in a relatively short amount of time.

Still, NARTH has affected the public perception of lesbians and gay men in other ways. Primarily, they have provided a scientific front for the perpetuation of stereotypes and bigotry. Here are the greatest areas of concentration for NARTH under Nicolosi's stewardship:

- Trade group protection
- Opening the ex-gay movement to Jewish people
- Opening the ex-gay movement to a more intellectual crowd
- Portraying conservative psychiatrists and ex-gays as victims
- Proving that homosexuality is not genetic

Trade Group Protection

The primary reason that NARTH was founded (other than labeling gays sick) was to protect the reparative therapy industry from attempts to ban the practice. Reparative therapy is a cash cow that allows unscrupulous practitioners to make small fortunes and achieve notoriety at the expense of their clients' mental health and well-being. For instance, Nicolosi charges his patients $125 a session, and he recommends two one-hour sessions a week (one individual and one group). Nicolosi's practice has afforded him and his wife and son a lavish lifestyle that includes a ranch-style home with a pool in an upscale suburban Los Angeles neighborhood.[13]

Nicolosi would seem to have a fairy-tale life, except for the uncomfortable fact that former patients sometimes speak out about how their lives were miserably altered by reparative therapy. "I've never talked to anybody that made it to the other side," said "Jeff" (a pseudonym), a former Nicolosi client. According to *New Times Los Angeles,* Jeff spent roughly \$20,000 on ineffective treatment.[14] Jeff's disgust with Nicolosi led him to compile a list of fifty former patients who say Nicolosi's treatment failed, which is a significant number, considering he claims to have treated 400 gay clients.

I interviewed former Nicolosi patient Tod LoRusso, who concurs with Jeff and said that Nicolosi's reparative therapy simply does not work.[15] "I don't think anyone ever said [they were changing]," said LoRusso, who was under Nicolosi's care for a year. "He would say we were doing better. . . . My friend Andy . . . talked about changing and started dating women. . . . Of course, now he's totally gay."

The testimonies of these individuals are far from isolated cases. For some time, mental health professionals have heard the horror stories associated with reparative therapy and thought something should be done to stop it. Stories such as the one told by Jeff Ford of St. Paul, Minnesota, are commonplace:

> . . . I began seeing a psychologist who believed by using electric shock he could cure me of my homosexuality. . . . I went through 40 or more sessions twice a week during which the psychologist strapped electrodes to my arms and hooked me up to a "penile plythysmograph." . . .
>
> I can still remember the horror I felt every time I sat in that chair. I can still feel the shame and embarrassment of having wires hooked to my arm and penis while looking at pictures of naked men. Intermittently, the psychologist would give me an electric shock that would involuntarily catapult my arm several inches into the air. When leaving his office, I always felt embarrassed and tried to hide the burn marks the electrodes left on my arm.[16]

Other methods are also routinely employed to elicit "change." For example, a church in Dallas used unconventional "therapy" that induced nausea to help gays become straight. "We have them drop a mint-sized bitter pill in their mouth or open a small bottle of rotting hamburger," said the Reverend Terry Wier of Isaiah 56 Ministries. "We ask them to smell it and put their mind to God by singing a worship song."[17] Although Nicolosi claims he is opposed to this particular method, he has helped create a climate where homosexuality is considered so evil that almost anything goes in the attempt to "cure" gays.

Today, many reparative therapists avoid methods such as shock or aversion therapy, but they still are employed more frequently than most will admit. The most common abuse by reparative therapists, such as Nicolosi, is the sin of omission. They flat-out lie to their patients when they claim that there is no such thing as a happy homosexual. "I do not believe that any man can ever be truly at peace in living out a homosexual orientation," wrote Nicolosi in his book *Reparative Therapy of Male Homosexuality.*[18]

For the millions of openly lesbian and gay women and men who have led fulfilling lives, this statement is patently absurd. The impact of Nicolosi's words on a gay individual who has never met another openly gay person is, however, significant: "I spent decades in therapy because I was told that there was no such thing as a happy gay person," said Tom, who wished to be identified by only his first name, in our interview. "I was told all gay people were miserable, which I now know is not true. It really has ruined the majority of my life. I think of all of the time, money, and energy I put into reparative therapy and wish I could have put it into something more productive. I could be very bitter if I allowed myself to be."

As the horror stories mounted, the American Psychological Association moved to condemn reparative therapy. In 1997, members proposed a resolution that required therapists who undertake this practice to obtain "appropriate informed consent." In other words, patients should be told that the major mental health associations oppose reparative therapy and that no patient should be coerced into attending. Furthermore, patients should be advised that many lesbian and gay people live happy, fulfilling lives. According to University of Rochester clinical psychologist and assistant professor of psychiatry Robert Pollard:

> The question is, are you going into this knowing that homosexuality is not a mental illness, and knowing that you do not necessarily have a problem, and knowing that people who are gay and lesbian can demonstrate perfectly normal mental health?[19]

NARTH, the association that protects the profits of the reparative therapy industry, saw this resolution as a direct threat to their endless money pit. They fought this resolution vigorously, using blistering attacks against it. Nicolosi, in a fit of rage, called the resolution "intimidating and discouraging. It's like having a restaurant and having a big sign in the window saying, 'You might be poisoned, you might not be happy with the food.'"[20]

The reality is, though, that Nicolosi and his cohorts used deceit and guile to bully desperate people into reparative therapy. Nicolosi told gays who had never met another homosexual that they might get poisoned and might not be happy if they entered, what he termed, "the gay lifestyle." Although Nicolosi liked to play the victim, it was his own dishonesty and misleading of clients that made this resolution necessary. With 122 people voting in favor, one opposed, and three abstentions, the American Psychological Association passed the resolution demanding informed consent.

The "APA's resolution is extraordinary because it raises serious ethical questions about attempts to change sexual orientation," said Gregory Herek, a research psychologist from University of California, Davis.[21] According to Doug Haldeman, former president of the American Psychological Association's society for the psychological study of lesbian, gay, and bisexual issues:

> In the past 10 years, Christian fundamentalists have enlisted a coalition of old-style psychologists, psychiatrists and social workers who have become very visible in this country and internationally, and who have as a mission to "help" homosexuals get rid of their sexual orientation. . . . Our aim is not to try to stop them per se or interfere with anyone's right to practice [therapy], but we want to expose the social context that creates this market.[22]

Should reparative therapy be completely banned? Even many therapists who oppose the practice believe that patients should have the right to choose their own therapy, even if it is harmful. Critics ask, "If people do not want to be gay, shouldn't they have the option to try to change?" As someone who has repeatedly witnessed the harm done by reparative therapy, I emphatically disagree with this line of reasoning. To allow reparative therapy to continue, the mental health establishment is turning a blind eye to a therapy that is by definition malpractice. How many more lives will have to be shattered before it is made illegal?

My opinion on reparative therapy was backed by a June 2001 Amnesty International report that called for stopping torture and mistreatment based on sexual identity, repeal of antigay laws, and the discontinuation of forced medical "treatments" designed to "cure" homosexuality.[23]

People go to these "doctors" only because they are made to feel terrible about themselves. They are convinced that they will go to hell if they do not change, and many believe that suicide may be the only alternative. They are lied to—told that there are no happy, productive gay people and that the so-called gay lifestyle leads to only "death and destruction." These dejected individuals also fear that coming out will mean a loss of status, family, friends, and church.

Under such duress, how can one argue that these people are freely making the *choice* to change. The questions that should be asked are these: Would these people want to change if they were not subject to religious persecution, legally sanctioned discrimination, and social condemnation—if not outright physical danger? If discrimination and persecution play no role, why is there no therapy for those who want to change from straight to gay?

There is also the matter of coercion and forced participation. Although I have found no evidence of adults being forced to attend therapy, adolescents—and even toddlers—are often dragged into Nicolosi's clutches against their will. "The parents bring me kids who are unhappy," Nicolosi told *The Advocate* magazine. "It's my job to increase the possibility of a heterosexual future for these effeminate boys."[24] Some of Nicolosi's clients are as young as three years old. (The religious right accuses gays of recruiting?) No health expert I spoke with could point to an example of a three-year-old who was unhappy with his or her sexual orientation or, for that matter, a three-year-old who was even *aware* he or she had a sexual orientation.

Unfortunately, bad science has not stopped Nicolosi from convincing parents to force kids into his programs—for a price, of course. One young Nicolosi victim e-mailed the Human Rights Campaign begging for help:

> I'm seventeen and my parents are forcing me to go to a NARTH meeting this weekend. There is no way I am going to a place

where they can try to brainwash me and make me feel bad for who I am. I'm not sure if you are aware of NARTH but my parents have spoken to the group for a few months now and have become completely brainwashed by the members. They say they are against forced change and yet they are forcing me to go to this weekend of speeches and meetings.

A therapist's role is not to force toddlers and adolescents to attend antigay seminars or to help people make cosmetic behavioral changes to fit into society. If reparative therapy is allowed to exist, then all types of "therapy" that help the persecuted curry favor with the majority to avoid discrimination must be considered fair game. For instance, in some countries, such as South Africa, black people try to bleach their skin to attain social advantages. Should this type of "therapy" also be tolerated simply because people "want to change"? In fact, skin bleaching is less expensive, works more quickly, and has a much better success rate than reparative therapy. Similarly, should it be considered ethical for therapists actively to help self-loathing Asians who want to appear more Caucasian find cosmetic surgeons to round out their eyes?

To this author, skin bleaching, eye rounding, and attempts to change sexual orientation are all demented efforts to relieve oppression by helping the dispossessed mirror preconceived societal notions of the human ideal. In most cases, even where transformation is considered successful, these efforts will likely leave lasting psychological scars. Clearly, it is not the job of trained therapists to support efforts that increase or contribute to feelings of self-loathing, inadequacy, and low self-esteem or to treat the desire to assimilate to the majority culture as the most valiant of psychological goals. The sooner reparative therapy is banned, I believe, the better off society will be.

Opening the Ex-Gay Movement to Jewish People

The ex-gay movement is, for the most part, a Christian one. On the front page of the Exodus Web site is the tag line "Freedom from homosexuality through Jesus Christ." Antigay prejudice is, however, not limited to right-wing Christians. Bias against gays is so entrenched that it cuts across all theological, cultural, and socioeconomic lines. This leaves many Jewish parents in a bind because they have to choose between acceptance and allowing an evangelical Christian organization to help their children supposedly become straight. What if the conversion isn't to heterosexuality, but to Christianity?

This is where reparative therapy comes in. Although it is essentially Christian fundamentalism looking for validation through bad science, it does offer false hope for non-Christians through its veneer of secularism. This is why NARTH appears to have, according to my observations, a disproportionate number of Jewish supporters. NARTH is especially accommodating to Orthodox Jews and once brought in Dr. Laura Schlessinger as a keynote speaker at their annual conference.

In their 2000 meeting in Washington, DC, NARTH featured Rabbi Sam Rosenberg of Jews Offering New Alternatives to Homosexuality (JONAH). Rosenberg, according to NARTH, spoke about reparative therapy and Judaic biblical and Talmudic insights into the homosexual condition.

Opening the Ex-Gay Movement to a More
Intellectual Crowd

Unless one is raised in an evangelical or fundamentalist home, the ex-gay ministries will probably seem absurd. Facing everything from exorcisms to fasting, your average nonreligious person simply will not identify with their dubious methods. "The nonbeliever has great difficulty understanding ex-gay ministries, because we are talking about a supernatural transformation that God brings about," said Michael Johnston, a prominent ex-gay and president of Kerusso Ministries. "Overcoming homosexuality is not about rational thought or rational discussion."[25]

Yet, many nonreligious people are gay or have gay children and want them to change their sexual orientation. NARTH's pseudoscience is a perfect solution for these more intellectual individuals who can't buy into the silly superstitions and religious mysticism provided by the ex-gay ministries.

In the social strata of reorientation programs, the ex-gay ministries are trailer parks for the blue-collar working class while reparative therapy is an exclusive country club reserved for white-collar yuppies. One reason for this is the high cost of reparative therapy, but there is also the education factor. The rigorous mind games played by reparative therapists work better for smart people, while the white-knuckling prayer sessions appeal more to the uneducated.

Obviously, this does not apply to everyone in these programs, so please don't e-mail me with examples of Mensa members who took part in the ministries. There are smart people in the ex-gay ministries and those who are obtuse in reparative therapy, and a lot of people who are attempting to convert take part in both. On average, though, those in reparative therapy have more money and are better educated. My observation is backed by a 1997 NARTH study that showed 90 percent of people taking part in reparative therapy had college degrees. This is a much higher percentage than is found in the general population.[26]

Portraying Conservative Psychiatrists and Ex-Gays As Victims

The most common narrative told by members of NARTH is that liberal shrinks who supposedly hijacked the American Psychiatric Association in 1973 are persecuting them. Much of this has to do with their inability to accept defeat on scientific grounds. Here are three examples from Nicolosi's book, *Reparative Therapy of Male Homosexuality,* that highlight NARTH's attempt to portray members as victims:

> Militant gay advocates working in a small but forceful network have caused apathy and confusion in American society.[27]

> The combined effects of the sexual revolution and the "rights" movements—civil rights, minority rights, feminist rights—have resulted in an intimidating effect upon psychology.[28]

> Although the intention has been to end discrimination, one result has been discrimination for a different group of people—those men whose social and moral values and sense of self cannot incorporate their homosexuality. . . . Unfortunately, these men [ex-gays] have been labeled victims of psychological oppression rather than the courageous men they are, committed to an authentic vision.[29]

By playing the victim card, Nicolosi is a historical revisionist, blatantly twisting the pages of history into a fictitious narrative that conveniently fits his point of view. His effectiveness is limited at this time by the presence of psychiatrists who were active in the 1973 decision. The real danger of Nicolosi's revisionism, I'm afraid, will come twenty years from now when most people will have forgotten what really took place in 1973. Without diligence and commitment to historical integrity, future revisionists may try to reintroduce his flawed work as a legitimate viewpoint rather than treating it as the dishonest antigay propaganda that it is.

Proving That Homosexuality Is Not Genetic

Ironically, the biggest fear of both the antigay and progay movements is that homosexuality will one day be proven to be a genetic phenomenon. The antigay industry knows that if homosexuality is shown to be a genetic trait, acceptance of homosexuals will quickly follow. The progay side fears that if a gay gene is found, women one day may be able to abort fetuses destined to turn out as gay in adulthood. This may sound like science fiction, but recent technological advances make the prospect more realistic than people might imagine. " 'It's not a matter of whether' we'll find homosexuality's basic mechanisms, 'it's a matter of when,' " Dennis McFadden, a University of Texas scientist told the *Los Angeles Times*. "And parents are going to rush to influence them, possibly before a child is born."[30]

Of interest is the way both sides are handling the touchy issue. The progay side studiously avoids the topic, while the antigay side works feverishly to mislead the public regarding the truth about possible biological causes for homosexuality. NARTH is in the forefront of this right-wing supereffort to disprove the existence of a gay gene. To individuals such as Chandler Burr, author of *A Separate Creation: The Search for the Biological Origins of Sexual Orientation,* NARTH and others on the far right have good reason to attack the gay gene theory: "We all know that if a homosexual orientation is something you're born with, the Religious Right might as well pack it in right now. They've lost," wrote Burr in our interview.[31] "The American people just will not penalize people for what they are."

Public opinion seems to back up Burr's assertion. According to a May 2000 Associated Press poll, 59 percent of people who believe gays are born with a homosexual orientation support same-sex marriage, while 69 percent of people who believe gays choose their sexual orientation are opposed to same-sex marriage.

So what does the science actually say about homosexuality? "A lot of the science is in a bit of an unfinished state . . . a state of flux," former Salk Institute scientist Simon LeVay told me in a telephone interview.[32] "We can be pretty confident that there is a genetic component to sexual orientation, but it is not one hundred percent of the reason why one person is gay or straight."

Indeed, the modern era of looking for biological roots to explain sexual orientation began in August 1991 when LeVay announced in *Science* magazine that he had uncovered brain differences between gay and straight men.[33] His study, using corpses of AIDS victims, found that a cluster of neurons in the hypothalamus appeared to be twice as big in the heterosexual men than in the gay men. This led him to theorize that there may be a biological component to sexual orientation.

Another 1991 study pointed toward a biological component to homosexuality.[34] Scientists Richard Pillard and John M. Bailey studied homosexuality among brothers and found that 53 percent of (29 out of 56 pairs) of identical twins were both gay. Of the fraternal twins, 22 percent (12 out of 54) were both gay. In adoptive brothers, 11 percent (6 out of 57) were both homosexual. Of nontwin biological siblings, 9 percent (13 out of 142) were gay. This study clearly showed a biological/genetic component to sexual orientation, but the fact that not *all* of the identical twins were gay suggested that there may be more than just a simple genetic explanation for homosexuality.

"It is not really clear what that nongenetic influence might be, and it might be sort of just a random thing that occurs prenatally," explained LeVay in our interview. "Human development works kind of like a slot machine, if you will. It sort of circles and wheels and some random result just comes out. That's really quite a common thing in development, and it may be something like that, something we can't say is programmed; it just sort of happens developmentally."

Another study that made a lot of headlines was the National Institute of Health's (NIH) 1993 study by researcher Dean Hamer.[35] In his study, it was shown that some cases of homosexuality might be inherited from the mother by her sons through a specific region of the X chromosome (Xq28). Hamer demonstrated this by noting that 33 out of 40 pairs of homosexual brothers whom he studied showed the same variation in the tip of this chromosome.

Recently, new studies have provided further evidence that sexual orientation has biological or genetic components:

- University of Texas psychoacoustics specialist Dennis McFadden found that when measuring the way the brain reacts to sound, lesbians fell in between heterosexual men and straight women, suggesting they might be exposed to higher than normal levels of male hormone in utero.[36]
- University of Liverpool biologist John T. Manning found that the lesbians whom he studied have a hand pattern that resembles a man's more than a straight female's. Manning concluded from his study that this "strongly tells us that female homosexuals have had high levels of exposure to testosterone before birth."[37]

This is just a snapshot of some of the genetic and biological research that has shaped the debate on sexual orientation. Clearly there is more that we do not know than we do understand at this time. Still, this burgeoning scientific field has changed attitudes, shaped public perceptions about gays, and had a dramatic impact on public opinion.

This shift in attitudes was illustrated in a June 4, 2001 Gallup Poll that showed for the first time in American history, a majority of people, 56 percent, believed that homosexuality is something that "a person is born with." This was a significantly higher percentage than when the question was first asked in a 1977 poll, which reported that only 13 percent of Americans thought a person was born homosexual.

Those on the side of the religious right can also read the polls and realize that they will increasingly become marginalized unless they can reverse the present trend and convince America that homosexuality is not genetic. NARTH has been their pit bull in these efforts, flooding the country with a deluge of misinformation on the so-called causes of homosexuality. For example, in a "fact" sheet titled "Is There a 'Gay Gene'?" NARTH dismissed the recent scientific advances by making them appear to be nothing more than fabrications created by the supposedly liberal media: "In reality, there is no evidence that shows that homosexuality is simply 'genetic.' *And none of*

the research claims there is. Only the press and certain researchers do, when speaking in sound bites to the public."

This phrase illustrates how slippery NARTH really is. The statement is *technically* true because the research cannot show, at this point, that homosexuality is *simply* genetic, but NARTH's statement conveniently omits the incontrovertible fact that a growing body of research points to a possible biological component to sexual orientation. If NARTH were truly interested in education, rather than obfuscation, their statement would read more like this: "While there is no definitive proof that homosexuality is genetic, recent scientific advances show that there may be a biological component. More research needs to be done, but based on the science, the possible role genes may play in sexual orientation, including homosexuality, cannot be dismissed."

NARTH also misuses the incomplete scientific data to show that upbringing *must* play a part in homosexuality, but the inconclusive nature of the genetic science does not necessarily bolster NARTH's argument for nurture. It shows only that we don't have enough information to make an absolute determination of the root causes of sexual orientation. In fact, based on the limited amount of evidence, a better case can be made for nature than nurture. Although several studies show a potential genetic component to homosexuality, no credible studies exist that show sexual orientation is linked to a poor relationship with a same-sex parent, as NARTH postulates. And if such a study were to exist, I suspect the results would show that a child did not become gay because of a distant same-sex parent, but that the same-sex parent created distance because he or she could tell the child was born gay. Furthermore, there is no credible evidence that male sexual or emotional abuse against women leads to lesbianism, as reparative therapists often claim.

New scientific studies support that homosexual traits can be seen in children from an early age, regardless of class or background, which may lead to rejection by ignorant parents. According to J. Michael Bailey, a psychologist and sexuality researcher at Northwestern University in Evanston, Illinois:

> For . . . boys who show "pervasive and persistently" effeminate behavior, the odds of being gay lie at 75%. . . . That is a probability of homosexuality 20 times as high as that in the broad population of boys. . . . Among girls, this so-called gender-atypical

behavior also is a good predictor of later lesbianism, though the pattern is weaker.[38]

In other words, although NARTH claims a distant or absent same-sex parent causes homosexuality, it is more likely that the noticeable presence of homosexuality early in a child's life is what causes the perceived distance.

"Virtually every man I interviewed who admitted to having effeminate tendencies had some kind of nightmare story to tell: a father who disowned him, kept himself distant, or constantly compared him to his older, more masculine brothers," wrote Tim Bergling, author of the book *Sissyphobia,* in our interview.[39] Bergling's research suggests that gays are more likely to have a distant same-sex parent only when the parent recognizes his or her child is displaying effeminate behavior from an early age. That is, the chicken (effeminate behavior) does come before the egg (distant same-sex parent), which leaves NARTH with egg on its face.

Furthermore, if NARTH's unproven cause-and-effect theory were true, a distant same-sex parent could be found in the background of virtually all homosexuals, regardless of how masculine in appearance. This is not the case, however, and there is no proven common denominator in the backgrounds of homosexuals, as NARTH disingenuously claims. NARTH's nurture theory of a distant same-sex parent also flies in the face of an inescapable reality: Millions of gay men and women are close to their same-sex parents while millions of heterosexuals are not. The logical conclusion to be drawn is that a relationship with a same-sex parent seems irrelevant to the outcome of one's sexual orientation.

Inside Nicolosi's Lair

Tod LoRusso, twenty-eight, could not believe his eyes. He looked at the ad in a Christian newspaper and for the first time in his life he had hope. He read and reread Dr. Nicolosi's promising ad, claiming that he could help rid people of their homosexuality. If there were a way to become straight, LoRusso would do whatever was necessary.

To get to Dr. Nicolosi's office, LoRusso had to drive nearly two hours. He met with the doctor and thought that finally he had found a person who could understand what he was going through. After a few months, though, red flags began appearing. Most obvious was Nicolosi's sliding scale for "healing." He would tell some clients that healing could take place in as little as a year and then in the next session that healing was as long as five years.

This author directly encountered Nicolosi's shifty predictions on the time it takes for one to become heterosexual. On the *Hannity & Colmes* show mentioned earlier, he said that the average amount of time it takes to convert is 6.7 years. At other times, he told the *New Times Los Angeles* that "we're working two years here," and, in his book, that "change" is a "long-term process," and one that is "most probably lifelong."

Nicolosi's prognosis is so embarrassingly random that he couldn't even decide in his own book whether he offers a magical cure for homosexuality. At first, he distanced himself from the notion of a cure, warning that change is a more realistic goal: "Usually some homosexual desires will persist or recur during certain times in the life cycle," he wrote. "Therefore, rather than 'cure,' we refer to the goal of 'change,' a meaning shift beginning with a change in identification of self."[40] Later, in a spectacular breach of ethical conduct, Nicolosi flip-flops, referring to a cure while counseling a client: "That's an essential part of the *cure* . . . just seeing it through to the end and that futility," he told the patient.[41] Incredibly, this is the exact behavior he vigorously warned against on earlier pages.

It may appear that my parsing of Nicolosi's statements is, at times, captious, but it is nonetheless a necessary and worthwhile exercise in accountability. His insouciant game of musical cures, played at the expense of his clients, can cause grave psychological trauma. Thousands of people hang on his every word—through his practice, his book, speaking engagements, and numerous media appearances—and his semantic malpractice literally places people's lives at risk.

One must remember that for the reparative therapy client, each day—or hour for that matter—is an epic struggle. These individuals studiously avoid the love and intimacy that feels natural by adopting an agonizing regimen of self-denial, attending expensive therapy sessions, engaging in endless prayer, and maintaining long-term celibacy. A strong-willed person, with great difficulty, may be able to adhere to this ascetic lifestyle for two years—if promised this is how long it will take to attain heterosexuality—but how is the individual supposed to react when the two years are up and he or she is told the new time line is 6.7 years? Clearly, this is why many reparative therapy patients later call their so-called treatment psychological terror-ism. The constant revision of the cure time line led the American Psy-chological Association to report in a 1994 fact sheet terms that reparative therapy often leads to "depression, anxiety, and self-destruc-tive behavior."

LoRusso continued with therapy because he did see some im-provements in his life—the doctor helped him become a more asser-tive and confident person—but he, as with everyone else in his group, remained gay. In fact, Nicolosi's group therapy sometimes morphed into "grope therapy," as he encouraged his clients to socialize outside of the therapeutic setting. "Relationships went on outside the group as well, whether it be friendships or some guys, you know, would fool around a little bit and that would be dealt with in the group," said LoRusso. "Mostly it would be kissing, or some guy wanted to fondle the other guy, and like that."

Nicolosi, who quoted Colin Cook twice in his book—Cook, a star of "Founding Follies," if you recall, is the founder of Homosexuals Anonymous and famous for nude massages and phone sex—appar-ently struggled with issues similar to Cook's: "After I left, there was some oral sex thing that happened," LoRusso continued. "People [in the group] wouldn't tell about the situation or the thing that happened in private, and it was obvious that something had happened."

By the end of the year, LoRusso had seen enough; he packed his bags and moved to Texas. After a couple more years of trying to change at a right-wing church, he came out of the closet and has not looked back. "As a kid I was labeled . . . a 'fag' or a 'queer,'" said LoRusso. "But now I'm like 'Yeah, I'm a fag, and I love it. And don't ever take it away from me.' . . . My advice [to someone thinking of en-tering reparative therapy] . . . is just love yourself."

The Scientificization of Stereotypes

The first time I saw Nicolosi in person was at the 2000 NARTH conference in Washington, DC. My first impression was that this was a not particularly macho man who was trying very hard to look mas-culine. For instance, he didn't simply walk to the stage but deliber-ately sauntered. Once he reached the microphone, he puffed up his chest like an angry parakeet and audibly strained his voice to make it sound deeper than it was naturally. Instead of coming across as genuinely masculine, however, he looked like a buffoonish caricature of machismo—I pictured him crooning the hit "Macho Man" by the Village People.

To understand Nicolosi's work is to realize that creating this cartoonish persona is central to his program. In his practice, he has narcissistically set himself up as the ideal of masculinity, and his therapeutic goal is to turn homosexual men into replicas of himself. Being the paragon of masculinity that he believes himself to be, he laments in his writings that often patients fall in love with him.

After Nicolosi presents himself as a Ramboesque figure that all men should aspire to be, he breaks the world down into neat categories and puts people into little boxes depending on their gender or sexual orientation. His entire body of work is based on stereotypes and outdated assumptions on what it means to be a man, a woman, or a gay person. It is as if Nicolosi made a list of every outrageous stereotype and gave each one a scientific label—the "scientificization of stereotypes," if you will.

Nicolosi's ludicrous generalizations don't begin with gays, but with differences in the sexes. For example, the "nurturance of the mother is more likely to be unconditional; however, since the father mediates between the boy and reality, his nurturance is more likely to be conditional."[42] Since when is a father's love more conditional than a mother's, and, more important, why can't a mother mediate between a boy and reality? Nicolosi also casually dismisses paternal instincts: "most fathers have felt ill-at-ease handling and caring for a fragile newborn boy."[43] He represents mothers as a stabilizing element of the feminine influence, while fathers automatically "symbolize strength, independence and mastery of the environment."[44] Also, through the father, "the boy learns that danger can be fun and exciting."[45] Another Nicolosi generalization: "Men tend to view their bodies in terms of strength, agility and action, and they need to relate on a physical level. Unlike men, most women can relate in a static manner by sitting and talking face-to-face."[46]

Nicolosi's view of masculinity has always been skewed, if not downright screwy. In his book he theorizes, "Nonhomosexual men who experience defeat and failure may also experience homosexual fantasies or dreams."[47] Armed with this useful tidbit of knowledge, perhaps gay men could start hanging out by the locker rooms of losing sports teams in hope of catching a hot athlete in a weak moment of "defeat and failure."

I tested this theory on the National Basketball Association's (NBA) Washington Wizards, who have failed for years. In fact, if defeat causes homosexuality in straight men, by now the Wizards' uniforms should be lavender Speedos. To my dismay, the experiement failed; none of the players seemed remotely interested in me as I stood outside the locker room batting my eyelashes.

With his anachronistic view of women and bizarre image of men, it should be no surprise that the doctor has a fairly twisted view of family relations. In Nicolosi's surreal universe, a cabal of sneaky little gay boys and their subversive mothers are busy surreptitiously undermining fathers: "Later in childhood he [the gay boy] will indirectly express his anger by ignoring father and denying that he has any importance to the family, conspiring with mother in collusion against father."[48]

This sentiment was echoed later in Nicolosi's book in conversation with a client, "How many times have homosexual sons told their mothers to leave Dad!" he exclaimed. The client responded, "But why?" "Because you left Dad a long time ago. Now you want Mom to do the same. You identified with her against him."[49] Amazingly, the possibility that Dad might be a negligent husband and abusive father who deserves to be abandoned never crossed the doctor's mind. It couldn't be Father's fault when Nicolosi has his usual scapegoats— women and gay men—to blame.

Nicolosi's War Against Gays

Nicolosi's preposterous stereotypes of straight men and women are nothing compared to how he generalizes about gays. The world's leading reparative therapist once told a crowd at an antigay seminar that gay men are "disconnected" from other people and live in an unreal world and that's why they like theater.[50] Nicolosi also swears that gay men cannot play sports. Of course, he ignores that gay sports leagues have proliferated in most major cities in Western civilization and that there have been several gay professional athletes, such as ex–big leaguer Billy Bean and former National Football League (NFL) player David Kopay.

Another stereotype that Nicolosi propagates is that heterosexual relationships last, while gay relationships are destined to fail. "I think that the homosexual condition has certain limitations to it," he once remarked on CNBC's *Equal Time*. "I think that two men in a relationship have difficulty and two women would have difficulty where there's a certain compatibility between male and female." Upon hearing this ridiculous stereotyping, cohosts Stephanie Miller and Mo Gaffney put him in his place: "I'm only laughing, because I've had such trouble in relationships with men," said Gaffney. Miller followed up, "We speak for heterosexuals everywhere when we say Ha, ha, ha, ha!"[51]

It seems that Nicolosi's main tactic in his efforts to degrade homosexuals is to throw enough stereotypes against the wall in hopes that some will stick. Nicolosi, however, should heed the old adage that one shouldn't lie unless one can remember what one has said because, in his quest to defame gays, he contradicts himself quite often. For example, in his book he claimed, on the one hand, gays suffer from "a deficit in sense of personal power," and, on the other, "[m]ilitant gay advocates working in a small but forceful network have caused apathy and confusion in American society."[52] One might wonder how a group of pathetic, weak people suffering from a "deficit in personal power" can manipulate the world's only superpower.

Clearly, Nicolosi is insincere, alternating between calling gays weak and all-powerful depending on the point he is trying to prove. Since very few people who are not in reparative therapy follow his work, he likely figures he can get away with this dishonesty and exploitation. Nicolosi also counts on people not remembering what he wrote from one page to the next. For example, "A deficit in assertion and sense of personal power [for gays] almost invariably lead to difficulty in making major life and career decisions."[53] Yet, five pages later, homosexuals "may work unusually hard in business."[54] Thus, on one hand, homosexuality leads to career paralysis, and, on the other, it leads to career success. Oddly, he never considers that a gay person's achievements or disappointments may have nothing to do with his or her sexual orientation.

Nicolosi also seems to blame any mental health issue a gay person might have on his or her sexuality. In his book he blamed one man's "fear of tall bridges" on the client's sexual orientation. Another client's "phobia of the phone" was somehow traced back to his homosexuality. The prescient medicine man even claimed gay men are more likely to be "pee shy" and have trouble urinating in public places.[55] This led Nicolosi to astute observations:

> Psychodynamically, urination is a form of assertion, of symbolically letting go with other men. The above client made the insightful connection between not being able to "flow" in conversation and having difficulty "flowing" (urinating) with other men.[56]

Real Dudes Drink Gatorade

The easiest way to prove that reparative therapy is nothing more than repression that fails to change sexual orientation is to have people read Nicolosi's book. In 315 pages, he trots out an endless parade of victims, none of whom is the slightest bit "cured," or changed, for that matter. The only reason anyone comes back, it seems, is because Nicolosi twists his or her brain into a knot that would make a Boy Scout troop leader proud. These hapless victims are run through an exhaustive obstacle course of psychological voodoo that plays hocus-pocus with their fragile minds.

The first thing the good doctor does is turn the world upside down, confusing his clients through perverse word games and cognitive tricks. Even though they are still attracted to the same sex, he has them identify as "nongay homosexuals," claiming "gay" is a political term. In other words, if one afternoon a male client of Nicolosi's has sex with five men in a sex club, he is not considered gay—unless he marches in the gay pride parade after he is finished having sex. Is this not psychologically manipulating people to distance themselves from their true feelings? Is this not the epitome of denial?

Imagine how ludicrous this semantic dissembling would seem if it were directed toward any other minority. Would not the world laugh if there were a psychological trade group who promoted the curious notion of "non-Jewish Hebrews" or "non-black African Americans?" Yet, the continuing societal stigmatization and marginalization of homosexuals allows Nicolosi and NARTH to offer these bizarre theories, and to have them taken seriously by otherwise sober conservative commentators.

Nicolosi's twisted view of reality often rubs off on his clients, distorting their perceptions as well. For example, one of Nicolosi's patients visited a bathhouse and had sex with a man he clearly was interested in. Yet, he told Nicolosi that he wasn't turned on by the guy:

> Yeah, I wasn't at all interested in the guy I met there. In fact he said, "I'll be calling you." You know, it felt like a threat, like blackmail. That would normally scare me, but this time I felt like I didn't care. Because I know this person who goes to bathhouses isn't really me.[57]

This is simply denial. The client claimed he wasn't interested in the guy he partnered up with, yet he still had intercourse with him. Next, the client declared to Nicolosi that he was mortified by the thought of the man calling him, but, obviously, he gave his number to the man. Finally, he claimed this behavior "isn't me," yet there he was at the bathhouse engaging in sex with a man. Nicolosi applauded this as progress.

Another client of Nicolosi's, Will, was having an affair with Tom, a "straight" married man. Most people would look at this unhealthy situation and conclude that Tom is a conflicted individual who may be a married, closeted gay man. In Nicolosi's surreal world, however, Tom is a success and Will is simply trying to achieve heterosexuality vicariously through sex with him. Here's how Nicolosi advised his client:

> So here you are, you're not feeling quite capable of performing sexually with women. So Tom, for you, is a transitional object—an object linking you to the feared woman. You feel close to Tom, so if Tom can be successful with women, then maybe through association, you can be successful with women too. Through identity with Tom, you might gain that male power. Through him, you have one foot in the other world you seek.[58]

I believe that the majority of people might conclude the opposite. It is much more likely that Will is Tom's link to coming out, rather than Tom being Will's link to heterosexuality. Only in Nicolosi Land would Tom be held up as a shining example of heterosexual functioning. Oddly, Nicolosi never questioned what would drive this married "straight" guy to have an adulterous affair with a man. It seems as long as a person engages in sexual behavior with the opposite sex, he or she is labeled straight, regardless of how he or she actually feels inside.

Nicolosi's mind games appear to have no limits and the things his clients will say and do to become straight can be downright comical—if it all weren't so sad. Nicolosi constantly encourages his clients to increase their masculinity as a prerequisite to heterosexuality. This often creates theater of the absurd, with hilarious examples of men desperately groping for signs of machismo. "I played racquetball the other day, then we got the usual after-game drink, Gatorade. . . . That's what you're supposed to drink. It felt good to be sweaty,"[59] one client told Nicolosi, updating him on the progress of his burgeoning masculinity. Another client told the doctor, "When you hear a bunch of straight guys speak to each other, they say things like, 'Hey, bud,' and 'Hey, dude.' (*laughs*) I used to think that sounded so stupid. But you know, now I really like being called that."[60]

With such a quacklike approach to changing a person's sexual orientation, it is not surprising that Nicolosi studiously avoids keeping statistics on his failure rate. A *Newsweek* reporter once asked him why he keeps no statistics. "I don't have time," he replied.[61]

The Ringmaster's Legacy of Lunacy

Joseph Nicolosi is the undisputed ringmaster of the reparative therapy industry. Yet, we have seen that his work is dishonest and consists of nothing but the regurgitation of outdated stereotypes disguised as science.

In this author's view, reparative therapists are detestable, money-hungry con artists who lure and bamboozle susceptible people with misleading promises and false hope. One reason these quacks practice their chicanery is to cash in on this lucrative industry, but one cannot dismiss raw hatred as the primary motive that drives these charlatans to extreme lengths to denigrate lesbians and gay men.

Although the newer, more polished and politically savvy, antigay "doctors" have avoided the overt invective that doomed Paul Cameron's career, they are, nonetheless, just as radically antigay. As diligently as they work to spruce up their images, they still occasionally slip up, the unvarnished truth seeping through their lips.

In 1998, the gay-bashing murder of University of Wyoming student Matthew Shepard shocked the entire nation. Even the most vocal antigay activists in America felt compelled to express their regrets. This outpouring of sympathy did not include Nicolosi, however. After he was forced to move a NARTH meeting to an alternate location because of protesters angered by Shepard's death, he icily dismissed Shepard's murder: "A kid gets killed in Wyoming, and we can't even have a scientific meeting," said Nicolosi, revealing his true colors.[62]

Unfortunately, Nicolosi and NARTH have spawned a small but growing pool of reparative therapists to carry on his legacy of lunacy. Instead of relying on objective science, these individuals subjectively pick and choose only the elements that back up their religious views. According to leading psychiatrist and author Jack Drescher:

> They are like creation scientists. What science offers to confirm what they believe they will take. What science offers that disconfirms what they believe is to be discarded or to be rejected. So sometimes it looks like you are having a scientific conversation, but you really are not because it's two different dialogues going on at the same time. One is about science; one is about belief and faith.[63]

Chief among NARTH's new reservoir of "talent" is Maryland counselor Richard Cohen, Nicolosi's understudy and the future of the lucrative reparative therapy industry. Nicolosi's main talent is organizing disgruntled psychoanalysts and repackaging their outdated theories as new. Cohen's strength, on the other hand, is supplanting the obsolete ideas of psychoanalysis with a wide array of modern ideas. With Cohen rapidly gaining influence, today's reparative therapy techniques are as likely to come from a cult's compound as from a shrink's couch. As you will see in the following chapter, modern reparative therapy has become nothing more than an incoherent witch's brew of fundamentalism, pop psychology, and New Age mysticism.

Radical Richard

Bizarre Sex Cult Tied to Reparative Therapy

On Easter Sunday 1977, a group of sixteen families, led by their charismatic pastor and his wife, packed their belongings and moved from Ingleside, Illinois, to the West Coast to start the Wesleyan Christian Community Church.[1] The group bought fifty-eight acres on Vashon Island, not far from Seattle, and built an insular compound where they could practice *inner healing,* which supposedly helps people overcome addictions, sexual problems, and family abuse.

However, these were not your average Christian missionaries, but exiles booted out of their Illinois church for taking part in peculiar sexual practices that could be found nowhere in scripture. Only three months before their pilgrimage to Vashon, the Reverend Louis Hillendahl and his wife, Mary Lou, made the news after they were exposed, literally, for practicing nude therapy sessions inside the Ingleside United Methodist Church. According to reports, sexual "experiments" with more than twenty participants "spontaneously" erupted inside the church, including "therapy sessions" during which men, women, and children breast-fed on women who had stripped to the waist.[2]

Reverend Hillendahl enthusiastically confirmed the news reports. "We were trying to find some way for our children to withstand the onslaught of sexuality that is stressed in advertising, television programs and in other ways," explained Hillendahl about his unconventional therapy. He claimed the questionable physical contact actually improved people's lives: "Some of the participants came to our coun-seling program with their lives in pieces," said Hillendahl. "The ther-apy helped put them back together again."[3] The nude sessions were such a smashing success that they were expanded to include a week-end retreat at a motel in Kenosha, Wisconsin.

Methodist officials were not amused by the discovery. When they said that they wanted congregants to get to know one another in the biblical sense, this was not exactly what they had in mind. So, the shamed Hillendahl was sent packing, only to resurface in Washington State months later, where he formed his commune for inner healing.

The new group was an eclectic mix of puritanical Christianity, pop psychology, and survivalist dogma. Alcohol, drugs, and smoking were strictly forbidden, as were outdoor pets, without community ap-proval. All decisions were made by unanimous agreement of the en-tire membership, after each person had been heard. Group members were expected to build their own houses from scratch, as well as a 7,000-square foot community center. To do this, they had to hand over a minimum of $300 per month, and those who were more afflu-ent were expected to give "as much cash as they had available."

It took five years to build the mysterious compound, which had fourteen housing units and a group center. During this period, Hill-endahl's followers lived in army tents with no running water or in-door plumbing. The reverend thought the harsh conditions were ideal for fostering an environment of family values: "We realized that liv-ing in big suburban homes with a private room for each person, each coming and going with his or her own activities, had created a situa-tion in which family members really didn't know one another," wrote Hillendahl on his Web page.[4]

As in Illinois, however, it turned out that Hillendahl's followers were getting to know one another a little too well. In 1983, three fol-lowers were charged with sixteen counts of rape and other illegal sex acts against boys and girls, ages two to thirteen. Those charged with the crimes claimed that the children testifying against them had been brainwashed. In retaliation, those implicated for child abuse, as well as two other former cult members, filed suit against the church, say-ing it fostered bizarre sexual practices in the community.[5] The suit ac-cused some of the group's members of engaging in nude fondling ses-sions, breast-feeding of adults, and abusive discipline of children. In addition, the commune was blamed in the suit for requiring forced labor and separating children from their parents. In 1984, the three cult members were convicted of sexually abusing the children.

This cryptic commune should have been no more than a footnote in cult history, but their zany, if not dangerous, "therapy" is today linked with a key reparative therapist, Richard Cohen, who joined the group in 1988. Though he has long since departed that group, Cohen now traverses the nation promoting gay conversion through—you guessed it—"inner healing" and "touch therapy." Although no evidence has yet surfaced of nude therapy sessions, clearly the group left an indelible imprint on Cohen's model for "healing" homosexuals, which is fast becoming the rage in mainstream reparative therapy circles. In fact, Cohen is a regular speaker at NARTH conferences and has promoted his brand of "therapy" in high-profile media such as *Larry King Live, The Ricki Lake Show, The Sally Jessy Raphael Show,* and *20/20.*

It is frightening that a disciple of Reverend Hillendahl is a leader in the modern reparative therapy movement. Unfortunately, thousands of people are unaware of Cohen's eccentric background and willingly submit themselves to his twisted treatment. Even scarier, however, NARTH—representing more than 1,000 therapists nationwide—has wholeheartedly embraced Cohen and peddles his methods as advances in treating homosexuality. "NARTH is open to the exploration of therapeutic approaches to treating homosexuality," Cohen told me in our interview at the L Street Borders Books in Washington, DC. "[Nicolosi] is changing now his therapeutic approach. . . . So he's changed a lot."[6]

In their embrace of Cohen, Nicolosi and NARTH have willfully elected to elevate a man whose life has swung like an out-of-control pendulum from one extreme to another. This not only is moral malpractice and ethical turpitude but also unwise for an organization that already rests on the shakiest of scientific foundations.

In addition to NARTH's support, the controversial talk show host Dr. Laura Schlessinger endorses Cohen's methods; she even wrote the foreword for his book, *Coming Out Straight: Understanding and Healing Homosexuality.* "With intellect and care, he [Cohen] offers invaluable insight into the reason for same-sex attractions and, for those willing to brave it, he illuminates a challenging journey from isolation," wrote Schlessinger.[7]

Of course, Dr. Laura's ill-informed opinion might come from the fact that she is simply a physiologist, not the psychologist most people think she is. In fact, when it comes to mental health issues, she has about as much credibility as Dr. J. or Dr. Seuss. I will wholeheartedly agree with her on one point: Anyone who follows Cohen is, no doubt, "braving it."

The following is the story of Richard Cohen,[8] Nicolosi's heir apparent, Dr. Laura's most prominent ex-gay advisor, and the future of reparative therapy in America. Cohen swears gays can change into heterosexuals. And if anyone should know about "change," it is the protean Cohen, who has worn a thousand masks and whimsically mutated into countless creations. Who is the chameleon-like Richard Cohen? Does he even know? Strap yourself in because we are about to go on the wild ride that is Cohen's life story. Read on and decide for yourself if this is a person who should be allowed to treat anyone, much less be the standard bearer for a dubious form of therapy that is backed by some of the most powerful political forces in America.

A Man of Many Incarnations

Richard Cohen grew up in Lower Merion, a suburb of Philadelphia, and was the youngest of three children in a Jewish family. It wasn't a happy upbringing: "Most often, my dad would come home from work and scream at us," wrote Cohen in his book *Coming Out Straight*. "There was constant fighting and tears in the Cohen household." When his father wasn't busy berating him, Cohen's brother Neal would beat him up. When things got out of hand at home, Cohen would act as the clown, "trying desperately to relieve the tension that was in the air."[9]

Beginning in middle school, Cohen began sexual experimentation with school friends, but he was also cognizant of social pressures and began dating girls to "act normal." At seventeen, Cohen's unhealthy way of dealing with his sexual orientation began to surface when he described his need for a man as an "obsession" and admitted his sexuality continued to "haunt" him. Later that year, Cohen had his first real sexual encounter with a man he met in his father's health club. It is clear from this experience that the young gay lad was having an unusually difficult time accepting himself:

My body and spirit felt ripped in two. Afterwards, I left his apartment and took the subway home. When I was underground waiting for the train, I walked into a dark corner and deeply sobbed. I felt so violated and disappointed. . . . What I experienced felt like rape.[10]

Shortly after, he confessed the experience to his father, who didn't take it too well, feeling his son had embarrassed him. The distraught teenager begged his father to let him see a therapist to help him change—the first in a parade of shrinks in what very well may have become a psychological dependence on therapy.

In 1970, Cohen escaped the bondage of his youth, matriculating at Boston University. Freedom from his oppressive home environment didn't seem to help, however. At BU he found *another* shrink and went through three years of what he described as an "excruciating time of pain." He also went to his first gay bar but claimed he didn't "like the scene" and found it to be a "meat market" where he felt like a "commodity on a shelf."

Fortunately, Cohen did not have to feel like an expired can of Spam at the meat market for long. He found a boyfriend, Mike, but he was still a miserable wretch because Mike "suffocated" him. Cohen's despair eventually reached such depths that he attempted suicide, downing a bottle of Bufferin. He survived, but the episode forced Cohen to re-think his life, so he dumped suffocating Mike and switched his major from music to theater.

It is indisputable that the portrait Cohen paints of himself in his book is of a young man deeply troubled by his sexual orientation. Yet, in our interview, Cohen took great pains to show that, although out of the closet, he was unusually comfortable with his sexuality: "I was out to my family and I was out to my friends," said Cohen, staring directly into my eyes and talking in a hypnotic tone. "I had no shame nor remorse nor guilt about it. My parents accepted me. . . . I was very relaxed, comfortable in a way in that world."

Either Cohen has a remarkably different definition of self-acceptance than most people or he was disingenuous in our interview. First, if he was happy, why was he seeking "intensive therapy," as he called it, to change his sexual orientation? Second, do happy, well-adjusted people attempt suicide or feel "raped" because of a consensual sexual experience? Finally, Cohen contradicted himself: in his book he wrote that his father was "embarrassed" by his sexuality, but then in our interview he said his parents were "accepting" of him. This duplicitous talk is a hallmark of Cohen and other reparative therapists who must dissemble in order to hold together their crumbling sandcastle of misinformation against a rising tide of education and understanding.

Things finally started to look up for the troubled college student when he met Tim, whom he described as a "dream come true." The two men dated for three years in what Cohen called a "roller-coaster" relationship in which he was the "pursuer" and Tim was the "distancer." Unfortunately for Cohen, Tim became even more distant: he got hooked on Christian fundamentalism and began believing their relationship was sinful. At first, Cohen "persecuted him for his belief" but eventually "apologized," realizing Tim was "right." Soon after this revelation, Cohen joined the Episcopal Church in Roxbury and began teaching Sunday school. Realizing that homosexuality was not compatible with God's word, Cohen and his partner eliminated the physical part of their relationship.

Not long after his switch from Judaism to Christianity, Cohen, as well as Tim, discovered the Unification Church and, in 1974, became full-fledged Moonies—marking Cohen's third religion in four years. At times it appeared that Cohen tried on religions like some people try on clothes—a perfect fit today, only to be discarded tomorrow for a new, better-fitting name brand. "I had always been on a spiritual quest, trying to find the meaning and purpose of life," wrote the ever-metamorphosing Cohen. "I tried so many kinds of faiths and ways: Judaism, Buddhism, and therapies."[11]

Cohen immersed himself in the Moonie subculture to repress his sexual desires and stayed celibate for nine years. He even joined the church choir and traveled through Asia, where he met a young Korean woman, Jae Sook, whom he eventually married. This marriage seemed doomed to failure, however, because Cohen, despite his efforts to be straight, was still a gay man. As his repression mounted he became a self-described "rageaholic" who verbally abused Jae Sook. At times, Cohen's verbal abuse erupted to the brink of violence. "I projected onto Jae Sook all the pent-up hostility I had previously felt toward my mother," wrote Cohen. "My rage got so bad that I even felt like killing her at times. . . . At home, Dr. Jekyll turned into Mr. Hyde."[12]

All that changed late one evening after he and his wife had finished copulating. Suddenly, he felt as if his "spirit had jumped out of my body" and out of nowhere he came to the ghastly conclusion that he had "experienced some kind of abuse in early childhood. My hypothesis was that there was an incestuous relationship between my mother and myself," wrote Cohen.[13]

Cohen was beside himself, fuming over the thought of his mother's impure actions, so he did what any well-adjusted rageaholic would do. He picked up a tennis racquet and pounded a pillow to release all of the "pent-up anger and frustration." He pounded and pounded uncontrollably until he had a "flashback": "All of a sudden, I saw male genitals coming toward my mouth. I screamed. I felt shocked. I felt horrified."[14] The accused perpetrator was obviously not his mother, but a friend of the family, "Uncle" Dave, who allegedly molested him between the ages of five and six. "I cried and the tears flowed for the next few years, as I worked through memories of sexual abuse. . . . I learned that to be close to a man I must give him my body."[15]

To afford his expensive therapy sessions, Cohen had to labor as a waiter four nights a week, on top of working for a theater company. During this period, he and his wife also had their first child. In his ongoing quest for help, he one day went to an ex-gay ministry in the area, but as with many others, he actually found that it was an XXX-gay ministry. "[T]he director approached me to have sex with him. This created more pain and feelings of hopelessness."[16]

Soon after the ex-gay ministry debacle, the dam burst and Cohen had another life-changing revelation:

> I decided I couldn't take it anymore. . . . So, I told God, my wife, and several friends that if I couldn't find what I needed through godly men, then I would go back into the homosexual world to find someone who was willing to be with me.[17]

Cohen, never a man of subtleties or half measures, delved into the gay scene with reckless abandon. For two and a half years, Cohen endlessly trolled the seedier New York City gay saloons while deserting his wife and son for long stretches of time. In the midst of this domestic fiasco, his wife gave birth to a daughter, their second child. "It was a very bizarre time," wrote Cohen. "I was out running around New York City with my boyfriend, and she was at home alone taking care of our son, knowing her husband was out with a man."[18]

Amazingly, while in the epicenter of this homosexual maelstrom, Cohen found his way back into heterosexuality. He accomplished this by meeting a straight Christian man named David who gave Cohen all the nonsexual loving and care he never received from his abusive father. Through this relationship, he supposedly began to heal his past so-called homo-emotional wounds. "God is just," wrote Cohen. "It was Dave who abused me at five, and it was David who helped me heal at thirty-five!"[19]

With the same astonishing ease with which he swapped religions, Cohen vacillated back and forth between sexual orientations. He went from openly gay college student to celibate Moonie, from miserable heterosexual husband to homosexual barfly, and then ultimately reemerged as a Christian family man. "I sobbed for about an hour in David's arms," wrote Cohen. "In those moments of release I found freedom from same-sex desires. Cutting this neurological connection to the sexual desires freed me from thirty years of relentless pain and endless pursuit of men."[20]

Following his triumphant breakthrough with David, Cohen once again reinvented his identity, unveiling his latest incarnation as an ex-gay man at the Exodus national conference in 1987. At the symposium, he prayed that God would give him guidance and reveal the next steps in his "healing journey." When God ignored his calls for direction, Cohen became annoyed, went to a nearby lake, and *ordered* God to provide him with a plan: "OK, God, it's showdown time! I'm not moving from this spot until you tell me what to do and where to go," Cohen insisted. "Even if I die sitting here, so be it. I await your guidance." God, sufficiently alarmed that Cohen might expire lakeside, dutifully dropped whatever he was working on and instantly submitted to Cohen's demands: "Then the directions came clearly: 'Move to Seattle, receive help for your marriage, get an education, and then reach out to help other people.'" Knowing God was at his beck and call, Cohen had the chutzpah to ask for verbal confirmation, as if God were a travel agent: "I asked, 'Would you please repeat that one more time?' The words came one more time, exactly as I had heard them before."[21]

Who was Cohen to argue with God? Following this divine revelation he packed an eighteen-foot truck and moved his family and their precipitiously positioned belongings across the country. Cohen initially thought God wanted him to move to Seattle to get more involved with the ex-gay ministries, so once in town he promptly visited the local group. Once again, however, he was let down by Exodus when the group's director fell off the heterosexuality wagon and resumed life as a gay man. After his disastrous stint in the local ex-gay ministry, Cohen was lost and thoroughly confused. He had relocated thousands of miles—and for what purpose, he wondered.

God works in mysterious ways, though, and Cohen soon found his calling with a peculiar group of Christians who had backgrounds every bit as surreal as his own. On January 1, 1988, the Cohen family discovered the Wesleyan Christian Community Church—the exiled cult on Vashon Island who were kicked out of their Illinois church for conducting nude therapy sessions. He wanted to move his family there but was thwarted by anti–divine intervention. "We tried several times to get there, but each time some accident or event stopped us," explained Cohen. "Jae Sook said, 'Maybe it's God saying don't go.' I realized that it was not God but the other side trying to stop us!"22

Through raw determination Cohen persevered, foiling Satan's master plan and moving his family to the salacious commune. Once there, Cohen flourished in what turned out to be a marriage made in heaven. The sect gained a loyal, enthusiastic follower and Cohen had the opportunity to learn Reverend Hillendahl's "therapeutic" techniques, which are strikingly similar to the ones he employs to this day to help gay people change their sexual orientation. Cohen recalled in our interview, "We lived there for a while [six months] and then got counseling for two and a half years. . . . We did group therapy a lot. They worked with my wife and I a lot."

After Cohen left the secretive island sect he went back to school to become a counselor to "help people leave homosexuality." He also worked for three years as an HIV/AIDS educator for the American Red Cross but ran into trouble there because he allegedly began proselytizing to sick patients. "The Gay and Lesbian Task Force of the mayor's office in Seattle requested that the American Red Cross fire me," wrote Cohen, apparently flummoxed that anyone would take offense to his fire-and-brimstone routine. "Their reason was that I was homophobic and spreading hate. Many in the homosexual community have felt threatened by my work. I understand their fears and pain."23

Cohen's deathbed "church lady" act had its limits, and eventually he had no choice but to strike out on his own. He started the International Healing Foundation, under the guise of which, for the past twelve years, he has trotted around the globe boldly claiming to have "counseled and taught thousands of men, women, and adolescents" how to become straight.[24]

His claim of changing "thousands" is quite an impressive boast. How does he do it? What are his astonishing techniques? Even more remarkable is that he does this work without a degree in either psychology or psychiatry—he is simply a counselor. His secret must lie in his offbeat, Hillendahl-inspired work, which has catapulted him to the pinnacle of reparative therapy. Let's explore that next.

The Symptom Synthesizer

When I was in grade school we would play a game called "Punch" at recess in which two friends would stare directly into each other's eyes to see who would blink first. The loser would receive a solid punch in the arm—hence the name. When interviewing Cohen, I again felt as if I were playing this puerile dare game, albeit without the punitive arm whack for the loser.

Cohen, when talking or listening to me, looked directly into my eyes with a penetrating stare meant to mesmerize and intimidate. He never looked down or blinked and the raw intensity was palpable, if not unbearable. His eyes were like lasers piercing my soul and probing for any weaknesses or insecurities he could exploit. As he tried to penetrate my mind, he fired off countless personal questions about my background, seemingly trying to figure out how to gain a psychological advantage.

An acolyte of Moberly's, Cohen is a fervent believer in her theories of same-sex ambivalence and insists that *all* gays have either been abused or had a poor relationship with a same-sex parent. As I was setting up for our talk, Cohen relentlessly grilled me on my background, hoping to find a tidbit of information that he could point to as the *cause* of my homosexuality. I threw a monkey wrench into his calcified philosophy, however, by disclosing that I was very close to both my mother and father and that I had never been molested. To which an incredulous Cohen responded, "I don't believe that you or anyone else can have same-sex attractions and have successfully attached to both Mom and Dad. It's an impossibility and I do not believe it can be true. So even though you may *say* you have a close relationship, . . . somewhere back there . . . [was unsuccessful attachment]."

There are no ambiguities in Cohen's black-and-white world where he unequivocally knows all of the answers. I had been with the man less than an hour and he had, in essence, diagnosed me as having repressed memories of childhood abuse or as suffering from subconscious parental neglect. The amazing part is that Cohen was so convincing that I actually felt compelled to delve into my past later that evening and dredge up possible events that might correspond to his theories. Alas, I came up empty-handed and concluded my childhood was every bit as happy as I remembered it.

Cohen's magnetism and ability to make people buy into his outlandish, unproven therapies partly derives from his use of hypnotic intonation. While cunningly using his eyes to capture one's undivided attention, he talks in deliberate tones, lulling the listener into a trancelike state. I had never experienced anything quite like it before, and it was downright scary.

Ultimately, Cohen is successful and dangerous because he fully believes his own rhetoric and, hence, is able to make others follow him. As we have seen, the diaphanous Cohen casually switched personas and religions with astonishing nonchalance. Of note is the fervor and absolutism with which the ever-changing neophyte approached every conversion. Each time he found a new faith, it was *the* way, in fact, the *only* way—until he found the next faith. This distinctive ability to become fully engrossed with a particular belief at a given time makes Cohen a terror to those susceptible to his techniques.

Cohen's book, in this author's opinion, is probably the most well-written ex-gay book ever published. Though loaded with pseudo-scientific data, it is a remarkably easy read for the layperson. The text is chock full of amusing charts and graphs that show the ways in which one supposedly becomes homosexual. Cohen even trumpets an exciting new term for the condition, *same-sex attachment disorder,* with an exciting new acronym, SSAD, which is supposed to represent how out lesbians and gay men feel. Of course, one can persuasively argue that this functions also as a disclaimer because this is the way most of his clients will feel when they are done with his therapy and left to wonder what black hole sucked in all of their money.

The ideas in Cohen's book are not new. Similar to his mentors Socarides, Moberly, and Nicolosi, Cohen offers zilch in the way of advancing scientific understanding of sexual orientation. His ideas are a veritable stew of outdated psychoanalytic techniques and New Age fads. Cohen's talent lies in taking this hodgepodge of quirky ideas and wrapping them in a pretty package and serving them to the public as a new creation.

However, his new creation is more like a Frankenstein monster, causing potential harm to those who stumble in its path. The first hint that something is wickedly awry is Cohen's convoluted attempt to show causation of homosexuality. Cohen asks, "If homosexuality is a normal sexual orientation, why is only 1 to 3 percent of the population homosexual and not 50 percent?"[25] Concluding that homosexuality is abnormal because 50 percent of the population isn't gay is as irrational as saying that left-handedness is an abnormal trait because it also is not shared by half of all human beings.

In his book, Cohen states often that "homosexuality is an acquired condition." Of course, he drew his flawed conclusions from the discredited works of Bieber, Socarides, Moberly, and Nicolosi. Cohen takes causation several steps further than his mentors, however, offering a stunning new array of explanations for homosexuality. At times Cohen casts such a wide net that it seems miraculous that *all* people haven't turned out gay.

According to Cohen, if a "hypersensitive" child is thrust into a variety of situations or events, the child has a chance of turning out homosexual. Cohen acknowledges that this "sensitivity" is a God-given trait, but if sensitivity is inborn, or genetically determined, then why can't homosexuality be inborn? Furthermore, couldn't the child be sensitive *because* he or she was born gay? These are important questions that Cohen readily dismisses because they don't fit neatly into his cause-and-effect model. When challenged, Cohen spouts off simplistic notions and prosaic biological explanations of why inborn homosexuality is not a possibility: "The penis and the vagina fit together. Two penises, two vaginas, they don't work."[26]

Other times, such as at the NARTH meeting discussed in "Historic Injustice," he illustrates the implausibility of homosexuality by partaking in live magnet demonstrations: "Simple science demonstrates that opposites attract," said Cohen, holding two magnets while speaking before the crowd at the NARTH conference. "When you have two magnets of opposite polarities, they naturally gravitate toward each

other. If you have two magnets of the same polarity, they naturally re-
pel one another."

After Cohen establishes the hypersensitive child theory, he lists the
stimuli that may cause one to be gay. For instance, he claims that the
mother "may have directly or indirectly criticized the father." Is there
a family in existence in which the mother at some point has not criticized the father? Does Cohen know of families who never fight? Can
he himself say his wife has never criticized him in front of their three
children?

Another theory he expounds is that a sensitive child may see an opposite-sex sibling or parent receiving more attention and love, and
therefore the child tries to attain the same level of attention by emu-
lating the opposite sex. "The son may take on a more feminine appearance to win the affection and approval of his father," wrote Cohen. Once again confusing gender identity with sexual orientation,
Cohen also wrote that "if a parent expresses disappointment with the
child's gender, . . . he may then take on the characteristics of the opposite gender in order to obtain his parent's love and acceptance."[27]

This strategy makes a lot of sense. In our culture a boy is certain to
win the love of a distant father by donning a pair of heels and
prancing around the living room—preferably when Dad's beer buddies are over watching a football game. Although this behavior may
earn the boy the attention he craves, it will most likely not be positive
reinforcement. For Cohen to espouse this absurd theory suggests that
he is grossly out of touch.

Other situations that Cohen believes cause homosexuality are divorce, a death in the family, adoption, and even religious experiences
that cause a child to feel rejected. Cohen's bizarre causation model
goes beyond familial situations and meanders into what he calls
"body image wounds." If a sensitive child is overweight or extremely
thin, he or she might turn out gay. If a person is too short or too tall or
has some kind of physical disability, homosexuality might also be
in the cards. Cohen also blames "social or peer wounds" for sending
sensitive young men and women running off to the nearest gay
bar. These gay-inducing wounds arise from name-calling and put-
downs—goody-goody, teacher's pet, nonathletic—as well as lack of
rough-and-tumble for boys and too much rough-and-tumble for girls.
Of course, there isn't a child in the world who has not experienced

these so-called wounds. To say they contribute to homosexuality is baseless and scientifically bankrupt.

Cohen reminds me of a fortune-teller in New York City who once suckered me. Leaving a bar drunk late one evening, I went to an all-night clairvoyant with a few friends for laughs. The fortune-teller, who was dressed in a flowing robe and looked like a stoned genie, peered into her crystal ball and said, "Let me guess, you were born in June."

"No," I replied.

"I know, December!"

"Sorry."

"I see a vernal tint to your eyes. You must be April's child."

"Not exactly."

She guessed three more times before she finally said "July." When I nodded in concurrence, she looked at me with a twinkle in her eyes and exclaimed, "See, I knew it!"

This is very much how Cohen and others of his ilk operate. A person comes for succor and Cohen supplies a myriad of reasons why he or she is gay. When one "symptom" doesn't fit he introduces another. Since everyone has had something unpleasant happen—from incidents as severe as child abuse to the relatively innocuous put-down—Cohen is able to manufacture a custom-made, gay-causing trauma for each patient. The more people he and others can get to fit into the ever-widening model, the more money there is to be made. He is a veritable symptom synthesizer.

"There is no one size fits all," Cohen explained to me. "You are not going to find the same symptomology with all of the people. There are homosexualities, not homosexuality." This explanation falls short, however, when one considers the spandexlike elasticity of his model and the glaring contradictions in his book. More than anyone, he hedges his bets to make sure virtually anyone is a potential patient. For example:

- "There seem to be two polarities involved [with homosexuality]: inferiority or grandiosity."[28] That certainly covers the spectrum.
- Gays often are "teacher's pets" and "goody-goodies" who suffer from "good little boy syndrome,"[29] but *"[o]ppositional behavior*

is an integral part of homosexuality."[30] He even coined a heart-warming phrase for his support group: "Nice Sucks."

It seems Cohen wants to have it both ways, ensuring that he can line his pockets by justifying homosexuality through any conceivable human behavior.

A final example of his penchant for prevarication involves several pages in his book where he explains that a *distant* father is the primary cause of male homosexuality, only later to discuss a patient who is gay because he is *too close* to his dad. Cohen claims to have helped the gay patient in "successfully separating and individuating from his father." Once again, Cohen gives new meaning to the term *bisexual,* offering two completely separate and conflicting reasons for a person's sexual orientation.

B-SADD

Once Cohen explains the supposed origins of homosexuality to clients, they are introduced to his special brand of therapy. Cohen's therapeutic paradigm consists of five different techniques. To be consistent, we'll stick with Cohen's phraseology and label his plan B-SADD (pronounced "be sad"):

Bizarre techniques
Seduction
Aversion
Disassociation
Distraction

To keep the techniques in chronological order, we'll start with seduction and end with bizarre techniques.

Seduction

In this phase, the objective is to create a mosaic of half-truths and all-out misrepresentations designed to make a potential client believe change is possible, if not probable. If change does not occur, the therapist usually blames the patient for not trying hard enough.

Where Cohen diverges from many in the ex-gay ministries and reparative therapy is his absolute certainty that *all* people have the ability to become heterosexual. From the title of his book, *Coming Out
Straight,* to his oft-quoted catchphrase, "Born gay, no way," Cohen
leaves little room for ambiguities or shades of gray. "I'm very certain
that people who have same-sex attractions [suffer from] arrested development," Cohen boldly asserted in our interview. "For those who
wish to make this transition from homosexual to heterosexual, I am
certain that it is possible. . . . I knew that God did not create me this
way."[31]

Each chapter in his book begins with a stunningly tacky picture of
a deliriously happy man and woman locked in an intimate embrace,
implying, not so subtly, that Cohen's expensive therapy sessions will
give the client an opportunity to become like the people in the por-
traits.

Aversion

The flip side to seduction is aversion. If a therapist cannot convince a client to change based on the merits and marvels of heterosexuality, he or she will usually try to persuade clients to become straight
by invoking the supposed evils of homosexuality.

The goal is to compound existing fears a client may have about his
or her sexual orientation. The therapist does this by relentlessly
degrading and dehumanizing homosexuality while simultaneously
glorifying heterosexuality. Most of this is subtle, evidenced in the
disingenuous way therapists, such as Cohen, assign emotions or shortcomings that all humans share or experience as exclusive to gay people. For instance, Cohen wrote, "A man with same-sex attractions
may have a chameleonlike nature" or suffer from "impatience or lack
of self-discipline."[32] To suggest that these behaviors are in any way
unique to gay people shows obvious bias by the therapist, calling into
question any observations he makes on the lives of gay people.

Cohen also carefully chooses his words to subconsciously diminish
lesbian and gay sexual and romantic relationships. For example, gay
people never seem to lose their virginity in a willful and pleasurable
manner. Instead, they are always "introduced" to homosexuality, usually through a lecherous older person or scheming friend. On the
other hand, all heterosexual relations are described in loving, roman-

tic terms. When gays are through with sex, they feel "empty, alone, frightened, deceitful, guilty, [and] dirty,"[33] whereas virtually all examples given of heterosexual sex note that it usually ends with the participants feeling whole or complete.

In fact, gay life isn't really life at all, according to Cohen and other reparative therapists. While marriage and heterosexual life embody contentment and fulfillment, gay life is reduced to a "lifestyle" or a "scene." Thus, a client is presented with a false choice between a happy straight *life* and a miserable gay *lifestyle*. These semantics are systematically employed to play on the insecurities of those who are unhappy because they have made bad relationship choices and are looking for a scapegoat for their own personal failures.

Of course, there is a "gay scene." There are people who choose to go out to nightclubs every evening of the week and party with illegal drugs until dawn. Some heterosexuals do this as well. To submit that this is a gay lifestyle is either a willful attempt to slander an entire class of people or proof that those making such allegations have no experience in the "heterosexual scene." Perhaps they should get out more before making such generalizations.

When reparative therapists are not busy denigrating single gay men for their supposed lifestyle, they are busy trying to tear down gay relationships. Sure, some gay people often do have empty, failing relationships, but so do heterosexuals, and it is common knowledge that more than 50 percent of straight marriages in the United States end in divorce. This portrayal of heterosexuality as a paragon of stability while gay relationships are doomed to fail is folly. Unfortunately, some gay people are so preconditioned and beaten down by society that they buy into this egregious myth. I've heard, on many occasions, forlorn gay men—and less frequently women—bemoan the fact that gay relationships fail simply because they were unceremoniously dumped. Well, guess what? Straight people get dumped every day too. It's not gay relationships, but all relationships, that are difficult to build and maintain.

Even with the imprimatur of society and all of the rights and benefits that come with legal marriage, straight relationships often don't make it. Taking into account that children rightfully keep many couples from divorcing, without children as the glue, the heterosexual divorce rate could skyrocket. If one considers the lack of societal and governmental support for same-sex relationships and that most gay people—especially men—do not have children, the success rate of gay relationships is quite impressive.

Sadly, however, most reparative therapists never tell clients or the public the truth about lesbian and gay relationships. Not only is this immoral, but I believe this is malpractice. Any therapist who blatantly misleads by saying that *all* gays are promiscuous or unhappy or that *all* gay relationships are doomed to failure should lose his or her license and no longer be allowed to practice.

Instead of deliberate misleading, similar to many therapists of his ilk, Cohen reverts to old-fashioned scare tactics. For gay men, this usually involves the veiled or overt threat of contracting HIV/AIDS. After a health threat is established, these unethical therapists describe how homosexuals are depraved human beings who are a menace to society, especially children. Cohen does this by citing none other than the notorious Paul Cameron and his bevy of statistics on child molestation.[34]

In a desperate attempt to convince clients that homosexuality is destructive, Cohen stoops so low as to twist suicide statistics on gay youth. He points to a 1989 report by the U.S. Department of Health and Human Services' Task Force on Youth Suicide which showed that one-third of all youths who attempt suicide are lesbian or gay. The study named societal pressure and fear of rejection as the reasons these adolescents tried to kill themselves. In Cohen's twisted version, these young men and women wanted to die because they suffered from homosexual problems. Perhaps this is true, but their "homosexual problems" are that people such as Cohen spread hate and ignorance, making their lives unbearable. In reaching his conclusion, Cohen conveniently ignores studies that show many gay youths are often victims of harassment and violence. For instance:

- One major study showed that 18 percent of male respondents said they had physically assaulted or threatened someone they thought was gay, and 32 percent admitted they were guilty of verbal harassment.[35]
- An MTV poll found that nearly one-third of students surveyed acknowledged having said "something negative . . . about another person for being gay, of a different race, for their gender or for being disabled."[36]

- In another prominent study, nearly half of America's brightest high school students admitted they were prejudiced against homosexuals.[37]
- In an analysis of teen behavior by the Massachusetts Department of Public Health, it was found that while 10 percent of all teens attempted suicide, 40 percent of gay and bisexual students tried to take their own lives. "They are no more mentally unstable than other students, but they are susceptible to victimization by their peers," said Ellen Connorton, coordinator of violence prevention and injury at the Massachusetts Department of Public Health.[38]

When you also consider that many of these same teens are abandoned by their families and condemned by their religious institutions, is it any surprise that many see suicide as the only escape? Cohen never considers any of these cultural factors and instead blithely concludes that these teens are committing suicide because homosexuality intrinsically causes people to want to die.

Cohen's conclusion that homosexual feelings can cause suicide is implausible. Sexual orientation consists of sexual desire and feelings of love, two of the most exhilarating feelings and emotions known to mankind. In a normal, unbiased setting, these feelings, whether heterosexual or homosexual, are cause for celebration, not suicide. The potential for suicide occurs only after teens are told that to be accepted by God, family, and society they must live their entire lives without love or passion. Facing such a future creates depression, hopelessness, and an insurmountable conflict wherein suicide may be viewed as the only way out.

Once Cohen and his cohorts convince clients that they can "change" and that homosexuality is a detestable, melancholy way of life that leads to the ineluctable outcome of AIDS or suicide, the real therapy begins.

Disassociation

A central part of reparative therapy and the work of Cohen involves isolating patients from society. The theory is that in order for lesbians or gay men to abandon their old identities, they must undergo a radical transformation that includes shedding nearly all vestiges of their past.

To accomplish complete disassociation, however, Cohen and other reparative therapists suggest some rather draconian measures. For example, to eschew homosexual temptation, Cohen advises avoiding anyplace one can engage in homosexual activity, such as bars, bathrooms, and parks. Of course, this makes it difficult to enjoy simple pleasures, such as sharing a picnic lunch with friends or relaxing by a pristine mountain stream in a park. Imagine what a burden avoiding public rest rooms might be when driving a long distance on an interstate. Cohen's version of disassociation also includes strongly encouraging clients to "[c]ut ties with homosexual friends and partners." So gays are encouraged to desert friendships cultivated over many years and to form new bonds with Christians, whose only qualification for friendship is that they unequivocally condemn homosexual behavior.

Now that you have no friends and you can't venture into public places where homosexual activity might occur (i.e., anywhere), at least you can sit home and read, right? Well, actually, you can't do that either. Cohen advises to temporarily (one to two years) avoid reading newspapers and magazines and listening to news reports that support and encourage homosexuality. In reality, this means you must abstain from nearly all movies, television programs, magazines, and newspapers because they all run stories dealing with gay issues. Plus, all entertainment and fashion magazines contain countless ads with luscious models of both sexes that would cause temptation for anyone, let alone someone trying to deny his or her sexuality. You can still read and socialize, of course, but the books and friends have to be certain handpicked ones. Predictably, immersion in Cohen's expensive ex-gay literature and audio/videotapes is hunky-dory.

In essence, Cohen puts people seeking change on an island surrounded by a sea of fundamentalist or evangelical literature and like-minded cohorts. Cohen's model is a warped version of the FOX television show *Temptation Island*, but instead it is *Temptation*less *Island*. The gay person seeking change is isolated, taken away from all that is pleasurable, and assured that no dissenting point of view can be heard.

The numerous former ex-gays I have talked to say that these techniques can be temporarily effective at slowing libido, which can sometimes be misconstrued for a change in sexual orientation. They also say that sexual orientation ultimately does not change, and once you leave Temptationless Island for the real world, the repressed sexual feelings return, often with greater intensity.

The larger question remains: Is this brainwashing? I believe it may be, and, if not, it certainly comes close to crossing the line. Is it not cultlike to ask *adult* patients to withdrawal from lifelong friendships, read certain books, see handpicked shows, hear only Christian radio, and limit socializing to religious-based activities with Christian fundamentalist friends? I know of no other form of therapy that sequesters its patients and essentially asks them to excommunicate from society, even to the obsessive point of avoiding public rest rooms. The extent of the mind control reparative therapists sometimes exert over their clients is best expressed by Cohen himself: "Mentally, the brain needs reprogramming."[39]

Distraction

Once patients are sufficiently isolated, it is imperative that reparative therapists offer various ways to distract them from having to think about their lonely existences. If a patient has time to think, then the reality that change has not occurred is likely to surface. So reparative therapists such as Cohen devise a plethora of tactics to keep patients' minds on anything but their sexual attractions. The irony, however, is that, to change sexual orientations, the patients' entire lives must become focused exclusively on their homosexuality—the very entity that they are trying to forget.

Cohen offers the most comprehensive distraction tactics of any antigay therapist I have encountered, but with key boosters such as Nicolosi, his methods are gaining much wider acceptance in reparative therapy circles. The first thing Cohen tells patients is that, to change their sexual orientation, they must alter their diets and get in shape. Cohen believes that working out and eating healthy are essential elements to becoming straight. Apparently, he has never visited a gay gym or been to a circuit party. The reasoning for the new diet and gym routine, according to Cohen, is that most gay people "act out" sexually when they are feeling tired or run down. Eating right increases energy and therefore decreases the chances of a gay sexual tryst. Cohen advocates that homosexual "strugglers" eat at least five to six small, well-balanced meals each day. Cohen also advises clients to work out at the gym: "A big part of the homosexual condition is a poor self-image. Developing a sense of physical well-being is very important in the process of recovery."[40]

In our interview, I brought up that ex-gay John Paulk contradicted his healthy diet theory when Paulk wrote in his book, *Not Afraid to Change,* that part of becoming straight was packing on extra poundage:

> My weight started to increase, and I found little desire to keep on a strict diet in order to stay fashionably slim. My very appearance was changing; I was looking less and less gay. And I was perfectly happy about it.[41]

Cohen became visibly piqued and animated over Paulk's hypothesis: "Because somebody had an obsession with being thin, it is not healthy to let oneself go and just become fat," said Cohen, whose sinewy build revealed that he was physically fit. "They're both actually shadows of the same wound."

Cohen's road to heterosexuality also includes quitting caffeine completely because even small amounts of caffeine increase anxiety, anger, fear, and the prevalence of dysfunctional thoughts.[42] Remembering this, I felt a little guilty inviting him to our interview in the Borders café. I wouldn't want a whiff of Irish Cream to give him any impure thoughts.

Cohen, citing Dr. Christopher Austin, offers myriad activities that clients should partake in daily to help make them straight:

- Prayer (five to fifteen minutes)
- Inspirational/scriptural reading (five to fifteen minutes)
- Journaling (five to fifteen minutes)
- Meditation/relaxation (five to fifteen minutes)
- Accountability/confession: talking to friends on a rotating basis (two or three friends)
- Serving/giving (two to six acts of kindness daily)
- Socially connected: talking to people about the lighter things in life (one to two contacts)
- Recreation (thirty to ninety minutes)
- Visualization: picturing positive outcomes of reaching your recovery goals (five minutes)

- Sleep (eight hours)
- Gratitude: recognizing pleasant things in your life (fifty to five hundred daily)[43]

Although many of these activities are undoubtedly healthful, no evidence suggests that they can lead to a change in sexual orientation. Instead evidence shows that they can keep people busy enough to limit the amount of time they have to think about their sexuality. If a person really did all of these things on a daily basis, his or her entire life would be overwhelmed with ex-gay-related activities. From diet to sleeping patterns, there is not one aspect of a client's life that Cohen does not seek to influence or control.

The most vivid example of the all-consuming therapy is his promotion of performing fifty to five hundred gratitudes a day. Examples include enjoying the small, pleasurable things in life, such as pets, tasty food, or urinating. This positive thinking is healthy in realistic doses, but if one were actually to perform five hundred gratitudes a day—in the sixteen hours Cohen recommends one be awake—this would amount to a gratitude every two minutes. Who could partake in this regimen and hold a real job? And reparative therapists call homosexuality a lifestyle?

Following Cohen's formula for success means the client will have little or no time to do anything but be an ex-gay. From early morning to late evening, Cohen and others in his field try to create the illusion of heterosexuality through the monopolization of a client's personal time.

Bizarre Techniques

As discussed in "Historic Injustice," reparative therapy is rooted in outdated and disproved psychoanalytic thought. Some, such as Socarides, still practice these anachronistic ideas, but they are being replaced in NARTH by more contemporary methods that mix the old psychoanalytic discipline with an eclectic stew of New Age experimental medicine.

Cohen is in the forefront of the movement to introduce modern guru-style treatments to the traditionally staid reparative therapy industrial complex. He enjoys talking about bioenergetics and touch therapy and peppers his seminars with swami hip phrases such as "keep balance between light and dark energies."

Currently a heated struggle is going on between old-line psycho-analytic practitioners of reparative therapy and the newer therapists who embrace pop psychology. Cohen and his supporters vociferously argue that their methods are more effective in changing sexual orientation: "Socarides is even longer than Nicolosi," said Cohen in our interview, referring to the time it takes to "cure" homosexuality in patients. "He's strictly psychoanalytic, lay down on the sofa three times a week. That's ad infinitum . . . because that approach is laborious and antiquated."

A key part of Cohen's New Age therapy is what he calls *inner child* work. Much of this involves recovering painful memories that could potentially have made a person gay. Ex-gay leader Leanne Payne, author of the *Broken Image,* is also a major advocate of memory healing. Although jarring repressed memories to reveal subconscious trauma is possible in some rare cases, Cohen takes this controversial process several steps further. The counselor insists that he can help people recover traumatic memories from as far back as when they were in their mothers' wombs. He calls these memories *intrauterine experiences.* According to Cohen:

> If the mother was experiencing difficulty in her relationship with her husband . . . or if she felt rejected, unloved, or unwanted . . . or she experienced any other painful feelings during pregnancy, the unborn child within may have experienced these thoughts and feelings as though they were directed at him or her.[44]

Cohen, in his book, illustrates his unique ability to help patients recover these early memories through recounting the story of a client named Alan who never bonded with his parents and felt "unloved and unwanted." Cohen brought this man back to the womb during therapy and helped him leave homosexuality through the retrieval of an intrauterine memory of having experienced "intense pain and anguish":

> [H]e spoke to his mother [about] . . . those nine months . . . she carried him in her womb. She told him that his dad was having an affair with another woman at the time, and she felt unwanted and unloved. In an instant, Alan realized that he had internalized and personalized her feelings.[45]

This author spoke with several renowned memory experts on the efficacy of intrauterine memory recovery, and they all scoffed at Cohen's ideas, saying that recalling these early memories was impossible:

- "It's ridiculous," said one noted memory expert and psychiatrist from the Philadelphia area. "I don't think anyone reputable would use this sort of treatment. Many therapists who use these techniques also fail to deal with a patient's real problems."[46]
- "Few if any respected psychologists would believe these are authentic memories," wrote Dr. Elizabeth Loftus, University of Washington psychology professor and author of twenty books, many of which are on memory.[47]

The skepticism from these experts stems from the irrefutable fact that it is biologically impossible for human beings to remember specific memories before two years of age, with most people unable to recall memories before the age of four. "There is no scientific evidence that people can recall events that happened to them in infancy and very early childhood," wrote Pam Freyd, executive director of the Philadelphia-based False Memory Syndrome Foundation. "The term used is 'childhood amnesia' and it is one of the more robust psychological findings."[48]

Even Cohen recognizes that the idea of recovering intrauterine memories seems unlikely, saying in our interview that it is "highly improbable sounding." Yet, it is a central doctrine to his work in "curing" homosexuals.

In another example of unearthing homosexual origins through recalling fetal trauma, a NARTH seminar instructor helped a client realize that an abortion attempt may be the reason he had unconscious hostility toward his parents and subsequently became gay:

Ivan's mother attempted an abortion while in her second trimester. The attempt failed and Ivan was born. He always felt an animosity toward his mother and distance from his father. He felt as if he didn't belong, did not fit in, and was not meant to be alive. Until he questioned his mother about his birth experience, he never knew about her attempt to abort him.[49]

Cohen helps people dredge up past memories through a technique called *bioenergetics*. This is the practice of supposedly unlocking a repository of unexpressed emotions and memories in the musculature of the body by pounding a pillow with a tennis racquet. Cohen's belief in bioenergetic exercises goes back to his own recovered memories of child abuse: "It was through this pounding of bioenergetic work that I had a flashback and all of a sudden saw genitals flying at my face," said Cohen in our interview. While pounding the pillows, Cohen has his patients take deep breaths and verbalize their pent-up anger and frustrations. "I have them say, 'Dad,' 'Dad,' 'Dad,' 'Dad,' over and over, using proper diaphragmatic breathing," wrote Cohen."[50]

If this method helps with anger management, then great! However, no evidence shows that people can recover memories from infancy through this technique, nor can it lead in any way to a person changing his or her sexual orientation. That doesn't stop Cohen, though, who almost requires the retrieval of lost memories for a patient to become straight. If he were to capsulate his work on a bumper sticker, it might read, "Once you flashback, you'll never go back."

Cohen's reliance on flashbacks raises some difficult ethical questions. For instance, Cohen insists that a childhood disturbance is a prerequisite for homosexuality and that *all* gays have had at least one event that caused a detachment from one or both parents. But if a client can find no such event, is he or she pressured into manufacturing a crisis? In other words, are clients encouraged to troll for trauma that may not have taken place? Cohen vehemently denied sending his clients on potentially devastating fishing expeditions in both his book and our interview.

This may or may not be true, but evidence suggests that some of Cohen's clients who thought they had great relationships with their parents reversed course after recovering memories of abuse during therapy and ended up blaming their parents for their homosexuality. One client said, "My childhood, in my eyes, had been perfect,"[51] but after therapy sessions with Cohen, he discovered myriad family abuses that had made him gay.

Without access to his list of clients, there is no way I can examine whether Cohen manufactured these subconscious family conflicts or whether relationships were permanently damaged by his work, but there is ample evidence to suggest that fishing for facts which don't exist can lead to what is called false memory syndrome:

> In the 1980s and '90s, thousands of people . . . entered psychotherapy for treatment of depression, anxiety, eating disorders, sexual dysfunction and other problems, and were told that their troubles were due to repressed memories of childhood sexual abuse. These painful memories, they were told, lay festering in their subconscious, causing their symptoms. It would be necessary for the patient to "recover" the memories in order to heal their current ailment.
>
> There was no credible scientific evidence for any of this: no evidence that people who had experienced years of abuse ever repressed it; no evidence that forgotten memories caused the symptoms experienced; no evidence that "recovering" memories relieved the symptoms. Nevertheless, during the course of therapy many of the patients came to believe that they had repressed memories of abuse. On the basis of these memories, many of the accused found themselves facing criminal or civil charges for child abuse, and some of them went to jail. But it turned out that in most of these cases, the events people "recovered" during therapy never actually happened.[52]

Cohen is careful to guard himself against such allegations and even places a boxed-in disclaimer in his book. However, it is incontrovertible that the memory techniques used by Cohen—when administered inappropriately—can have disastrous, life-destroying effects. In fact, there have been several high-profile court judgments and settlements against therapists, with plantiffs awarded punitive damages in millions of dollars, with one award exceeding $10 million.[53]

One reason I wrote this book is to help those struggling with their sexual orientation make informed decisions about whether to enter reparative therapy. I would adamantly warn anyone who elects to experiment with reparative therapy to be aware of the potential pitfalls of false memory syndrome. Many of these therapists are highly trained individuals who are adept at manipulating minds, especially if a patient is vulnerable and open to suggestion. If a therapist provides guidance toward the discovery of a particular past trauma, *get out* of the session as quickly as possible. Your life may depend on your ability to recognize that psychological abuse is occurring.

Another technique promoted in Cohen's endless grab bag of therapies is called *family constellations*—which he claims can heal so-called generational wounds. Drawing from the work of Bert Hellinger, Cohen proposes that a gay man can experience recovery by examining his family structure and "experience great insight and relief from these hidden influences that have impacted his life." As proof, in his book he points to a client named Neil who felt "he did not belong in his family" and believed "he was adopted." During therapy, he created and participated in a family constellation that included not only his immediate family members and their significant others but also "his father's war victims and buddies from World War II" who had died:

> Neil realized that he had taken on the energy of the dead soldiers and war victims. He thought his father loved them more than himself; therefore, he would become like them and willed himself to die. In this way he would finally obtain his father's love.[54]

If a client's parents did not cause homosexuality, Cohen speculates that gayness may have been acquired through the avenging, bitter spirits of dead ancestors. The counselor cites Dr. Edith Fiore's book *The Unquiet Dead,* which, according to Cohen, shows how an opposite-sex spirit influenced each of her homosexual clients. "I believe these spirits were connected in some way through the lineage, either direct ancestors or those who were hurt by their ancestors. Generally, the influencing spirits are seeking revenge, retaliating for wounds inflicted upon them."[55]

Once a particular trauma or nettlesome spirit is uncovered, Cohen tries to heal the wounds through a variety of methods. Most of them are patterned after Elizabeth Moberly's work, such as developing same-sex, nonerotic friendships or teaching gay men to play catch. Sometimes, Cohen's therapy amazingly leads to a born-again straight athlete. Such was the case with a fifty-year-old man burdened since the age of twelve with lack of hand-eye coordination, an inability to throw a ball, and feelings of being "less than the other boys and less than a man":

I paired him up with a friend of mine who was willing to play ball with him. Within a few days, a new man was born. He *could* throw a ball! He just needed some practice and a sympathetic man to show him the ropes.[56]

The signature part of Cohen's routine is *touch therapy.* This method of healing involves long periods during which a same-sex heterosexual holds and pets a gay person in a nonsexual way. The goal is to make a person lose attraction to same-sex individuals by receiving the mentor's so-called healthy touch. Obviously, this creates the potential for sexually abusive situations to occur. So, though "touch therapy" can help, it also can be detrimental if placed in the wrong hands, so to speak.

Remember, reparative therapy changes sexual *behavior,* not sexual *orientation.* People can learn to act straight and repress their sexual urges, but they rarely, if ever, change their fantasies, attractions, or capacity to fall in love with members of the same sex. People may think they are straight, but engaging in touch therapy could unleash a tidal wave of repressed feelings and emotions on unwitting clients. For example, as noted in "Founding Follies," Homosexuals Anonymous founder Colin Cook had to resign after giving dozens of nude massages to clients he was supposed to be helping overcome homosexuality. He lured the men by saying he was trying to desensitize them to pleasures of the flesh.

To his credit, Cohen—unlike Nicolosi—says that therapists should not be mentors, though he does acknowledge the difficulty in finding straight men who are willing to sit on a couch or bed for hours petting gay men, or straight women who are willing to cuddle with lesbians. With a dearth of heterosexual participants, chances are the duties will fall back to the therapists or supposedly healed ex-gays, opening the door to Cook-like situations in which a "touching" session digresses into a therapy that heals an entirely different set of needs.

Cohen Repeats Sins of the Past

With such an eccentric potpourri of outlandish therapies, why would any *reasonable* person use Cohen as his or her therapist? They rarely do, judging from the generous samples of clients sprinkled throughout his book. Cohen's clients appear to suffer from one or more mental disorders, including phobias, paranoia, delusions, depression, sexual dysfunctions, substance abuse, and alarmingly low self-esteem. Nearly all of his clients seem to be fragile individuals who engage in destructive binges or spiral into depression following the slightest provocation or incident. For instance, consider the story of Jerry, a Cohen client who abandoned God because he broke one of his mother's favorite vases after receiving Communion for the first time:

> Jerry was perfectionistic. If he only got it right, then he would be accepted and loved. . . . He never forgave himself for that mistake, and consequently grew more distant from God and his parents' religious beliefs. . . . To him, God became his ultimate accuser and judge.[57]

Another patient, Kevin, was under Cohen's care to change his sexual orientation, though it appears his real problem was random panic attacks:

> Kevin was sitting all alone in an office waiting for an appointment. . . . He waited and waited. Suddenly, he felt as if the walls were caving in on him. He ran out of the room, forgetting about the appointment altogether.[58]

The behavior exhibited by Jerry and Kevin is the rule, not the exception, in Cohen's book. I could provide a laundry list of Cohen clients who are chronic masturbators, junkies of every imaginable stripe, the unstable, and the infirm, but their stories would be redundant. The bottom line is that Cohen's patients seem to be suffering from a variety of genuine disorders that would benefit from professional help. Instead of getting assistance for their real problems, however, they are erroneously blaming their maladies on their natural sexual orientation and trying to change that. By using the mentally impaired to represent all homosexuals, Cohen is repeating the sins of the past. He is no different from Bergler or Bieber, who labeled gays sick based upon their flawed studies of patients diagnosed with various psychological disorders, such as schizophrenia or neurotic behavior.

No Statistics on Failure Rate

So, how well does Cohen's therapy work? He claims a 75 to 80 percent success rate but admits—as did his mentor Nicolosi—that he does not keep precise numbers and never conducts follow-up studies. He ultimately blames the medical and mental health establishment for his lack of data—although there is nothing stopping him from corresponding with his own clients.

Cohen may say he wishes he could keep statistics, but anecdotal evidence suggests that his excuses are nothing more than an elaborate cover-up for monumental failures. It is remarkable that, for a man who claims to have helped thousands of gays become straight, the majority of patients used as examples in his book acknowledged that they were not totally healed. One would think that his book would be a veritable showcase of his work, with every single client cited a raging hetero. Yet, the vast majority of patients who are trotted out, such as Bonnie, admit, "There is still work to be done." Slade, another patient, says he isn't completely straight but has seen a "dramatic decrease in my sexual fantasies," and Steve admits, "Although I have not fully healed my same-sex attractions, the strength and power of the feelings have diminished as a result of consistent work on my heart."59

If the best Cohen can do is show partially healed clients in his book, one wonders about the fate of the *thousands* of men and women whom he did not elect to highlight as "success" stories. Of course, Cohen has a ready-made answer for this question to absolve him of his failure: "A lot of the people I've worked with . . . don't want to come forward," said Cohen in our interview. "So many people don't want to be seen or heard. They've moved on. That's like their past. . . . So these men [and women] were courageous enough [to share their stories]."

It is amazing how the majority of clients with the courage to come forward were still "struggling" to be straight. Equally astonishing is the difficulty Cohen had in finding clients to plug his therapy who are now completely and unequivocally heterosexual. It reasons that clients who experienced total success would be the ones most inclined to offer testimony. For example, the people in Weight Watchers who are most likely to promote the program are the ones who lost the most weight. Similarly, you don't see ads for nicotine patches with users claiming, "I'm down to only one pack a day!" Only in Cohen's inverted world is the opposite true: the people achieving the least success are the ones who step forward with bravado.

Of course, it is ridiculous to compare sexual orientation to addictions or eating disorders. The love expressed by millions of people worldwide is not an addiction. Sexual orientation is a deep-seated, unalterable part of who people are; it runs as deep as the soul; it is the very core of being.

The only addiction, it appears, belongs to the reparative therapists, whose avariciousness allows them to abuse mentally thousands of men and women. Unfortunately, as long as some lesbians and gay men are made to feel ashamed, and therefore desperate to change, the unethical practice of reparative therapy will continue unabated. This nasty habit will be kicked only when our world fully accepts lesbians and gay men, treating them equally, with dignity and respect. Until then, the tears of self-flagellating lesbians and gay men will provide a river of money that keeps the evil industry of reparative therapy afloat.

The Iron Cross

In 1998, a coalition of religious political leaders discovered reparative therapy and the ex-gay ministries, eagerly coopting both in an effort to deny gay people equal rights. The religious right needed the ex-gay ministries to convince ultrareligious people that gays and lesbians could change, and they also needed the unreliable statistics from NARTH to convince secular Americans that change was possible.

Working the three in concert resembled a giant iron cross bound by religious conviction. At the top of the cross, religious political leaders called the shots, turning NARTH and Exodus into willing political puppets. On the left flank of the cross were the ex-gay ministries, who, by embracing the far right, got the attention they long desired at the expense of their independence and integrity. On the right side of the cross was NARTH, whose affiliation with the political right gained them a deluge of new clients willing to pay for their expensive theocratic therapy. At the bottom of the cross, of course, was the GLBT community, getting pummeled by all three antagonists. In Act III, we will examine how these predatory groups converged into a major political force intent on crushing GLBT equality.

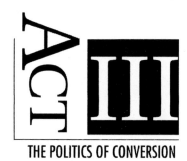

ACT III

THE POLITICS OF CONVERSION

The Puppeteers

Man's evil love makes the crooked path seem straight.

Dante, "Purgatorio"
The Divine Comedy

Going Nuclear

"It wouldn't matter how many hoops of fire we jump through, it is never enough for him," a frustrated GOP operative bitterly complained.[1] The Republican official was referring to the all-powerful James Dobson, head of the Colorado Springs–based right-wing group Focus on the Family. Dobson had long been respected by the right for his books and broadcasts helping families with pedestrian matters such as changing diapers or using corporal punishment to discipline children. In the spring of 1998, though, Dobson conspicuously thrust himself into the political arena in a midterm election year to discipline what he saw as a new batch of errant tykes: Republican leaders on Capitol Hill who, he believed, were not sufficiently promoting his ultraconservative agenda.

Right-wing adherents were euphoric when Representative Newt Gingrich (R-Georgia) stormed into Washington in 1994 to claim his throne as speaker of the house. Many in the religious right—which played a crucial role in the GOP takeover—thought that Gingrich's Republican revolution meant that they would have free rein to pass ultraconservative laws. What they did not count on was that Bill

Clinton would badly outfox Gingrich, leading the speaker to close down the government in 1995. A reinvigorated Clinton and his congressional allies worked together to help stymie the more nutty GOP proposals that appealed to Christian conservatives, such as shutting down the Department of Education.

While the savvier right-wing warriors were realistic about the GOP leadership's ability to enact their broad socially conservative agenda, purists in the movement became increasingly frustrated. The "perfectionist wing," as Gingrich called them, felt betrayed, believing that they were not receiving their just rewards for placing Gingrich and his far-right buddies at the wheel. Dobson became infuriated by what he saw as Congressional inaction and began publicly scolding the GOP leadership.

As the nation's most powerful Christian conservative, with radio and television broadcasts seen weekly by 28 million people, Dobson, aka King James, was a major player in the GOP, so when he warned the GOP to start aggressively promoting right-wing social issues or he would consider "going nuclear" against the party, Republican leaders visibly quaked. On March 18, an aggrieved Dobson met with twenty-five conservative House Republicans in the basement of the U.S. Capitol to have an emotional "Come to Jesus" meeting. "If I go," Dobson threatened the lawmakers, "I will do everything I can to take as many people with me as possible." He later stated, "I really hope you guys don't make me prove it, because I will."[2]

Dobson's admonitions were taken to heart and several meetings were set up with obsequious House leaders to discuss his agenda. House Majority Leader Dick Armey (R-Texas) even asked subcommittee chairpersons to examine how Dobson's demands could be met. Thus, the deadly 1998 "Summer of Hate" began.

The GOP Responds to King James

One of the first casualties of Dobson's threatened eruption was openly gay San Francisco philanthropist James Hormel, who was nominated by President Clinton to be ambassador to Luxembourg. Even though Luxembourg officials welcomed Hormel with open arms, Republican Senate opponents placed a hold on his nomination, saying he wasn't fit to serve because he would promote the "gay agenda" in an overwhelmingly Catholic country. Conservative GOP

Senators knew Hormel had more than enough votes to win and if they had allowed Hormel to be confirmed, Dobson surely would have walked. Their hold effectively halted the vote on the nomination.[3]

The real fireworks, however, began on June 15, 1998, when Senate Majority Leader Trent Lott (R-Mississippi) appeared on the sparsely watched cable TV show hosted by conservative Armstrong Williams.[4] On the broadcast, Williams asked Lott whether he thought homosexuality is a sin. Lott replied:

> It is. My father has a problem, as I said, with alcoholism. Other people have sex addiction. Other people are, you know, kleptomaniacs. I mean, there are all kinds of problems, addictions, difficulties, experiences of things that . . . are wrong, but you should try to, you know, work with that person to learn how to control that problem.

An Associated Press reporter wrote a story about Lott's comments, which led to a volley of attacks and counterattacks between gay and antigay groups. Representative Dick Armey backed Lott by saying, "The Bible is very clear on this. . . . Both myself and Senator Lott believe very strongly in the Bible." White House Press Secretary Mike McCurry caused the right wing to go apoplectic when during a press briefing he called Lott's remarks "backwards." Around the same time, religious political broadcaster and Christian Coalition founder Pat Robertson warned Orlando, Florida, of hurricanes, terrorist bombing, tornadoes, and meteors for allowing gay pride flags to be flown along city streets in recognition of that city's gay pride festival.[5]

A landslide of antigay legislation soon followed the hateful rhetoric, including the Hefley Amendment, which unsuccessfully aimed to overturn then-President Clinton's May 28 executive order banning workplace discrimination based on sexual orientation.

A Sinister Cabal of Conservatives

Ostensibly, this barrage of antigay rhetoric and legislation was spontaneous, but it was becoming increasingly clear that something more sinister was at work. These offensive words and deeds were not isolated incidents, but part of a secret strategy by the religious right to appease Dobson and motivate conservatives to vote in a heated midterm election year.

In January 1996, several of the religious right's most notable leaders huddled together in the cellar of a Christian church in Memphis to strategize on how to derail the GLBT movement. They called this clandestine cabal the National Pro-Family Forum. Their first foray into politics was wildly successful. They designed the Defense of Marriage Act, which banned gay marriage in the United States, and it was easily passed by Congress and signed into law by then-President Clinton.

Emboldened by their early achievement, the group, consisting of about twenty-five right-wing powerhouses, such as the Christian Coalition and Focus on the Family, sought to expand their scope. The group met again in June 1998 at Focus on the Family headquarters to strategize on how to mobilize conservative voters and make the biggest impact in the upcoming elections. They knew they needed a fresh antigay issue to rally the troops but were flummoxed as to what it should be. A relative newcomer to the coalition, the crafty Janet Folger, director of the Fort Lauderdale–based Center for Reclaiming America for Christ came up with the answer they were seeking.

The Ideological Entrepreneur

When Janet Folger was seven, she won first prize in a Cleveland, Ohio, Fourth of July costume contest dressed as a cleaning lady with a sign that read, "Clean up the world." Since that day, she has never looked back, scrubbing away at what she perceives as social decay and moral filth with a puritanical streak that has unnerved friends and foes alike.

Folger, born in Parma, Ohio, grew up in an authoritarian household led by her parents Jim and Beth Folger, along with three brothers, two of whom barely speak to her now. Folger found her calling in a high school health class when an antiabortion presenter showed a picture of a plastic trash bag spilling over with fetuses. From that moment on, she became an antiabortion warrior, doggedly pursuing the goal of outlawing abortion.

Her first job was at a Christian radio station in Cleveland, where she worked part-time while earning bachelor's and master's degrees in communications at Cleveland State University. In 1988, immediately following graduation, Ohio Right to Life brought her on as a state lobbyist, a brilliant move that made the group a major force in state politics for years. Her abrasive—bordering on abusive—lobbying style won her few friends, but it did earn her a flurry of impressive legislative victories. In 1997, largely through Folger's efforts, the state legislature passed a measure to force minors to get at least one parent's consent or that of a judge before obtaining an abortion. Many legal experts considered it the toughest antiabortion law in more than a decade.

Folger, an intense, fast-talking hurricane of a woman, always ready with a sarcastic quip, became widely respected but also feared by Democrats and Republicans alike. Hauling a plastic fetus around the Ohio capitol building, she would torment lawmakers, often barging into their offices unannounced to deliver blistering, wild-eyed sermons if they planned to vote against her abortion position. This antagonistic behavior earned her many bitter enemies. In 1994, her Porsche 924S was set ablaze. No charges were filed, however, despite an FBI investigation. She also earned the enmity of several members of the Ohio legislature who viewed her as a mean-spirited, manipulative bully:

- "She literally made some of us sick," said Representative John Garcia (R-Toledo), a prolife advocate. "She got me so angry that I was ready to vote for abortion just to get her out of my hair."[6]
- "She likes to intimidate legislators," said Representative June Lucas (D-Mineral Ridge), "and to make threats."[7]
- "There aren't too many people I don't like, but Janet Folger is one of them," said Representative Joan Lawrence (R-Columbus). "I don't like and I don't trust her. She will say or do anything to accomplish her goals."[8]

Indeed, Folger's ideas and behavior have simultaneously awed and angered gay activists. She once, for example, wrote in the conservative magazine *Insight on the News* that the militant gay group ACT UP was partially responsible for pressuring the American Psychiatric Association in 1973 into removing homosexuality from its list of mental disorders.[9] There is one problem with Folger's polemic. ACT UP is the acronym for the AIDS Coalition to Unleash Power. That no one had even heard of AIDS prior to the early 1980s makes it difficult for ACT UP to have protested the APA in 1973. Of course, this inconvenient fact meant little to Folger. She was interested only in using

ACT UP's militant reputation to evoke images of radical homosexuals to scare conservative readers of *Insight*.

Although Folger did not start out her career as an antigay advocate, she became an avowed homophobe after she was hired in August 1997 to direct the Fort Lauderdale–based Center for Reclaiming America for Christ. This group is the political arm of the antigay Coral Ridge Presbyterian Church, led by televangelist D. James Kennedy. Folger's emergence as an antigay powerhouse came as a shock to many people and has led to repeated charges that she is an unabashed opportunist:

- "It's very odd to all of us," said Susannah Sagen, former executive director of the National Reproductive Rights Action League in Ohio. "Never once did she say anything about gays. I think she thinks this is where the bread and butter is, that this is the way to galvanize the fundamentalists."[10]
- "Janet is an example of what I like to think of as an issue entrepreneur," said former Executive Director of the Christian Coalition Ralph Reed. "Some entrepreneurs try to figure out what new hot stocks are. Janet is the ideological entrepreneur, someone who tries to pick new hot issues."[11]

Folger was astute enough to realize that gay rights was the issue du jour, and, from reading polls, that people were much more likely to support gay rights legislation if they believed homosexuality was innate. Therefore, the key to reversing the gay rights movement was convincing a majority of Americans that homosexuality was a choice. With this is mind, Folger shrewdly changed the right's entire paradigm of attacking gay civil liberties by devising the new and exciting strategy of promoting the ex-gay ministries. This innovative model allowed conservatives to say they loved homosexuals while working to take away their rights. It seemed to be a brilliant idea, and the other members of the National Pro-Family Forum leapt on the ex-gay bandwagon without hesitation.

The group decided it would launch a series of full-page ads in major daily newspapers promoting the ex-gay ministries. The ads would promise homosexuals "hope for change." The print campaign would be followed, they decided, by a million-dollar television campaign later in the year. "Moving in the ex-gay direction was the obvious place to go," said Human Rights Campaign Executive Director Elizabeth Birch in our interview at the Wall Street Deli, below HRC headquarters in Washington. "The lesson of the nineties for the extreme right is the up-front, hard-core extreme gay bashing was actually costing them a price," she continued. "So they began to move strategically into more sophisticated ways of implanting the same messages, but inside more creative Trojan horses."[12]

The Normandy Landing

On July 13, 1998, I was sitting at my desk when Birch came storming through the office hallways holding a full-page *New York Times* ad with the large headline "I'm Living Proof That the Truth Can Set You Free." The ad featured a close-up photograph of a smiling, well-made-up Anne Paulk who described herself as a "wife, mother and former lesbian." In addition to Paulk's own words as testimony in the ad was the following plug for ex-gay ministries:

> Thousands of ex-gays . . . have walked away from their homosexual identities. While the paths each took into homosexuality may vary, their stories of hope and healing through the transforming love of Jesus Christ are the same.

Overnight this campaign made the term *ex-gay* a household word, a sensation in the popular media, and the talk at gyms, office coolers, and subway stations. Ex-gays became a ubiquitous topic on the American cultural landscape.

Before I could finish my morning coffee I was hustled into Birch's office for a series of intense conference calls with the leaders of several national gay and lesbian organizations. We soon discovered that this first ad was part of a $600,000 campaign, warmly named "Truth in Love," sponsored by fifteen arch-right groups with an incredible history of gay bashing. The Family Research Council's Bob Knight called the campaign the "Normandy landing in the larger cultural wars." Quite frankly, it did feel as though we were under siege by hostile forces, with media requests skyrocketing and calls and e-mails pouring in from rattled members.

As news reports rolled across the airwaves, people were genuinely frightened by the right's latest attack. This new assault was particulary threatening because the hatred was veiled under the guise of love. In many cases, gay people who had long been out and thought they had been accepted were asked by family and friends to consider submitting themselves to the ex-gay ministries. The ad campaign brought a lot of unnecessary stress and humiliation to untold numbers of lesbian and gay people nationwide.

Within forty-eight hours, a coalition of twelve national gay groups, led by the Human Rights Campaign and the Gay and Lesbian Alliance Against Defamation, had responded with a powerful full-page ad of their own in *USA Today*. The coalition's ad featured Dave and Ruth Waterbury, Republican, churchgoing, Minneapolis parents, and their lesbian daughter, Margie. In the ad, the Waterburys made an appeal to the American people to treat their daughter with dignity and respect so she can live her life free of discrimination.

As a result of the dueling ad campaigns, the American Psychological Association assailed the efficacy of reparative therapy, with APA Executive Director Dr. Raymond Fowler saying:

> For nearly three decades, it has been known that homosexuality is not a mental illness. Medical and mental health professionals also now know that sexual orientation is not a choice and cannot be altered. Groups who try to change the sexual orientation of people through so-called "conversion therapy" are misguided and run the risk of causing a great deal of psychological harm to those they say they are trying to help.[13]

Despite the harsh condemnations by gay groups and the medical and mental health community, the Truth in Love campaign marched on with full-page ads in *The Washington Post, USA Today, Los Angeles Times, The Wall Street Journal, Chicago Tribune, The Miami Herald,* and the *San Francisco Examiner.*

One ad featured a large group of ex-gays smiling while huddled together under the explosive headline "We're standing for the truth that homosexuals can change." The not so loving text read, "There are problems for homosexuals even condoms can't fix. Studies also show a high degree of destructive behavior among homosexuals, including alcohol, drug abuse and emotional and physical violence."

In yet another full-page ad, this time in *USA Today,* full-time football star and part-time hate preacher Reggie White was featured. Earlier in the year White had been harshly criticized in the media for his crude remarks about homosexuals. The headline in White's ad screamed, "In Defense of Free Speech." The ad painted this behemoth of a man as a whimpering victim of the media and liberal interest groups. In the ad, White pontificates on a laundry list of absolute "truths" that he had apparently been handed straight from God:

> *The truth about the non-genetic roots of homosexuality* . . . and how nurture, not nature, is the real cause of homosexual behavior.

> *The truth about ex-gays* . . . and how thousands are leaving their homosexual identity for sexual celibacy, and even marriage.

> *The truth about homosexual recruitment in public schools* . . . and how activists have misused AIDS funding to promote homosexuality to elementary-age kids.

> *The truth about raw political power* . . . and how homosexual activists are creating laws to mandate acceptance of homosexual behavior in every facet of life from work to school to religion *and making it a criminal offense to dissent.*

> *The truth about sexual sin* . . . and the powerful hold it has on homosexuals and heterosexuals alike and the only way to find real hope and healing.

A final full-page ad was placed in the *Miami Herald* with the bold headline "From innocence to AIDS. One mother's plea to the parents of homosexuals." It pictured ex-gay Michael Johnston as a little boy blowing out candles on a birthday cake. In the ad text Johnston's mother, Frances, tells a simplistic tale of how her son got caught up in the so-called gay lifestyle that resulted in his contracting AIDS. In the ad, Johnston thanks his mother while disparaging homosexuality:

> I am so grateful I can look my parents in the eye today and say, "thank you for loving me enough to tell me the truth." I will always regret the pain and sorrow I caused them—just so I could pursue my own selfish desires. It was the truth that set me free.

A Not So Truthful Campaign

"Truth" may have set Johnston free, but it wasn't anywhere to be found in the ads. Dr. Robert Garofalo, a noted pediatrician who conducted a study of gay teens, was cited in many of these antigay advertisements. According to Garofalo, "It's a complete misrepresentation of what the research actually says." Garofalo told *The Boston Globe,* "It was taken completely out of context. It comes to the complete opposite conclusion of what the paper actually concluded." Garofalo told *The Globe* he was "horrified and angry" about the misappropriation of his work, calling the interpretation by the group a "divisive and destructive forum":

> It's just an awful and very destructive message. It alienates them [gay teens] and makes them further feel isolated and alone. That's the very thing that leads to suicide, and leads to the behaviors that were reported in my paper.[14]

Despite these inaccuracies, the media reported on the ex-gay campaign as if it had some validity, instead of recognizing it as a promotion of discredited, scientifically bankrupt programs. The nadir of the media coverage was the notorious *Newsweek* cover story picturing the Paulks in their kitchen under the catchy headline "Gay for Life?" "The *Newsweek* cover absolutely exploited the whole story," GLAAD's Executive Director Joan Garry said in our interview.[15] "It's about what's hot and what's going to sell that magazine on that newsstand."

It was more than hot. It was sizzling, and it became almost larger than life. For a time, one could not turn on the television or open a newspaper or magazine without coming across stories on the ex-gay ministries. Once obscure ex-gays, such as the Paulks or Anthony Falzarano of Parents and Friends of Ex-Gays (PFOX), suddenly became highly sought after minicelebrities.

The Right Wins Round One

From the start of the print campaign, the antigay leaders behind it adamantly claimed they loved homosexuals and that the campaign was about prayer, not politics. Examining the ads, the people behind them, and their real motivations, however, clearly shows that this was a politically based campaign strongly motivated by hate and discrimination.

The first sign that these ads were not about love were the contents of the ads themselves. If the Christian right had stopped with the first two ads—featuring Paulk and the group shot of former homosexuals—their campaign would have been more convincing because these ads had the veneer of love. The third ad, featuring Reggie White, however, was their first strategic misstep. Astute commentators wondered aloud what made White, an inarticulate defensive tackle for the Green Bay Packers, an expert on genetics and the causation of sexual orientation. If this ad were truly about converting gays to Christianity, why was part of the text dedicated to attacks on gay "political power"?

Most important, White, although a hero of the right wing, was not a sympathetic public figure to most Americans. On March 25, 1998, White delivered a jaw-dropping speech to the Wisconsin State Assembly in which he called homosexuality a sin and asserted that it was a chosen "lifestyle." He equated gay people with "liars and cheaters and malicious and backstabbers." And he didn't stop there. In this infamous sermon he rattled off enough stereotypes to have earned him a standing ovation from former KKK Grand Wizard David Duke, had he been in attendance. White claimed blacks were gifted at worship and celebration, whites were good at tapping into money, and Native Americans weren't enslaved because they knew the territory and "how to sneak up on people." He also claimed that Hispanics are gifted in "family structure" and can put twenty to thirty people in one home, and that the Japanese and Asians are inventive and "can turn a television into a watch."[16]

It is baffling how the antigay political coalition thought they could win the battle of public opinion by promoting White as a martyr. Their argument that gay activists were stifling White's right to free speech seemed preposterous. It was not that White wasn't allowed to speak; it was that most people were repulsed by what he had to say. He was not viewed as a victim, but as a bigoted ignoramus who seemed excessively opinionated on topics about which he appeared to know little.

The White ad was also part of a nasty strategy, which ultimately failed, to split the traditional progressive Democratic base by turning economically liberal, yet socially conservative African Americans against gays. The message the antigay coalition was hammering home every chance it got was, "Gay men and lesbians are hijacking the civil rights movement." According to Folger, "It's preposterous, trying to take an inborn characteristic [race] and relate it to the behavior of homosexuality. There are thousands of former homosexuals. That cuts into the premise that gays need special rights."[17]

Aside from White, the antigay coalition praised gospel singers Angie and Debbie Winans for their controversial 1998 antigay song "Not Natural." They even brought on board conservative Alveda King, the niece of the late Martin Luther King Jr., to push their sinister agenda. "I have met former homosexuals," said King, "but I have yet to meet a former black."[18]

The right's penchant for overreaching and spewing vitriol also came blasting out in their final ad featuring Michael Johnston and his mother, Frances. The juxtaposition of the sweet picture of a child blowing out birthday candles with the noxious headline "From Innocence to AIDS" was widely considered contradictory to their claim of compassion and seemed jarring to the reader. Although not a knockout punch, this ad did erode the campaign's believability and message of "love."

The most obvious clue that this campaign was a wolf in sheep's clothing was the people in charge of running it. If Exodus had sponsored it, the campaign would have appeared more credible, but instead, its leaders were those who had already earned long-standing reputations as virulently homophobic, right-wing zealots.

Did the Family Research Council's Bob Knight have love in his heart when he said, "Just look at the human body. You can't fool nature. The rectum was not made for sexual activity. It's an exit ramp, not an entry ramp."[19]

Was Don Wildmon of the American Family Association full of compassion when he cautioned his members, "Since homosexuals cannot reproduce, the only way for them to 'breed' is to RECRUIT! And who are their targets for recruitment? Children!"[20]

Was America really supposed to believe that the Christian Coalition's Reverend Pat Robertson suddenly loved gays? Was this the same man who once said, "Many of the people involved with Adolf Hitler were Satanists, many of them were homosexuals, the two things seem to go together"? [21]

Perhaps the biggest refutation of the ad sponsors' assertions that they love gays came from the fact that D. James Kennedy, leader of Coral Ridge Ministries, was intimately involved. Kennedy is a powerful man with astounding reach in right-wing circles. His sermons reach more than 3 million Americans and are carried on 550 TV stations, reaching 25,000 cities and 200 countries. His church, which is so tall it has airplane warning lights, has an annual operating budget of $60 million and includes 10,000 members. His fund-raising ability is legendary; he's been known to collect more than $1 million during Sunday services. To fire up his flock and keep the money flowing, Kennedy needed to invent enemies, and enemy number one, since the fall of the Soviet Union, is homosexuality.

Kennedy has long been tied to radical theocratic groups, known as the reconstructionist movement, which claims the Bible calls for the stoning to death of gays. In fact, the ideas behind the Truth in Love campaign that Kennedy deputy Janet Folger reportedly thought up may have actually come from George Grant, a former high-level Kennedy staffer known as a reconstructionist.

In 1987, religious activist/author Grant wrote an influential book, *The Changing of the Guard,* which called on fundamentalist Christians to replace America's democracy with a theocracy. Instead of condemning these crackpot views, Kennedy hired Grant in 1991 as executive director and vice president of Coral Ridge Ministries. Grant's tenure ended in 1993, but his vision of using ex-gays as weapons with which to bludgeon the lesbian and gay community were penned in his 1994 book with Mark Horne, *Legislating Immorality: The Homosexual Movement Comes Out of the Closet.* The book begins with the story of an ex-gay named Lance, who ends his testimony by saying, "People can change. There really is hope. I'm living proof."[22]

Remember, the Anne Paulk ad read, "I'm living proof the truth can set you free." Is this just a shockingly eerie coincidence, or was the Truth in Love campaign directly inspired by a man who believes the Bible calls for capital punishment of gays?

Reverend Kennedy's ties to the fringe extend beyond his intimate association with Grant. The late reconstructionist founder R. J. Rushdoony and Gary North, another key member of the movement, had been frequent guests on Kennedy's weekly television show. In effect, Kennedy has continually offered a platform for homicidal extremists to express their twisted views.

Despite recent attempts to appear moderate by hiring spin doctor Janet Folger, Kennedy keeps the reconstructionist influence alive and well to this day at Coral Ridge Presbyterian, showing his lack of respect for religious pluralism by demeaning the separation of church and state:

> If we are committed and involved in taking back the nation for Christian moral values, and if we are willing to risk the scorn of the secular media and the bureaucracy that stand against us, there is no doubt we can witness the dismantling of not just the Berlin Wall but the even more diabolical "wall of separation" that has led to increasing secularization, godlessness, immorality, and corruption in our country.[23]

Folger echoed this sentiment: "The secret they [the courts] don't seem to understand is that there is no separation of church and state in the Constitution or in any of our founding documents."[24]

Incredibly, when I attended Coral Ridge Presbyterian's February 1999 Reclaiming America for Christ conference—in the midst of the Truth in Love campaign—Kennedy was still actively promoting Grant's antigay books.

Clearly, the election year ad campaign was never about love, nor was it really about changing gay people, but rather about changing laws to ensure gays and lesbians would have no legal protection from discrimination. To sell their message, the far right had to shroud their true political intent and claim the campaign was about assisting only those gays who "wanted help" to become straight. "Why is it wrong to give these people some hope?" Folger asked.[25]

Occasionally Folger would slip up, as she did on National Public Radio, and reveal her true political motivations: "That [ex-gays exist] shatters the foundation of the homosexual movement. That foundation of all their arguments is based on the myth that homosexuals are born that way and change is impossible."[26] If that wasn't bad enough, the antigay coalition campaigned to have punitive sodomy laws enforced so that gay people could be incarcerated.

Washington writer Andrew Sullivan brilliantly exposed Folger's true, frightening agenda on ABC's *Nightline,* hosted by Forrest Sawyer, in one of the greatest on-air performances in gay and lesbian history.[27] Using classic debate techniques, Sullivan allowed Folger to hang herself with her own words. Folger claimed repeatedly that the ads were not political and that the antigay coalition loved gay people. Sullivan trapped Folger, however, forcing her to admit that she and her cohorts actively support laws that would punish gay and lesbian Americans for consensual sex in the privacy of their own homes:

SAWYER: Ms. Folger, forgive me. He [Sullivan] is asking the direct question, do you support laws that advocate the imprisonment of people who engage in homosexual behavior?
FOLGER: I guess if you're looking at sodomy laws, there are sodomy laws on the books that I very much support.
SULLIVAN: Thank you. The answer is yes.

Revealing statements such as this show that when the antigay coalition "offers" so-called help to gays, it is like an "offer you can't refuse" from Don Corleone in *The Godfather.* Putting their PR spin aside, their real message is, "Take our offer to change, or we'll try to force you to change by passing punitive laws to make your life difficult, including locking you up in the pokey."

By talking not just about Jesus, but jail, it was clear that the ad campaign wasn't about persuasion, but persecution. The ads talked about conversion, but their real purpose was coercion. They claimed to be about education, but their real aim was intimidation.

Although the ad sponsors were shady theocrats bent on outlawing homosexuality, this was a difficult message for gay activists to sell to the public. The coalition spent so much money and dumped such an unprecedented amount of misinformation in the public sphere that it was almost impossible to counter it all. Gay rights groups fought admirably but were losing the war. The right had successfully changed the ideological landscape to the point where much of the debate among the unenlightened shifted from gay and lesbian equality to discussions on nature versus nurture. "I think [the campaign] was successful from the standpoint that it got them publicity. . . . It got people talking about it," said writer and ex-gay expert Natalie Davis in our interview.[28]

Like a panzer division zooming through the plains, it seemed nothing could derail the powerful antigay coalition. Gay and lesbian groups warned that the heated rhetoric in the ads and on Capitol Hill was creating an unusually hostile climate that could lead to violence. Unfortunately, this message fell on deaf ears, as our opponents dismissed our warnings as classic liberal victim mongering.

Drawing the link between hate speech and hate crimes was a difficult message to impart to the American people. Time and again I would bring up this connection in radio or television interviews, and right-wing hosts or callers would inevitably say, "Show me the proof." There was never an absence of hate crime cases and I, along with others, would vigorously cite them, but since these hapless victims were unfamiliar to the public, citing their misfortunes had little impact.

When I play pickup basketball in rougher neighborhoods there is a well-known saying: "No blood, No foul." Unfortunately, America needed to see blood before they would acknowledge that verbal gay bashing and antigay ads might create an atmosphere where evil could take root and flourish.

Dueling Press Conferences

It was early in the morning at the Human Rights Campaign's headquarters as I feverishly traversed the maze of hallways to corral members of the eclectic group of ex-ex-gays, mental health experts, and organizational leaders who were to participate in a major press conference in Washington's National Press Club.

"This is the order of speakers," I said, as the group huddled around a conference table. "Let's go through one dress rehearsal so we can be ready for the real thing."

The "real thing" was our October 8, 1998, media event designed to counter the National Pro-Family Forum's press conference where they were going to unveil their much-anticipated, $250,000-to-$4-million ex-gay television campaign.[29] Their event was also to be held at the National Press Club, one hour before ours. The dueling press events made for great theater and therefore attracted a hoard of media.

On a big-screen TV the antigay coalition played two sixty-second television commercials. The first was a takeoff on their *Miami Herald* print ad featuring the Johnstons. In the TV ad, Michael thanks his mother, Frances, for helping him "walk away from homosexuality," while the two sit side by side. According to the ad:

> I love my son very much. I always have. Even when he told me he was using drugs and involved in homosexuality. But just because you love your children, doesn't mean you approve of everything they do. Sometimes they make bad choices.

My son Michael found out the truth. He could walk away from homosexuality, but he found out too late. He has AIDS. If you love your children, love them enough to tell them the truth. There is hope for change, hope for the future.

The second ad featured a group of former homosexuals and their spouses who spoke of their conversions to heterosexuality through Jesus Christ: "The dream I thought could never happen, having a wife and kids, has come true," said a smiling ex-gay in the ad.

Both ads ended with the hair-raising tag line "It's not about hate . . . It's about hope," which was interesting because the right was tacitly acknowledging that a significant number of people saw the original print campaign as motivated by hate. While the tag line had a nice ring, it was too clever. After all, when is the last time a harmful product advertised what it was *not* about? For example, Ford never ran an ad for the Pinto saying, "It's not about the exploding engine, it's about the smooth ride," and Phillip Morris has never run an ad for Marlboro saying, "It's not about the cancer, it's about the smooth taste."

Immediately following their press conference, several members of the antigay coalition, including John Paulk, Janet Folger, Bob Knight, Anthony Falzarano, and Michael and Frances Johnston, sauntered into our press conference uninvited as it neared completion. The mutual loathing was palpable; the air was thick with tension and the atmosphere poisoned with unbridled contempt. They saw us as the Infidel and we saw them as the American version of the Taliban. There seemed to be no middle ground, and the situation threatened to spiral out of control, as seemingly mortal enemies came face-to-face, seething from wounds that had occurred in battles during the Summer of Hate.

After our press conference ended, passions on both sides overflowed, spilling into the hallways. Janet Folger traded pointed barbs with Elizabeth Birch. I engaged in a hostile exchange with Michael Johnston. Even my mother—who spoke at the press conference as a representative of Parents, Families and Friends of Lesbians and Gays (PFLAG)—was in the face of Frances Johnston.

Though cooler heads eventually prevailed, clearly the situation had changed dramatically. In the past, we had politely mingled with our opponents, whom we knew personally from appearing together on various television shows, but the summer's events had unleashed a torrent of fury and rage that undermined civil discourse and degenerated into base emotion and savage disdain.

Little did the right-wing coalition realize at the time, but this maelstrom of antigay ferocity that they had helped to create had been brutally unleashed on a young man in Wyoming two days before their press conference. Within forty-eight hours, the whole world would know the name of Matthew Shepard.

Judgment Day

On the night of October 7, 1998, twenty-one-year-old University of Wyoming student Matthew Shepard went out for a drink at the Fireside Lounge in Laramie, Wyoming. While at the bar, Shepard— all 5'2" and 110 pounds of him—made the acquaintance of two local burly high school dropouts. After finding out Shepard was gay, the boisterous Aaron McKinney and his quiet sidekick, Russell Henderson, lured Shepard into their pickup truck.

The two men drove him to a remote field, repeatedly pistol-whipped him, and left him to die, tied to a wooden fence in near-freezing temperatures. Two motorcyclists found him unconscious with a smashed skull the next day. Dried blood stained his face, except where tears had streamed down his visage. They originally thought he was a scarecrow because of the way he was situated on the fence.

Shepard's parents, Judy and Dennis, immediately flew home from Saudi Arabia—where Dennis worked—to be by their son's bedside. Shepard died October 12, while on life support in a Fort Collins, Colorado, hospital.

Police quickly arrested Henderson and McKinney after they found a bloody .357 magnum in the pickup truck and Shepard's wallet in McKinney's house. McKinney's girlfriend, Kristen LeAnn, tried to help her boyfriend by implausibly accusing the diminutive Shepard of being at fault for his murder. She said he supposedly made a pass at McKinney, a brawny, intimidating construction worker.[30]

Unlike the legions of hate crimes that get little attention, Shepard's murder vividly captured America's collective imagination and received astonishing amounts of media coverage. There was something mystical, if not transcendent, about the Shepard incident that is hard to elucidate. By all accounts he was an articulate, gentle young man filled with noble aspirations and boundless dreams. This starkly contrasted with the empty, dead-end lives of the brutish thugs who left him for dead in the harsh elements of the Wyoming prairie.

This event was so much more than a simple story of good versus evil. Shepard's death held up a mirror to America, and the vast majority of people didn't like the cruel image they saw staring back at them. It caused a seismic shift in public opinion and was nothing short of a monumental cultural awakening. Many heterosexuals with gay family members and friends were radicalized and came forth as vocal supporters of lesbian and gay equality. To borrow the old ACT UP slogan, they realized that, in some cases, silence did equal death.

For the first time in history, antigay violence was in the forefront of American consciousness. Antigay rhetoric no longer seemed innocuous and homophobic jokes no longer seemed quite as funny. The reverberations of Shepard's death changed the way many Americans viewed their behavior toward lesbians and gay men, and the aftershocks can still be felt today.

Much of the Shepard phenomenon had to do with the fact that his death occurred in the midst of the most sustained, premeditated, political and cultural antigay attacks in modern history. The homophobic volume had been ratcheted up to near ear-splitting decibels and now the right wing had to face the music. Through this tragedy, the public finally understood that there was, in fact, a link between hate speech and hate violence.

"We didn't know who Matthew would be, but we could have certainly predicted that there would be some very, very tragic violent deaths over the summer," HRC's Birch told Katie Couric on the *Today Show*.[31]

Race and class also played into the extraordinary legacy more than most people would like to admit. That Shepard was an attractive, college-educated, white guy who looked like the boy next door was a crucial factor in the story's escalation. It was not so much that people were racist, but the majority of people in power—white and middle class—could identify with Shepard more than they could a black kid or a white boy from a trailer park. Whether a member of Congress or a grandmother in the Midwest, these folks saw in Shepard a friend or family member they loved and respected.

Candlelight vigils in honor of Shepard were held across the nation. A vigil on the west steps of the U.S. Capitol, organized by GLAAD and HRC, drew more than 5,000 people, including Senator Ted Kennedy (D-Massachusetts), former Senator Alan Simpson (R-Wyoming), and House Minority Leader Dick Gephardt (D-Missouri). Actresses Anne Heche, Ellen DeGeneres, and Kristen Johnston, from *Third Rock from the Sun,* also attended the rally.

"I can't stop crying. I am so devastated by this. I'm begging heterosexuals to see this as a wake-up call to please stem the hate. We shouldn't be asked to change who we are," said DeGeneres, taking a not so veiled swipe at the ex-gay ad campaign during the Washington vigil.[32]

Overnight, the right wing went from victor to vanquished in the culture wars. The success of their ex-gay campaign essentially evaporated into thin air. Author and religious right expert Chris Bull wrote in *Perfect Enemies* that Shepard's death turned their ex-gay crusade into a "public relations hit, perhaps the most damaging to date," and reduced their apparent victory to "ashes."[33]

Adding to the antigay coalition's woes was the fact that Shepard's death brought crazy, wild-eyed extremists out of the woodwork. Reverend Fred Phelps, pastor of Westboro Baptist Church in Topeka, Kansas, and his followers picketed Shepard's funeral, carrying large signs with such slogans as "God Hates Fags," "AIDS Cures Fags," and "Matt in Hell." The right-wing ad sponsors' contorted attempts to distance themselves from the hate-mongering troglodytes only further entangled them in the mess. As eloquently stated by HRC's Birch:

> [T]hese kinds of crimes never happen in a vacuum. They happen because people's minds have been twisted with cruel stereotypes about gay and lesbian people. And this ad campaign has been pumped out all summer presenting gay and lesbian people as defective, as less than, as not fully human. And young Matthew Shepard made one mistake, and that's that he happened to fall into the path of someone that had been fed this rhetoric and came at him full of rage and hate.[34]

Shepard's death marked a turning point in gay and lesbian history. The right's overt war against gays was no longer considered politically acceptable. The blowback was so severe that the antigay coalition delayed their ex-gay television campaign seven months, and due to public opinion having turned so violently against them, it ultimately flopped.

Despite their failure, the antigay coalition, once again, inadvertently exposed their political agenda when Bob Carter, spokesperson for the Center for Reclaiming America for Christ, said the ads first ran in Washington because "that's where the policymakers are."[35] "Based on Carter's comments, the ads' sponsors are either trying to reach gay policymakers to help them change, or they want to influence policymakers so they will pass antigay laws," quipped HRC Communications Director David M. Smith.[36]

A year after Matthew Shepard was murdered a Hollywood hotel ballroom was filled with dozens of glamorous celebrities and the entertainment media. They were there for the screening of two HRC public service announcements (PSAs) promoting love and acceptance, featuring Matt's mom, Judy Shepard. In an ironic twist, the television war began with the voice of one mother, Frances Johnston, who was sadly unable to accept her son's sexual orientation, but it ended with the accepting voice of Judy Shepard, who finished one of the PSAs by softly intoning, "I loved Matt just the way he was. Just the way he was." With such authentic love, there was no need to tell the audience, "It's not about hate, it's about hope." They already knew the truth.

Who Says Fundamentalists Don't Believe in Divorce?

> They [the antigay coalition] didn't do what maybe we thought they would do. We were a picture they wanted during that period of time.
>
> Alan Chambers, Exodus Executive Director

When the leaders of the ex-gay ministries were first approached by the antigay political coalition with the idea of starring in an ad campaign, ministry leaders were ecstatic. For decades they had considered themselves outcasts, the ultimate minority within a minority—rejected by the fundamentalist church and scorned by the gay community.

By and large, the fundamentalists treated the ex-gays with substantially more hostility than the gay groups. Whereas the lesbian and gay community's response was usually supercilious laughter, the fundamentalists were often full of fiery condemnation. Most conservative church leaders could not understand why anyone would want to base their identity on an "ex-sin" any more than they would want to base it on a current sin. Calling oneself an ex-gay was, to them, as absurd as a person publicly identifying himself or herself as an "ex-adulterer." Once there was a cessation of the sin, they reasoned, stop talking about it and move on.

Discomfort also surfaces in most conservative churches when having to deal with ex-gays who still behave in a stereotypically homosexual manner. Although these individuals claim to have changed, they simply don't appear believable to conservative church leaders: "If you've changed, how come you still look queer?"

Suddenly, out of the blue, the most powerful fundamentalist Christian groups in the world were vigorously courting Exodus leaders, and these pariahs were unexpectedly rubbing elbows with preachers they had admired only on television. It was as if the captain of the high school football team and the head cheerleader were begging the nerds to sit with them at their exclusive table in the school cafeteria. These perennial lepers were starstruck and enraptured by the unexpected shower of praise and attention. The orphan of the right-wing Christian church was suddenly the favorite son, and the temptation to partner with the religious right was irresistible.

Furthermore, the vast financial resources of such groups as Coral Ridge Ministries and the Family Research Council would give the ex-gay ministries the mainstream attention they had long craved but were able to get only by appearing on talk shows such as *Jerry Springer.* "It's the biggest breakthrough for us in the past twenty-five years," exclaimed one ex-gay leader of a South Florida ministry, capturing Exodus's initial euphoria.[37]

The ex-gay ministry leaders soon learned, however, that running with the right-wing big boys had strings attached. The relatively apolitical Exodus leaders were now forced to become political operatives, acting as acquiescent shills for virulently antigay organizations. Instead of prayer as their focus, politics took center stage. And what a stage it was. The media cyclone swirling around the campaign created a situation in which the less nutty ex-gay leaders were shoved aside by outrageous, spotlight-hogging stage horses. The media had little interest in humble ex-gays who were honest about their incomplete transformations and spoke of repressing their sexuality through prayer. The media, especially television, preferred wild, prurient tales of sex-crazed homosexuals who gave up bathhouses after Jesus personally spoke to them. This allowed the most shameless, self-promoting, psychologically unbalanced ex-gays to become the public face of the ministries. Although Exodus leaders were excited that their story was finally being told, they never anticipated that they would lose control of who was telling it.

The ex-gay ministries soon became synonymous with the "truth-telling impaired," such as Falzarano, the confrontational leader of PFOX. His bizarre background and zany rhetoric were ready-made for the circus-act-hungry talk show circuit that thrived on the controversial, not the contemplative. Falzarano, a former male hustler with more than 400 sex partners, once was the joy boy of the infamous Roy Cohn. While "dating," the two partied nonstop, snorting lines at some of Manhattan's finest, homosexual, A-list bacchanals.[38] Although Falzarano found this wild lifestyle intoxicating—in more ways than one—he abruptly abandoned it after God pulled him aside and asked him to go straight.

Falzarano's account of how and why he became an ex-gay is contradictory, though, if not outright incoherent. Writer and ex-gay myth-buster Mark Pietrzyk, in an article for *Independent Gay Forum,* noted that, "at times, it might appear that Falzarano is two different people." According to Pietrzyk's article, Falzarano spoke in 1997 at an antigay seminar at Georgetown University. During his testimony there, he griped about how miserable he was in gay life and that, at his low point, the ambitious male prostitute had twelve different sexual conquests in a single night in a bathhouse.[39] Yet, on an episode of *The Roseanne Show* (February 1999)—in which he appeared with me—Falzarano claimed he was "really, totally happy" and had "no reason to change" until God commanded he do so. Whether gay life was fulfilling or forgettable seems to depend on what mood Falzarano is in on any given day.

Falzarano has also given incongruous stories about why he entered the ex-gay ministries. In one version, God said in an audible voice, "Anthony, I've been patient with you long enough. If you don't give up the homosexual lifestyle now, you will die of AIDS." According to

Falzarano, at the time of this divine intervention, the number of AIDS cases in the nation was insignificant. He said on *Roseanne,* "God pulled me out of the lifestyle before AIDS hit." In another rendering of his tale on *Good Morning America,* he left gay life because of the ravages of the AIDS epidemic. "I just realized, when I began to see thirty-five of my friends die of AIDS, that I probably made the wrong lifestyle choice."[40] So, did he "leave the lifestyle" before AIDS or after it became a devastating epidemic? In Falzarano Land, the lines of fact and fairy tale are often blurred.

Even though Falzarano was guilty of serial storytelling, the Family Research Council (FRC) put him in charge of turning the ex-gay ministries into a political arm of the religious right. Armed with an $80,000 grant from FRC, Falzarano became the group's political puppet, traversing the nation to use his ever-changing testimony in hopes of undermining gay rights legislation.[41] For instance, he spoke against a measure in Maine that would have outlawed job discrimination based on sexual orientation. He also lobbied to keep an antigay sodomy law on the books in Louisiana.

Another ex-gay leader who emerged as a media star—at the expense of the less nutty ex-gay leaders—was Michael Johnston of Virginia-based Kerusso Ministries and star of the right-wing television ad campaign. Reverend Jerry Falwell was Johnston's meal ticket, and the two teamed up, with Johnston sycophantically parroting Falwell's antigay pabulum.

From my encounters with Johnston, he appears to be a somber, particularly cynical individual who is far to the right of most leaders in the ex-gay ministries—which is difficult to do. All fire and brimstone and bereft of compassion, Johnston has little tolerance for other people. He once barked, "There is unfortunately a live and let live attitude [in America]."[42]

Johnston described himself prior to his transformation as "habitually stoned" with a life that was a "revolving door of drugs, alcohol, and sex." In 1986, Johnston tested positive for HIV but never bothered to tell his boyfriend, potentially putting him at risk for contracting the disease. After that relationship ended, Johnston engaged in reckless, unprotected sex with hoards of men. A reporter once inquired if he may have infected other people during his wild period. "If it weren't for the fact that I knew I had the forgiveness of my Father in heaven, I would have a great deal of difficulty living with that,"

Johnston explained. "That forgiveness is what sets me free from the guilt."[43]

Now that Johnston has supposedly abandoned his homicidal lifestyle—guilt free—he spends his time telling others how to live. His resentment has added a particularly foul, acerbic edge to the ex-gay movement and helped sabotage their claims to love gay people. "Barney Frank is a pervert," Johnston once spewed during a screed about the openly gay Democratic Congressman from Massachusetts.[44] "You are not fortunate, you are cursed," he said about gay people during one speech.[45]

Extremist leaders with shrill voices, such as Falzarano and Johnston, essentially hijacked the ex-gay movement with the help of the antigay coalition. As time wore on, relatively mainstream ex-gay leaders such as Joe Dallas, Randy Thomas, and Alan Chambers, began to resent these screwballs who had defined the movement they had worked so hard to build.

Impatience with the erratic behavior of the more extreme "ex-gays" was taking root within the antigay political coalition. At first, the coalition loved its marriage of convenience with these radical dupes, seeing it as a brilliant strategic alliance, but the marriage made in heaven soon soured. The first fissure came early on after Exodus listed the wrong toll-free telephone number for the organization in a full-page ad in *The New York Times.* For this more than $75,000 expenditure, calls meant for Exodus were routed instead to an electrical contractor's office in Dothan, Alabama. The embarrassed leaders in the antigay political coalition were furious. They publicly blamed the inept Exodus leadership of supreme buffoonery and privately called Bob Davies, the ex-gay group's executive director, a bumbling dunce.

The fanatical ex-gays who were once so useful were beginning to become a burden, and some were loose cannons who could not be trusted to stay focused on Exodus's message. For instance, while the antigay coalition was reeling from criticism over Shepard's death, the unpredictable Falzarano called the frail, wispy Shepard a "predator to heterosexual men."[46] This was hardly the message needed to blunt criticism that irresponsible rhetoric from the coalition was partially to blame for Shepard's death.

Meanwhile, on the ex-gay side, the more conventional Exodus leaders were beginning to tire of the heavy-handed bullying of the religious right. There were whispers in Exodus that the political coalition was being led by mean-spirited political preachers, such as D. James Kennedy, who were using the ministries to line their pockets, while not giving enough back to the ex-gay groups, many of which lived in penury. They particularly despised Kennedy's deputy, Folger, whom they saw as a ruthless mercenary who cared more about her career than Christ. Several ex-gay leaders bitterly told me off the record—for they feared harsh reprisals if they spoke openly—that they thought she saw the ex-gay ministries as a PR gimmick that would elevate her status in right-wing political circles.

"I pray for the salvation of homosexuals, but I pray more for the salvation of Janet Folger. She'll need all the prayer she can get when she meets her maker," one ex-gay leader carefully whispered to me at the Exodus 2001 conference in Asheville, North Carolina. "She's a vicious person, almost like a shark, who knows only how to attack and kill. I really don't see much love in her heart."

Things began to turn truly ugly after the antigay coalition's television ads were rejected by the major Orlando television stations. To get her message out, Folger came up with the idea to fly an airplane over Disney World, trailing a large, streaming placard that read, FREEDOM FROM HOMOSEXUALITY: JESUS CHRIST. Folger further fanned the flames of hate by describing the annual gay event as "Gomorrah with rides."

Many of the less vitriolic Exodus leaders thought the sky banner smacked of intolerance. They said it would be counterproductive and turn many already skeptical lesbians and gay men away from their ministries. When the less hostile ex-gay leaders passionately urged Folger to reconsider her plans, sources say Folger exploded. They claim she became irate, launching into a fearsome tirade, threatening to cut off Exodus financially and freeze them out of the antigay political coalition. When the ex-gays stood their ground, she apparently retaliated and made good on her promise.

"One of the things that certainly Center for Reclaiming America did was, they kind of separated themselves from Exodus," said Alan Chambers, who was then the leader of Exchange, an Orlando ex-gay ministry.[47] "I think it was a direct result of some people like me who were outraged at the things that went on. Obviously, we're not partnering with these ministries anymore."

From the beginning, there was a Grand Canyon–size disconnect between the expectations of Exodus and the actual intentions of the political coalition. The ex-gay groups saw the coalition as a savior, launching them into the mainstream and giving them truckloads of money for outreach and expansion. They viewed the ad campaign as the beginning of an enduring partnership. Meanwhile, members of the political coalition jumped on the ex-gay bandwagon as merely a PR stunt to spruce up their images and change their reputations as mean-spirited Neanderthals. They also saw the campaign as a fundraising bonanza. The naive ex-gay leaders thought this was a symbiotic relationship, when it was actually parasitic. The political coalition extracted every bit of value from the ex-gay mine, and when the gold rush was over, they abandoned the project like a Western ghost town.

Disillusionment set in on the ex-gay side, and some of the leaders mutinied. On September 1, 1999, Falzarano held a press conference to denounce his once beloved benefactors as charlatans. "Many of us in the ex-gay movement feel we're being used," he said at the press conference. "The [antigay coalition] isn't coming close to responding to the needs of homosexuals. [We] did that very successful newspaper campaign last year . . . the Christian Coalition did not send us a dime. D. James Kennedy," he continued, "did not send us a dime. All we're asking for is possibly some money to pay for postage stamps."

Falzarano's rebellion followed a blistering attack in an essay by influential ex-gay leader Randy Thomas, codirector of Dallas-based Living Hope Ministries:

> My association with Coral Ridge has turned out to be more of a hindrance than a help to my ministry. I felt their motivation was to reach same-gender-attracted people. I don't feel that now.
> The hundreds of thousands of dollars the coalition spent on the advertising campaign could have been simply given to Exodus and much more could have been accomplished. But I guess

that means giving up control. Coral Ridge needs to stop using their videos to instill fear instead of redemption. They need to present a redemptive message and not a political one.[48]

In December 1999, popular Exodus ministry leader Tom Cole took a veiled swipe at Coral Ridge in an op-ed that ran in the *Sun Sentinel,* the hometown newspaper of the powerful Coral Ridge Ministries. "The conservative Christian Church, which is strident in its condemnation of homosexual behavior, seems to be in denial about targeted attacks on gay and lesbian youth."[49]

The leaders of the political antigay coalition were stung by the criticism and felt betrayed. This backlash was their own fault, however, a result of not doing their homework. In their haste to shed their reputation as bigots and to mobilize conservatives in an election year, they failed to inspect closely those with whom they were partnering. With their history of failure, and led primarily by flaky and impulsive former addicts, this mercurial relationship could easily have been anticipated.

The bottom line is that the members of the political coalition know that the efficacy of the ex-gay ministries is highly suspect, at best. Clearly, if the affluent right-wing groups truly believed Exodus had merit, they would have dumped tens of millions of dollars into expanding these programs, but they gave next to nothing. They were willing to fund only individual ex-gays who were willing to push their political message.

The ailing partnership completely unraveled after a series of high-profile humiliations rocked the ex-gay ministries. In a one-year period, Wade Richards came out publicly, John Paulk—the centerpiece of their ad campaign—was exposed in a gay saloon, and London's largest ex-gay star, Jeremy Marks, renounced the ex-gay ministries. "People inside the religious right are kind of leery of dealing with these wacky ex-gays," said Natalie Davis. "You don't know if the change took until the person dies. You really don't know. Anything can happen."

Normandy or Vietnam?

The "Normandy landing" of 1998 turned out to be more like Vietnam, a carnage-filled quagmire that seemed to offer no escape. It appeared that both sides learned a valuable political lesson: When you cut a deal with the devil, everyone ends up living in hell.

In retrospect, was the ad campaign successful?

The first obvious sign that it failed was the outcome of the midterm elections. In the House the GOP lost five seats and they picked up no seats in the Senate. That's right, a big goose egg. In an awe-inspiring display of Christian love, Dobson pointed his finger at Gingrich, blaming him for the debacle and demanding that he resign as speaker. Yet, the fact is that the public rejected nearly all hard-core, right-wing candidates in the election cycle, showing that it was actually Dobson who had a losing message, including his ex-gay rhetoric. Then, the lead star of the ad campaign, John Paulk, as we have discussed, was temporarily booted off the Exodus board following his high-profile scandal, and, in August 1999, Anthony Falzarano was unceremoniously canned as the leader of PFOX for unspecified reasons.

After Falzarano received the axe, he refused to leave PFOX's headquarters and changed the locks, according to Reverend Earle Fox of Transformation Ministries. After a humiliating standoff with the PFOX board, at the expense of the group's reputation, Falzarano slunk away in shame and disgrace. Not too soon after this debacle, however, a determined Falzarano reappeared as the leader of a new group that he started, Parents and Friends Ministries—an obvious takeoff on Parents and Friends of Ex-Gays. With the two groups divided into warring factions, both withered and became virtually irrelevant. PFOX, however, is staging a minor comeback, with the enterprising Richard Cohen as its board president.

Falzarano's ultimate rebuke came in June 2001 when the conservative Catholic University of America (CUA) canceled a conference by his new group, saying that Falzarano applied for use of the school's facilities under "false pretenses." "We do not rent space to people who misrepresent themselves," explained CUA spokesman Victor Nakas.[50]

Another blow to the campaign's success came when Robertson and Falwell, two key ad campaign backers, obliterated their claim to "love" homosexuals during an infamous episode of *The 700 Club* following the September 11, 2001, terrorist attacks on the World Trade Center and the Pentagon. During the broadcast, Falwell partially blamed gay men and lesbians for the terrorist attacks, drawing widespread condemnation, even from the extreme right. Pat Robertson apparently agreed with Falwell's assessment. On December 5, 2001, only months after this unprecedented debacle, Robertson resigned as head of the Christian Coalition.

When the Family Research Council's new president, Ken Conner, took the helm, he cleaned house and dumped his once powerful antigay division. Gone from FRC were Bob Knight, Peter LaBarbera, and ex-lesbian Yvette Cantu Schneider, all lead promoters of the ad campaign.

Janet Folger, shell-shocked by her dealings with volatile ex-gays, has used her entrepreneurial skills to search for additional issues. She has put much of her focus back on abortion. According to HRC's Birch:

> There is one thing that Janet Folger didn't bank on. And that was that the truth would eclipse the charade of the ex-gay ministries. What they hadn't banked on was how sophisticated the public is and how much they mostly believe, more than not, that someone was born gay—and, by the way, their cousin Joey is gay. I don't think the ads rang true.

Indeed, Birch's assertion is backed by a significant June 4, 2001, Gallup poll on American attitudes toward homosexuality. Taken more than two years after the ad campaign, the poll shows the coalition unequivocally failed. For the first time in twenty-four years, in response to the question of whether homosexuality is something a person is born with or due to other factors, an equal number of respondents indicated that homosexuality is genetic or environmental. This represents a major shift in public opinion from 1977, when environment was chosen as the more prevalent factor, at a four-to-one ratio. More revealing, since the ad campaign, polls show that the number of Americans who believe homosexuality is inborn has increased 6 percent—an absolutely stunning rejection of the religious right's failed efforts.

To be sure, many ex-gay leaders are still politically active in working with the right wing and will continue to do so in the future. Still, the vast strategic alliance of 1998, designed to crush the gay rights movement, was largely unsuccessful. The antigay coalition gave it their best shot, put their integrity on the line, and, as a consequence surrendered much of their credibility. "It got to the point where the right miscalculated how successful they were going to be. . . . They thought about public sentiment as if it were 1992 [the year of the antigay GOP convention in Houston], instead of 1998," said GLAAD's Garry. "The ex-gay ad campaign . . . really backfired on them."

A Topic with Nine Lives

Just when it seemed that the topic was fading from the radar screen, Dr. Robert Spitzer, a Columbia University researcher, thrust it again into the spotlight. His infamous study, released May 9, 2001, seemed to add weight to the ex-gay argument that sexual orientation for gay people could be altered through prayer or therapy. As we shall see, however, his study was just the latest attempt by the political religious right to gain legitimacy for their arguments by teaming up with a supposedly unbiased scientist.

The ex-gay ministries is a topic that seems to have nine lives. Until the day comes when science uncovers why people are gay—or straight—people will be intensely interested in this fascinating subject, for it explores the core of our being. Not only will this discovery reveal the mystery of sexual orientation, but it will demystify the nature of "love" itself.

The intense public focus on Spitzer's study shows the public's insatiable appetite for information on this topic. It is a shame that people care so much about this and can't simply accept people for who they are. The explosive nature of this subject means it will keep recurring and cut across generational lines. That is why it is so important to document the astonishing failures of reparative therapy and the ex-gay ministries. In the following chapter, we will examine the latest in the conversion wars by closely inspecting Spitzer's politically loaded study.

Political Science

The Significance of Spitzer

When I was three years old, in 1973, all I cared about was collecting plastic dinosaurs and toy soldiers. Little did I know that I, similar to all gay people at the time, was considered mentally ill by the world's most respected psychiatric organizations. All that changed, however, in this year, in part to the open-mindedness of one researcher, Dr. Robert L. Spitzer.

Similar to many psychiatrists of this time period, Spitzer never questioned why lesbian and gay people were considered mentally ill. He simply assumed that homosexuality automatically disqualified a person from basic sanity and mental fitness. His schooling reinforced these ideas by presenting the biased work of antigay psychoanalysts Bergler, Socarides, and others as undisputed fact.

Spitzer's view was unexpectedly turned upside down in the fall of 1972 while watching a presentation by the Association for the Advancement of Behavior Therapy, a group that specialized in electroshock "treatment" of gay people. Suddenly, the meeting was interrupted and overrun by screaming advocates from the Gay Activists Alliance (GAA) who stormed the presentation to protest the abuse of homosexuals by these psychiatrists. Aside from the activists in the room, nearly 100 protested outside the New York building, handing out fliers that asked, "Torture Anyone?"[1]

Spitzer was livid and wanted the protesters removed from the building, but, in the heat of the moment, he and gay activist Ronald

Gold began talking, and Spitzer for the first time listened to what the activists were saying. A married man with children and trained in the old school of psychiatry, it had never dawned on him that gays actually might be sane and grossly mistreated by the mental health establishment. According to the gay history book *Out for Good,* by Dudley Clendinen and Adam Nagourney, both reporters for *The New York Times,* the chance encounter between Gold and Spitzer proved to be of great significance. Spitzer was on the APA Committee of Nomenclature, the group responsible for revising the *Diagnostic and Statistical Manual.* As discussed in "Historic Injustice," only through revision of the DSM could homosexuality no longer be considered a mental illness.

For the next year, Spitzer intently listened to the heartfelt testimonies of lesbian and gay activists and educated himself on the issues and hardships facing these individuals. He was a sympathetic man who was willing to hear people who had previously been ignored. Through his willingness to listen to all sides of the issue, millions of homosexuals were declared sane in 1973. Because he challenged conventional wisdom and forced his counterparts to review science rather than stereotypes, the lesbian and gay community has long respected Dr. Spitzer.

"Get Me Out of This Mess!"

Fast-forward twenty-eight years later: "Wayne, help get me out of this mess," Spitzer begged me. "I'm being portrayed as a right-wing zealot. I'm getting hate mail. Even members of my family are calling to say they can't believe I've joined the religious right and that I'm antigay."[2]

What could this respected Columbia University psychiatrist who helped remove homosexuality from the DSM have done to put him in such a pickle with the lesbian and gay community?

Spitzer's conundrum stemmed from a study he released on May 9, 2001, in New Orleans at the APA's annual meeting, in which he claimed that *some* "highly motivated" gay people could become straight through prayer, therapy, and "mentoring relationships."[3] This was obviously huge news, considering what Spitzer had done for lesbians and gay men in 1973.

What was eerie about Spitzer's new and controversial ex-gay study was how, in a twisted way, the circumstances that led to it mirrored his decision to embrace the pleas of gay activists in the early 1970s. At the 1999 APA convention in Washington, DC, Spitzer encountered a small throng of ex-gay protesters holding signs with slogans such as "Maybe the APA can't heal a homosexual, but god can!!"[4]

"He came up and said, 'You guys are out here again,'" antigay activist and admitted former homosexual Anthony Falzarano told the *Washington Times*. "I asked him if he would consider taking us more seriously and attend our press conference. I told him some prominent ex-gays would give their testimonies. To my surprise, he came."[5]

Spitzer was so mesmerized by these stories that after the press conference he asked the participants if they could provide him with a list of several hundred ex-gays so he could study whether they had actually changed sexual orientations, rather than simply their behavior. So the man who gave a sympathetic ear to a despised and misunderstood minority in 1973 was offering his sympathetic ear to another despised minority in 1999. However, although ex-gay activist groups may be despised, unlike the homosexuals of 1973, they are far from misunderstood. Anyone with a rudimentary knowledge of the political groups behind these misguided individuals understands that they exist, not to change gay people, but to change laws that protect gay and lesbian Americans from discrimination.

Spitzer, a neophyte in this political arena, did not understand whom he was embracing. He saw parallels between gay and ex-gay protests where there were none. Whereas one group's sole mission in 1973 was to get the mental health establishment to look objectively at the science, the mission of the ex-gays in 1999 was to deny gay people their basic civil rights. Unfortunately, Spitzer was unable or unwilling to differentiate between the aims of these two groups and, in my opinion, was duped into associating with strange bedfellows.

No Hallucinogenic Heteros or Switch-Hitters

I wrote Spitzer a letter expressing the HRC's concerns about his project. Although we welcomed new scientific research, we admonished him to steer clear of some very dubious characters and problems that might plague his study. The following are the main points emphasized in the letter and in subsequent communications.

Birds of a feather. We made it abundantly clear that he should avoid coordinating with right-wing activists who held extremist antigay views. If these groups had anything to do with his study, it would be seen as biased and might affect the way it would be received by the scientific community, the media, and the public at large.

Ex-gay for pay? No way. We warned Spitzer that in the current political environment his sample must be beyond reproach. This meant avoiding research subjects who were active members of right-wing organizations. Most important, none of the research subjects should make their living off of antigay lobbying or have a career as an ex-gay. In other words, no one who was "ex-gay for pay" should have been allowed to participate in Spitzer's study. This was common sense and a methodology any scientist should follow, we thought, when researching a controversial subject.

Truth or dare. One indisputable fact about the ex-gay ministries and reparative therapy is that many of the people who claim "change" later recant and say they were always gay. Most of these individuals say they claimed they had changed only to find societal acceptance.

We told Spitzer that to do a study based solely on the testimonies of ex-gays is scientific suicide. Based on their history of double talk and double lives, any credible study on ex-gays must use objective data to see if the physical responses of subjects match their sworn testimonies. Two technologies would have enabled Spitzer to discern whether his subjects were truthful in their testimonies. The first is the polygraph, otherwise known as the lie detector test. Although this technology is not infallible, it is certainly more credible than relying on verbal testimony alone. The second technology is the penile plethysmograph, a test that checks sexual arousal by measuring blood flow into a subject's penis while he views erotic videos. University of Georgia psychologist Henry E. Adams used this technology in 1996 to show that men who were the most homophobic demonstrated significant sexual arousal to male erotic stimuli.[6] Taken together, the polygraph and the penile plethysmograph would have provided much needed physical data to supplement the ex-gay tales.

Seeing is believing. We urged Spitzer to get out of the ivory tower and visit, both as a guest and undercover, the ex-gay ministries. Only by visiting these places and meeting these people in their element could he understand that they are driven by fear and a desperate need to find acceptance in their churches and families. We also wanted Spitzer to talk to ex-gays who didn't know who he was, so he could get an honest portrayal of these ministries. We wanted him to see firsthand some of the bizarre techniques, such as exorcisms, touch therapy, and intrauterine memory recovery, that are a staple of the ex-gay ministries and reparative therapy. If he witnessed the insanity of these programs, we believed, he would see through the rhetoric and understand the reality of how these groups ruin lives.

Hallucinogenic heteros. To achieve maximum credibility, it was essential that Spitzer interview his subjects at great length to see whether they were mentally competent to take part in his study. Although he did ask his subjects questions about their sexual orientation, perhaps the most important question Spitzer should have asked was, "Have you heard demonic voices or seen visions of holy figures in the past twelve months?" As discussed in "Undercover," a sizable portion of the people who claim to have changed appear to suffer from mental disorders or their judgment has been impaired from rampant drug abuse. In other words, if a person believes that Jesus lives in his or her television set or that Satan is stalking him or her, then it isn't far-fetched to assume that the person's heterosexuality may be a hallucination as well.

No switch-hitters. We told Spitzer that if he was going to study the possibility of gay people becoming straight, he must use people who are exclusively homosexual. If he used people who could be perceived as bisexual, critics would justifiably wonder whether a change in sexual orientation occurred or whether the subjects simply sublimated their homosexuality in favor of their heterosexual side.

The crystal ball. We vividly laid out his study's potential consequences if he did not follow our advice. First, he would be excoriated by gay political organizations for biased work. Second, the scientific community would publicly upbraid him for shoddy research and unprofessional sampling methods. Third, the religious right would enthusiastically embrace the study and use it as an opportunity to bash homosexuals and say they are unworthy of equal rights. Fourth, the media would sensationalize it, leading to distorted news coverage of the study. Finally, the results would lead to an increase in harassment against gays and be used to pressure young gay men and women into harmful ex-gay programs.

According to HRC's letter to Spitzer, "What a shame it would be if countless individuals were subject to shame, indignity and examina-

tion when the only thing that needed further examination was your research."[7]

Creating a Gigantic Shadow of Doubt

It became clear during my travels in researching this book that
Spitzer had not heeded our advice and was cavorting with right-wing
extremists. No matter which ex-gay ministry I visited or reparative
therapist I spoke to, Spitzer's name inevitably popped up—and never
at my initiation. None other than Richard Cohen bubbled with excitement when he voluntarily brought up Spitzer's name. He told me that
he was personally supplying Spitzer with research subjects and that
he talked frequently with the Columbia University doctor. At the
2000 NARTH conference, Nicolosi also spoke frequently and in great
detail about his connections to Spitzer.

More astounding was discovering that Spitzer was using Dr. Laura
Schlessinger to solicit for subjects at the same time that she was embroiled in an explosive spat with the lesbian and gay community. Gay
civil rights groups were protesting Paramount Pictures for offering
Schlessinger a TV show after she referred to homosexuals as "biological errors." Despite the controversy, Spitzer went on her show and
espoused what can only be described as antigay views: "I agree that a
homosexual who is not able to be aroused heterosexually . . . I think,
implicitly, there is something not working," he told Schlessinger.[8]
Spitzer tries to come across as "Mr. Nice Guy" when talking to the
mainstream media or gay activists, but he was clearly singing an entirely different tune on Schlessinger's program.

In May 2000, the link between Spitzer and the extreme political
right was outed in a very revealing way. At the APA's annual meeting
in Chicago, Spitzer's seemingly objective panel discussion on the efficacy of reparative therapy was canceled after it was discovered that
NARTH was surreptitiously working behind the scenes with Spitzer to
organize the event. Nicolosi, in fact, had sent a clandestine letter
to NARTH members claiming that Spitzer was "in close contact with
NARTH officers about its implementation and the selection of speakers." The letter also said that Spitzer was "moved to rethink this issue,"
meaning he was reconsidering whether homosexuals should be labeled
mentally ill in the DSM.

The progay psychiatrists felt bamboozled with the uncovering of NARTH's secret involvement and wisely backed out of the ambush disguised as a scientific panel. Embarrassed by the revelation, Spitzer wrote a letter claiming that Nicolosi gave the "false impression" that NARTH had been instrumental in planning the debate, and that Nicolosi made "misleading statements" about Spitzer's position on the 1973 decision.[9]

One would think that once Spitzer had seen Nicolosi's underhanded methods in action he would have cut ties with the NARTH leader. Instead, he inexplicably joined forces with Nicolosi and appeared with him at a right-wing press conference to protest the cancellation of the debate. The press conference was orchestrated to show, according to Nicolosi, that "the gay and lesbian community does not tolerate discussion of scientific issues."[10]

In a breathtaking display of political naïveté, Spitzer sat alongside representatives from antigay organizations. Among those participating were Richard Cohen, John Paulk, the Family Research Council's Yvette Cantu Schneider, and Joseph Nicolosi. In a one-hour period of time, Spitzer squandered a lifetime of credibility and allowed his reputation to be sullied by teaming up with this bevy of antigay activists. After this publicity stunt, Spitzer's claim of working on an "objective" study was irreparably tarnished, and his stature in the scientific community greatly diminished.

Unfortunately, very few reporters at the time were paying attention—in either the mainstream or gay press. These disturbing facts would become meaningful only *after* Spitzer's study was unveiled a year later and it became necessary to show how Spitzer's work was predestined to find that gays could change. It is astonishing that he openly frolicked with antigay activists and believed that his study would still be taken seriously. It is almost as if Spitzer went out of his way to cast a gigantic shadow of doubt on his work. If that was his intention, this author congratulates him because that is exactly what he accomplished.

The Media Maelstrom

When the story broke, it did so with an enormous bang. The first report from the Associated Press (AP) set the sensationalistic tone the rest of the media pack eagerly followed when it called Spitzer's work "an explosive new study [that] says some gay people can turn straight if they really want to."[11] This report set off a forty-eight-hour media frenzy with worldwide reverberations. The story was prominently featured in every major newspaper the next day, and television reporters and talking heads breathlessly regurgitated the incendiary AP report.

As the details of the study emerged, it was clear that Spitzer had ignored the vast majority of our suggestions. He had simply called up 200 ex-gays (143 men and 57 women) on the phone and interviewed them for a mere forty-five minutes. He asked these people—without ever meeting most of them in person—if they had changed, and most said "yes." What else would they say? After all, they were the religious right's hand-picked sample, and many of them were professional antigay lobbyists.

"History has done some interesting twists," Spitzer said following the release of his study. "Some homosexuals can change, to varying degrees."[12]

The core of the study claimed that 65 percent of men and 44 percent of women attained what he called "good heterosexual functioning." A minority of subjects, 17 percent of the men and 54 percent of the women, claimed they had no gay attractions whatsoever, while 63 percent of the women and 29 percent of the men reported "no or only minimal" same-sex attractions. A staggeringly high 87 percent of the male and female respondents reported feeling more masculine (men) or feminine (women).

Lesbian and gay civil rights groups were quick to condemn the study. The National Gay and Lesbian Task Force called it "snake oil packaged as science."[13] The Human Rights Campaign assailed the research as "biased and unscientific."[14]

Meanwhile, right-wing organizations seized upon it as proof that homosexuals could convert to heterosexuals. Traditional Values Coalition Chairman Lou Sheldon said, "His research validates what we have been saying all along: That homosexuality is a behavior that can be changed."[15] Reverend Jerry Falwell said that "the results have suggested the unthinkable to homosexual-rights advocates who insist that they are born with a 'gay gene' or some uncontrollable element that leads to their homosexuality," and Nicolosi, who helped supply study subjects, trumpeted the report as "revolutionary."[16]

Many of Spitzer's colleagues distanced themselves from the study and made it clear that his work failed to meet basic scientific standards:

- "His sampling method was totally inadequate," said Dr. Lawrence Hartmann, a professor at Harvard and a respected researcher on homosexuality.[17]
- "For 30 years, Bob Spitzer may have been considered a careful researcher. But with this study, he no longer is. It is far from good science."[18]
- "There is no published scientific evidence supporting the efficacy of reparative therapy as a treatment to change one's sexual orientation," the APA's medical director, Dr. Steven Mirin, said in a statement designed to distance the venerated group from Spitzer.[19]

No one seemed surprised by the fallout except Spitzer, who appeared flummoxed over the hullabaloo. "I'm shocked at how my study is being used," he told me in a phone conversation. How could he have been shocked when HRC warned him more than a year in advance what would happen? At best, his feigning surprise was disingenuous, and, at worst, his reaction was a cynical maneuver designed to separate him from the damage he had done.

The only good thing the author can say about Spitzer's research was that it was so incompetently slapdash that even the average Joe or Jane on the street could see through it. For instance, I was in a cab the day the study came out and listening to a report about it on the radio. As the report ended, the driver said in broken English, "You've got to be kidding me. If a guy calls 200 people on the phone, that's more like a poll than a study. What a joke."

The Spitzer Study: Anatomy of a Failure

For society to move forward and evolve, we must embrace science and its conclusions, even if they are sometimes controversial. Spitzer had a great opportunity to use his study to examine the effects reparative therapy had on the individuals who took part in it. Thus, it is a shame that he did not conduct a rigorous study that embraced objective measures and included a control group of people who said that the therapy did not work.

The following examines where Spitzer's study failed to live up to accepted scientific standards and succeeded in drawing legitimate criticism from those critiquing his work. Interestingly, if he had followed HRC's original advice, he would have avoided the harsh reviews he received.

Birds of prey. Although warned that his credibility would suffer if he allowed the right wing to participate in his study, Spitzer made antigay organizations an integral part of his work. An astonishing 43 percent of his sample came from the ex-gay ministries, and 23 percent were referred through the notoriously antigay NARTH. Religious pressure also figured prominently in attempts to change, with 93 percent of subjects saying that religion was extremely important in their lives. Clearly, the fear of religious rejection or persecution may have played a significant role in some subjects falsely claiming change had occurred. The bottom line: This study was essentially meaningless because it had the right wing's fingerprints all over it.

Ex-gay or propay? Antigay activists who get paid to lobby against gay rights were a large part of his sample. Exhibit A is Anthony Falzarano, Director of the Parents and Friends Ministries. As has been pointed out repeatedly, Falzarano has lobbied on behalf of antigay legislation in Louisiana, Maine, and Maryland and in numerous national media appearances. Falzarano also makes a substantial portion of his self-proclaimed $65,000 a year salary from antigay political organizations, including a large grant from the Family Research Council.

He once told CBS that Satan "uses homosexuals as pawns and then he kills them."[20] Most people would agree that it would be unethical to use a person with such biased views in a supposedly objective study, but Spitzer never took these concerns into consideration. He laced his study with homophobic lobbyists, some of whom made their livings from activities surrounding the ex-gay ministries, with no less than 78 percent of his sample of 200 men and women having spoken out publicly in favor of conversion therapy.

This raises serious conflict of interest questions. Can people be objective about their feelings toward conversion therapy when referred to Spitzer by antigay political groups who help pay their salaries? I think the answer is a resounding "no." Although his entire sample was not on the dole, for his study to be taken seriously, *none* of his sample should have been paid lobbyists. In this case, even one bad apple does spoil the whole barrel, and there were many rotten apples in this crop.

When I asked Spitzer why he had used outspoken activists who might taint his study, he said he had done so because he "had trouble" finding nonactivists for his research. He also mentioned in his study that he had "great difficulty" finding nonreligious therapists to refer subjects. But if tens of thousands of homosexuals have become straight, as the right often claims, then it should have been a relatively easy task to find at least 200 people nationwide who were not affiliated with far-right political groups. The "great difficulty" Spitzer encountered suggests that the number of ex-gays has been significantly inflated, and that there aren't many in existence who are not on the religious right's bulging payroll.

The video killed the ex-gay star. Despite our insistence, Spitzer elected not to use physical evidence to corroborate the ex-gay testimonies. I asked him why he had refused to use either the polygraph or the penile plethysmograph on his subjects. According to Spitzer, "there was no way he could get his subjects to submit to such tests." It never seemed to dawn on Spitzer that these individuals were doggedly avoiding these truth-detecting instruments because they were not telling the truth.

"I'd love to see all the ex-gay types, who are often willing to talk about their conversions, submit to such a test—to basically relinquish their capacity to lie," said Dr. Larry Rudiger, a research psychologist from the University of Vermont. "Given the energy the Religious Right is willing to throw behind this subject, you'd think they'd be eager to cull such definitive proof."[21]

Spitzer said that some of his subjects felt these instruments were an "invasion of privacy." Hearing this, I countered, "Funny how some of your sample were not as concerned about 'privacy' when they spoke intimately about their sex lives on *The Jerry Springer Show.*"

See no evil, hear no evil. Spitzer did not do basic preliminary research by visiting the ex-gay ministries, either undercover or as himself. This deprived him of a firsthand understanding of the wacky activities that go on inside these places. For instance, Spitzer describes himself as an atheist Jew. Would it not have been good for him to watch the ex-gays debate whether the Jews killed Jesus? Might he be alarmed at watching a live exorcism? Finally, if he would have left his office and gone into the field, he would have heard the stories of people who are struggling to change but realize that these programs do not work. Unfortunately, he did none of this and relied solely on the well-rehearsed stories of ex-gay political activists.

Visions and voices. Anecdotal evidence suggests that some of the people used in Spitzer's study were mentally fragile, yet there were no psychological tests administered to ensure they were competent to take part in this study. For instance, an alarmingly high 43 percent of the men and 47 percent of the women were "markedly" or "extremely" depressed before conversion therapy, and a disproportionate number (37 percent of males and 35 percent of females) of the individuals who took part in this study were suicidal before attempting conversion. Unlike many gay teens who sadly view suicide as an option, all of the participants in the study were adults with a mean age of forty-three. That many of these men and women were *still* contemplating suicide well into adulthood implies that they suffered from a higher rate of instability than the population at large. Psychological factors should have been given greater weight by Spitzer when picking research subjects.

Whose team? Were all of the participants gay and was Spitzer cheating to pad his results? Of the sample, 47 percent of the men and 67 percent of the women admitted to having had heterosexual sex *before* they entered therapy, 21 percent of the men and 18 percent of the women were already married *before* therapy, and 54 percent of the men and 58 percent of the women acknowledged some attraction to the opposite sex *before* therapy. In addition, 15 percent of the male participants and 39 percent of the females had little or no sexual attraction to the same sex as teenagers, when sex drive is usually highest. Clearly, many of the "success" cases may have been bisexual or heterosexual prior to therapy.

The Study's Conclusion: Change in Sexual Orientation Is Highly Unlikely

The media reported the study as if Spitzer had shown that "highly motivated" individuals could, in some cases, change their sexual orientation. Upon closer examination, however, Spitzer's research shows quite the opposite. For more than a year the doctor solicited the majority of his subjects through right-wing political groups and media stars, such as Dr. Laura. Remember, these groups regularly boast in the media that they have helped hoards of homosexuals "escape the lifestyle." Yet, for all of their money, power, and braggadocio, the best these antigay behemoths could do was come up with 200 people, of which only 17 percent of the men and 54 percent of the women claimed to have changed sexual orientation *completely*. Moreover, 68 percent of the male subjects and 41 percent of the female subjects still had same-sex masturbatory fantasies after therapy! Most observers would not objectively define these people as "straight." As if these paltry numbers are not embarrassing enough, we must remember that the failure rate would be much higher if Spitzer had not chosen to lard his study with people who are arguably bisexual.

Activists and colleagues have blasted Spitzer's study, but it will be the subjects themselves who will, in the end, cause the study's eternal demise. Since his methodology was to rely exclusively on testimonies, if only one subject comes out of the closet, the entire study will be undermined, and the past shows us that several, if not a majority, of his subjects will come out or will be found out in the next decade. Spitzer may have briefly enjoyed his ephemeral moment of talking-head media glory, but I predict future stories will not be so kind. As sure as the sun rises and sets, this study will come back repeatedly to haunt him. It seems likely that one day headlines will read, "Spitzer Subjects Say They Lied, Validity of Entire Study Now in Question."

Damage Control

It was midafternoon and Spitzer's shaky voice on the other end of the line sounded a tad weary. He had taken a rhetorical beating and was beginning to have regrets about releasing such a profoundly un-scientific study. He was also feeling guilty that his study might be used to coerce gay people into therapy. He called me because we had kept in contact while he was conducting the study and I had warned him repeatedly on its ramifications.

"Wayne, the right's using my work to attack gays, and the left is calling me a bigot," exclaimed an exasperated Spitzer. "How do we get out of this mess?"

My inclination was to say, "This is *your* mess and you can clean it up yourself," but, although history will judge him harshly for this study, he still had played a role in giving gay and lesbian people one of their biggest victories of all time. So, I swallowed my pride and worked with Spitzer to help him mitigate the damage he had already inflicted.

Spitzer's idea was to write an op-ed and place it in *The Wall Street Journal* to clarify what his study actually showed. The first point would be that his research should not be used to justify discrimination, and the second would be to note that the vast majority of gay people could not change even if they tried. Although this effort was clearly inadequate, it did help offset some of the damage. As another concession, I interviewed Spitzer, and he offered HRC the following statement via e-mail:

> I anticipated some misuse of the study results, but I did not anticipate that some of the media would say such ridiculous things as that the study raised the issue of homosexuality and choice. Of course, no one chooses to be homosexual and no one chooses to be heterosexual. I did anticipate, and in my presentation warn, that it would be a mistake to interpret the study as implying that any highly motivated homosexual could change if they really were motivated to do so. I suspect that the vast majority of gay people—even if they wanted to—would be unable to make substantial changes in sexual attraction and fantasy and enjoyment of heterosexual functioning that many of my subjects reported. I also warned against the study results being used to justify pressuring gay people to enter therapy when they had no interest in doing so and I have already heard of many incidents where this has happened.[22]

The Motivation Behind the Madness

Despite Spitzer's efforts, some burning questions still bother me. Why did this respected scientist choose to ruin his reputation, undermine his credibility, and lower his status in the psychiatric community? Why did he elect to put his most unimpressive work under the biggest media magnifying glass he could find?

One theory is that Spitzer was reaching the twilight of his career and wanted his last hurrah. As the psychiatrist who said, "Gays aren't sick," he knew that releasing a study concluding that "some gays could become straight" was newsworthy. This was the classic "man bites dog" story. To Spitzer, this may have seemed a tantalizing proposition and an opportunity to go out with a bang. It had been a long time since Spitzer's name had appeared in bright, neon lights, and in this age of the great media circus, the temptation of achieving fame and recognition can be a powerful narcotic. It is alluring enough for some individuals to throw away a reputation that took decades to earn. "I'm willing to admit that I like controversy and to be in the center of burning debates," Spitzer told *The Advocate*'s Chris Bull.[23]

Perhaps Spitzer should have blazed a different career path and put his energies toward becoming a host on CNN's *Crossfire*. Although in many professions creating publicity is an advantage, Spitzer should be well aware that in the scientific arena it is best not to create "controversy." Legions of people in turmoil about their sexuality should not have to endure unnecessary trauma because of Spitzer's ego trip and desire to see his face on the little screen.

Another theory is that cunning members of the religious right manipulated Spitzer, using sympathetic ex-gay stories to dupe him into conducting a politically loaded study.

Most likely, Spitzer's foray into *political* science was a combination of the two theories. It is a fact that people such as Paulk, Falzarano, and Nicolosi recruited the scientist, who was known for his sympathetic ear, but in the process of this seduction, I believe, Spitzer realized that he could leverage a controversial study to line up media appearances and speaking gigs.

Unfortunately, Spitzer's attempts to minimize the damage came up far short of what was needed. Although I believe he never intended to hurt lesbian and gay people, there is no doubt that his sloppy work—whatever his true motivation—has caused unnecessary suffering. In fact, the day after his study was released, I received a call from a college professor who said an openly gay student was harassed and told by fellow students that she should seek change because Spitzer's study proved she could. I also got a call from a young man whose previously accepting parents had a change of heart and told him he could be straight if he would only "try harder."

In the end, however, the real loser is Dr. Spitzer. Whether he was an over-the-hill stage horse galloping toward the limelight or a court jester hoodwinked by a scheming religious right is unimportant. What matters is that Spitzer's embarrassing travesty of scholarship will surely go down as his defining work, a professional pockmark that will indelibly taint his once splendid career.

ACT IV

THE ENCORE

Future Follies and Failures

A New Direction

Since the founding of Exodus International in 1976, the organization has been plagued by incompetent leadership that has thankfully stymied the organization's ability to reach its full potential. Unfortunately, this may change, as the media-savvy and highly ambitious Alan Chambers of Orlando's Exchange Ministries has taken over as executive director. Not only will he move the group's headquarters from moderate Seattle to socially conservative Orlando, but he will also replace the impressively inept Bob Davies, who fruitlessly bungled at the helm for twenty-two years.

Chambers is highly organized and will ferociously use his skills to build the organization in ways Davies never could. Within the next few years, under Chamber's stewardship, I believe Exodus will experience growth both in the United States and abroad. His presence ensures Exodus will remain a force in popular culture and in the Christian fundamentalist world for many years to come.

Most alarming about Chambers is his focus on targeting vulnerable adolescents. Before taking over at Exodus, Chambers was the director of the Fringe Youth Outreach in Orlando, where he regularly counseled high school teens and maintained an e-mail list of 300 teens. According to an Exodus press release, Chambers claimed kids came from as far as a three-hour drive away to receive help and that the "need for reaching youth struggling with homosexuality is huge." "It's overwhelming," noted Chambers in the press release. "But I know God is in control and that helps ease my ache for the kids of this generation."[1]

"Ache" is an appropriate word for what many of these kids will experience in these harmful programs, according to leading experts. They say that programs such as the one Chambers ran in Orlando only intensify feelings of self-loathing. "When professionals tell parents and youth that they can change an adolescent's sexual orientation, it raises false hope," said renowned San Francisco State University clinical social worker Caitlin Ryan in our interview.[2] "It can increase distress, especially when they ultimately figure out that you can't really change someone's sexual orientation." Ryan continued, "I think it is damaging to make a child repress their inclinations and be something that they are not. . . . I think that, particularly when the youth is vulnerable and confused and feeling bad about him[self] or herself to begin with, it is only a prescription for misery down the line."

In October 2001, Exodus launched its new and dangerous Exodus Youth program, led by Jason Thompson, codirector of Portland Fellowship Ministries in Oregon. Chambers has worked with Thompson extensively on this program and will undoubtedly use his new position to expand Exodus Youth.

Chambers and his wife, Leslie, from my experience, are nice, decent people who hold sincere beliefs that happen to differ drastically from mine. Unlike many ex-gay leaders, Chambers appears to be mentally balanced and not a hateful individual. From our abundant conversations, it is clear that he is no fan of Jerry Falwell, Janet Folger, or Pat Robertson. Nonetheless, Chambers, though well-intentioned, may destroy many lives as he further confuses young people who need true acceptance, not false hope.

The New Frontier: Children

> They will continue to find vehicles that are closer and closer to children.

> Elizabeth Birch, HRC Executive Director

As Exodus and the religious right turn their attention to young gay men and women, their methods become increasingly sophisticated. For instance, Exodus has developed a slick CD-ROM, *The Map,* to lure adolescents. This production is light-years ahead of anything I have seen produced by the GLBT community.

The innovative device first captures the imagination of youth with an MTV-style video. It puts the young viewer in a racing car that careens around corners while questions pop up on the screen: "Where do these feelings come from?" "What would my family think?" "Can I change?" In the background is thumping dance music that one might hear at a gay nightclub on Saturday evening. I found myself unconsciously tapping my foot to the wild and exotic beat. At the end of the short video, against a black background, it reads: "Welcome to The Map. Go ahead, take the journey." The video is literally as good as any army recruiting video I have seen.

Following the fast-paced opening, an ex-gay appears on-screen and tells of the "eternal repercussions," "emotional consequences," and "physical ramifications" of homosexuality. The ex-gay host also offers his fundamentalist interpretation of scripture and dismisses gay affirmative theology by asking, "Do you want the Bible to fit your lifestyle, or do you want your lifestyle to fit the Bible?" *The Map* also includes more than twenty innovative minimovies that parade the requisite suicidal addicts who tell young people how dreadful gay life is.

Another group that aggressively targets youth is Focus on the Family and its traveling road show, Love Won Out, featuring Joseph Nicolosi and John Paulk. Focus has even appointed ex-gay leader Mike Haley to attract adolescents by appointing him to the position of youth and gender specialist. In January 2002, Focus officials announced they were doubling the number of Love Won Out conferences annually. "We are particularly concerned that only one perspective on homosexuality is allowed in the public schools," noted Focus spokesperson John Paulk in a Love Won Out press release. "These youth are not hearing the truth."

Paulk is interested in the truth? Somehow I think if he were allowed to speak in high schools he would omit the truth of what it is like for a married man to be sneaking into gay bars while out of town on a business trip.

One of the most insidious attempts to confuse parents and coerce youth into the ex-gay morass is an evil tract by Holocaust revisionist Scott Lively called *Seven Steps to Recruit-Proof Your Child*. The seven steps are as follows:

1. Get serious
2. Take authority
3. Inform yourself
4. Strengthen your family
5. Improve your parenting skills
6. Clean house (no pornography in the house, etc.)
7. Be active in your community[3]

Within these steps, Lively offers helpful advice and words of wisdom:

- Don't be intimidated by the word "deviant."
- Face the truth, gays recruit.
- Take your child out of public school (if you can).[4]

Equally sinister is the attempt to lure youths into ex-gay groups by using comics. The antigay, Mississippi-based American Family Association (AFA) recently took this new tact. In a partnership with the radical, Louisiana-based Tim Todd Ministries, the AFA went on a crusade to hand out 25,000 free *Truth for Youth* bibles in public schools. Inside each "bible" was a cartoon strip that dealt with a variety of social issues, such as abortion, pornography, rock music, evolution, and homosexuality, from a fundamentalist perspective.

Although the comic strip looks innocuous at first glance, its content is irresponsible, if not criminal, support for gay bashing. The comic begins with a young man at a gay disco lamenting the AIDS-related death of his older partner. The disco scene includes lurid images of wild sex and reckless drug abuse. What comes next is alarming. It depicts the young man walking out of a gay bar when, out of nowhere, a soda can smashes him in the face. As he nurses his smashed head, the gay-bashing teenagers who threw the object quickly drive away in their car while taunting the victim, yelling, "Fag!"

Instead of castigating the gay bashers, the comic strip has the young victim asking himself, "Fag, is that who I am? Is this my identity?" Not once in the children-targeted cartoon are the teens who aggressively assaulted the gay man held accountable for their criminal actions. What kind of message does this send to young men and women? That this is being handed out in public schools post–Matthew Shepard is incomprehensible.

At the end of the comic strip, the gay man receives a bible. He reads it, sees the light, and joins the ex-gay ministries. Linking the young man's decision to change with gay bashing suggests that physical violence and persecution are acceptable means to "persuade" a person to join the ex-gay ministries. I believe that any public school principal who allows these comics on campus should be immediately terminated.

Sadly, the AFA plans to intensify their programs geared toward youth. According to their promotions surrounding the comic strip, the organization confessed that the "AFA agrees with Tim Todd that our public schools are the biggest mission field in America."[5]

As if violence-promoting cartoons aimed at youth are not offensive enough, the ex-gay ministries have stooped so low as to aim their propaganda at toddlers. Richard Cohen has led the way with a children's book, *Alfie's Home*. The book, a bizarre crayon pictorial of Cohen's eccentric life, is clearly not fit for children. In the colorful book, Cohen discusses molestation and ex-gay counseling. In my opinion, the book is perverse, and Cohen should be committed to the funny farm for even imagining, much less creating, a lurid children's book such as this.

Clearly, children are the next frontier for the ex-gay ministries and the religious right, and statements by ex-gay leaders confirm this disturbing trend: "We have people as young as 11 contacting us, and it's mainly through our Web site (exodusintl.org)," former Exodus Executive Director Bob Davies explained. "Youth can go in there and find out all the information about Exodus and nobody else has to know."[6]

The main reason for the amplified focus on youth is money. Adolescents are coming out at earlier ages and parents are often desperate to make their children straight after they come out. These minors can be forced into these programs, with no way out, which allows therapists to keep getting paid, no matter how much children object to the quackery.

There is no easy answer to this problem, but, at the very least, the GLBT community should work to be as innovative as the ex-gay ministries. The GLBT community should use its resources and ingenuity to invent educational material to counter such specious products as *The Map*.

One such person who understands the need to offset the ex-gay propaganda targeted at children is Reverend Michael Piazza, pastor of the Cathedral of Hope in Dallas, the world's largest gay church. His 3,400-member church is looking at new ways to reach young people who are searching for answers. "We have to find creative ways to reach a younger generation and communicate in their language and their medium," Piazza told me in our interview.[7]

Perhaps the most promising development in recent years is the rise of the Gay, Lesbian and Straight Education Network (GLSEN, pronounced "glisten"), which bills itself as "the leading national organization fighting to end antigay bias in K-12 schools." GLSEN helps students create clubs known as Gay-Straight Alliances (GSAs) that battle discrimination and offer students a safe haven from harassment. The group also creates innovative videos to help educate teachers and guidance counselors on appropriate handling of gay students who are coming out at younger ages. There are now more than 1,000 GSAs in high schools across the country, meaning about one in every fifteen high schools has one. This amazing trend will do much to battle the destructive misinformation campaign by ex-gay groups, yet there is still much more work to be done to counter the intensifying focus on youth by Exodus and the religious right.

One of the biggest problems is that many health care providers do not have accurate information on GLBT resources. "A really good group to approach on this are pediatricians," said Caitlin Ryan. "Oftentimes when youth are confused about their sexual orientation or parents think that they might be gay they go to a pediatrician for advice, and the pediatrician really should be well informed about local referral sources, but they may not [be]," she explained. "I think, one, the [large] organizations like HRC really need to take this issue on and make sure that the national professional associations understand the kind of backlash that is occurring and how pernicious it is, especially for isolated youths and families," she continued. "They need to make the information readily available and on the local level, you know, with local provider organizations and school systems."

Globetrotting

Another frontier being vigorously explored by Exodus International is global expansion. The group currently claims to have ministries in seventeen countries, and Chambers vows to focus on international expansion.

This is particularly scary because fundamentalist Christianity is growing rapidly throughout third-world nations, particularly in Africa. Countries such as Zimbabwe, Uganda, and Namibia are fertile territory for the ex-gay ministries, especially since antigay groups such as Focus on the Family are broadcasting their poison in many of these countries.[8] Zimbabwe's leader Robert Mugabe has called homosexuals worse than "pigs and dogs," and Pat Robertson is deeply involved in business ventures with Liberia's scandal-plagued despot Charles Taylor.[9]

I also predict that within ten years Exodus will expand to Muslim nations, particularly in the Middle East. The rise of the ex-gay ministries in America was a result of the excesses of hateful people such as Paul Cameron who sought a perfect remedy that allowed for discrimination, but in the name of love. In the Middle East, currently, a genocidal war is being waged against gay people. For example, in January 2002, Saudi Arabian officials beheaded three men because of their sexual orientation. Any person who comes out publicly or is caught having same-sex relations in Saudi Arabia will likely suffer a similar fate as these men.[10] Also, in 1999, Egyptian officials raided a secret gay club in Cairo, convicting twenty-three men of "immoral behavior" and "contempt of religion" simply for being at the club.

In the aftermath of the September 11, 2001, terrorist attacks on the Pentagon and the World Trade Center, there has been increased focus on the Middle East. With this comes a tacit understanding and recognition that brutal, undemocratic regimes with repressive, fundamentalist policies are more likely to breed terrorists. With the eyes of the world on these Middle Eastern regimes, they will, at some point, need to moderate their draconian, seventh-century policies to avoid conflict with the West. Civilized countries will tolerate for only so long the beheading of gays, the subjugation of women, and the persecution of beliefs that differ from Islam. At the point where these countries stop their excesses, they will, I believe, promote some form of the ex-gay ministries. Exodus is already moving in this direction with a division called Exodus Africa and the Middle East, with active chapters in South Africa and Israel.

The very active Exodus contingent in Asia includes such far-flung places as Singapore, Taiwan, and the Philippines. Some of Exodus's most prominent leaders, such as Frank Worthen and Sy Rogers, have helped established these outposts of ignorance in Asia. This could be particularly problematic if China opens up and Exodus is allowed to fill the information vacuum in a nation where there has been virtually no open discussion of homosexual issues.

The more backward and uneducated a country is, the greater the threat Exodus poses. If groups such as Exodus and Focus on the Family gain strength in these regions, the world will be polarized between enlightened nations that grant gay people equality and countries that stigmatize and persecute homosexuals based on superstitions and stereotypes. The best way to counter this problem is for gay churches and more enlightened mainstream churches to engage in missionary work in these countries to present an option other than narrow-minded fundamentalism. Unfortunately, the antigay churches appear to be more zealous and may be winning this battle. Only by acting now will we save millions of people the plight of ostracism, prison, and, in some cases, execution.

Whistling Dixie

With Chambers moving Exodus to the Bible Belt, Exodus will be in a solid position to expand in Dixie, its natural stronghold. Amazingly, no Exodus ministries are in Mississippi or Arkansas and Alabama and Louisiana have only one apiece. This is a testament to the inept leadership of Bob Davies. Expect this to change as Chambers works to develop Exodus chapters in many Southern cities. Within five years, I believe, there will be more than a half dozen Exodus chapters in each Confederate state. A significant number of the residents, civic leaders, and church officials believe change in sexual orientation through prayer is possible. With minimal effort, these bastions of religious fervor should be teeming with John Paulk wanna-bes in the very near future.

Conversely, as acceptance increases in the more liberal and moderate areas of the nation, such as California, the Pacific Northwest, and the Northeast, expect the number of Exodus affiliates to decrease. To the majority of people in these regions, Exodus looks sillier by the day. The higher education levels and more accurate understanding of gay life common in these areas increasingly render the scare tactics of Exodus ineffective. This explains why Exodus has had difficulty maintaining vibrant ministries in metropolitan areas such as Washington, DC, New York City, and Boston.

A Moral Movement

While the elevation of Chambers creates new challenges, it also presents new opportunities to change the dishonest direction of Exodus. For far too long, Exodus has compromised its claim of moral authority by willfully and enthusiastically embracing hateful groups for the sake of expedience and growth. With their new leader—a professed detractor of antigay political organizations—Exodus can work toward becoming a moral movement.

Not that what they are doing is moral by any stretch of the imagination. What I mean by this is that Exodus can move in the direction of prayer, instead of politics, and abandon the use of obvious distortions about gay life to attract new converts. Their tactic to date has been to portray ex-gays as victims of a mythical gay lifestyle that brings misery and destruction to those who dare enter. Although this may attract some new members, it ultimately sullies the organization and makes it just another shrill voice willing to use scorched-earth tactics to gain political advantage. It is time for the group to spend less time with Caesar and more time with God.

Exodus leaders should aim to be what it is supposed to be, which is a group of gay people who believe homosexuality is a sin and want to change their behavior to conform to their fundamentalist version of scripture. The members are much like Catholic priests, abandoning their sexuality to serve what they believe to be their higher purpose.

Instead of sticking to these basics, however, Exodus has embraced phony statistics, pop psychology, nefarious haters, and a self-serving agenda that together are the antithesis of its stated Christian belief system. If the ex-gay ministries want rightfully to claim to be a movement based on solid values and integrity, these are the five clear steps they must take.

1. Stay out of politics. The most important thing Exodus can do to gain moral authority is to cut ties immediately with right-wing extremist groups such as the American Family Association and Coral Ridge Ministries. Although they are working less frequently together as a result of the infighting following the 1998 ad campaign, they are still loosely working together to deny gay people equality under the law.

Exodus leaders should make a formal statement that they will stay out of antigay political campaigns and no longer allow the group to be used as a tool to help the political right wing discriminate. Next, they should draft a written statement declaring that they generally support hate crime and antidiscrimination legislation. Just because Exodus leaders say that change is possible, why should that automatically make them oppose laws to protect gay people who hold different beliefs? Since these laws cover real and *perceived* sexual orientation, they would provide protection for ex-gays who still look stereotypically gay—such as John Paulk or Sy Rogers.

For the sake of argument, let's *pretend* Exodus or NARTH was actually successful at curing half of its clients. Why should the other half who were unable to change suffer legal and social persecution? Shouldn't these individuals be able to live free of discrimination and violence? To claim the moral and ethical high ground, Exodus should reexamine its ties to extremist groups and its reflexive opposition to gay rights laws. By taking this path, Exodus would also have the added benefit of not being targeted for exposure by gay groups. With no political agenda, activists would have little incentive to take pictures of Exodus leaders in gay bars.

2. Disassociate from NARTH. The ex-gay movement is supposed to be based on scripture, not psychology. Yet, in today's ex-gay ministries, the pseudoscience espoused by groups such as NARTH has become almost as sacrosanct as the Bible. The theories of Nicolosi and Cohen are touted as if handed down directly from God, but this idolatry of the mental health fringe has had a corrosive effect on the ex-gay movement. Exodus should ask why it turns to pop psychology for answers. The job of mental fitness should be left to the American Psychiatric Association, not ex-gay ministers who are not trained in this area.

Exodus also believes that a cure is possible through prayer, thus the motto "Freedom from homosexuality through Jesus Christ." If Jesus truly is the answer, though, then why has Exodus adopted the semisecular methods of NARTH? It appears as if Exodus suffers from a crisis of faith, as if having given up hope of healing through prayer, turning instead to the golden calf of pop psychology for answers.

If Exodus members are the true believers they claim to be, it should be enough to quote the Bible, yet Exodus dedicates much of its resources to efforts to debunk gay gene theories. Members also spend an inordinate amount of time espousing Moberly's and Nicolosi's ideas that support homosexuality being a result of a failed relationship with a same-sex parent or of molestation.

This acceptance of NARTH's work has turned nearly every ex-gay leader into a dilettante who offers clients shallow discourse on abstruse topics such as genetics and behavioral science. An ex-gay leader may work for minimum wage in a car wash by day and hold court on the intricacies of psychology by night. Is this what Exodus was designed to do? Although members call themselves conservatives, they act more like 1960s liberals, turning to psychology to explain and justify every human behavior.

At Exodus, unqualified amateurs seize tidbits of scientific information and use them out of context. This is how we end up with wacky theories such as the "rubber band technique" or "intrauterine memory recovery." Indeed, there is nearly as much experimentation with pop psychology in today's ex-gay ministries as there is prayer. Anyone entering these ministries is likely to end up on a couch getting psychologically analyzed by some unlicensed, unqualified ministry leader. This leader is likely to delve into this person's past to find the "root" cause of his or her homosexuality. There are no professional standards or ethical guidelines in place to oversee these leaders.

The biggest problem with Exodus aligning itself with NARTH is that it forces the ex-gay group to accept incoherent theories that it knows are not true. To accept NARTH's logic, Exodus must agree that molestation or a damaged parental relationship is a prerequisite for homosexuality. In the real world, however, many clients, if not the majority, who enter Exodus do not fit into this neat, preconceived sociological box. But because Exodus has invested so much in NARTH's philosophy, it cannot allow for any deviation from the chosen theories. So, if you come to Exodus and say you were neither molested nor have a rift with a same-sex parent, this can't be accepted at face value. Instead, a ministry leader will play shrink and endlessly try to pry loose a repressed childhood memory or some other phony, nonexistent trauma.

The truth is that Exodus has no idea whether homosexuality is genetic or not. The group is absolutely clueless—as is the rest of the world—on whether family dynamics play any role in sexual orientation. Group members are not biologists, psychologists, medical doctors, or researchers, although they often act as if they are. It should be enough to point to the Bible instead of relying on modern psycho-babble. With the Lord on their side, do they really need sham statistics and phony theories? It is time they took off their white lab coats and came back to church where the movement was founded. To do this, they must separate themselves from NARTH, whose main interest in propagating these theories is profit, not salvation.

3. Accurate labeling. Exodus dishonestly labels people ex-gay the moment these people get into its clutches, even though they still often have intense same-sex yearnings and little or no romantic interest in the opposite sex. Exodus also parades spokespeople around who are not totally "healed." This is misleading and false advertising.

Exodus leaders often make disingenuous statements, such as "I'm 50 percent healed." What exactly does this mean? Is the leader saying he can get half an erection? Let's face it, in human sexuality, one is either physically attracted to a person or not. Attempting to quantify this attraction through arbitrary percentages is a silly game that should have no place in Exodus or any other ex-gay group.

Playing semantic games with the meaning of "change" might serve Exodus well in the media, but it is not ethical. For Exodus to walk with any measure of dignity, it must begin to portray itself accurately. Only those who are 100 percent straight in both sexual behavior *and* fantasy should refer to themselves as ex-gay. If a person in Exodus does not change sexual orientation but chooses celibacy for religious reasons, the appropriate term is *celibate homosexual,* not *ex-gay.* If a person claims to be partially changed, the appropriate term is *struggling homosexual.*

Finally, no person should represent Exodus as a spokesperson unless he or she is completely straight, preferably for more than five years. If Exodus can't find enough of these people, shouldn't they begin to wonder if their program really works?

4. Be honest about the GLBT community. Just as it is unethical for Exodus to eschew the latest mental health information and label homosexuals "sick," it is immoral for the group to call gay life "unhealthy." Exodus has consistently portrayed gay life as a stew of drug addiction, unbridled promiscuity, rampant disease, and unhappy, broken people. Surely many gay people do take part in self-destructive behaviors and many are unhappy, but they are no more representative of a mythical gay lifestyle than female prostitution, alcoholism, divorce, and child abuse are part of a heterosexual lifestyle.

Exodus goes to great lengths to show that there are no happy, productive gay people in society, presenting gay life as a recipe for misery, depression, and loneliness. Exodus has little problem pointing to examples—many within its own ranks—of gay people who fit this stereotype ostensibly to prove the point. These examples prove nothing, however, other than an indomitable determination to demonize and stigmatize gay people.

It would be just as easy for a gay person to point out failed, miserable, heterosexual wretches who are embroiled in substance abuse, promiscuity, and instability and suffering from depression. In fact, I could walk out of my Washington condo and within fifteen minutes find at least a dozen heterosexual hobos. If I were evil-minded and wanted to distort reality, I could blame their failures on the heterosexual lifestyle. This would be a rather pernicious and irrational endeavor, just as it is when Exodus twists gay life to fit into its warped worldview.

It is time for Exodus to stop its destructive ways and abandon its crusade to misrepresent the lives of lesbians and gay men. If members want to believe homosexuality is sinful, I may vehemently disagree, but I can respect their right to believe it. This religious point of view should be their focus, not playing amateur Freuds or social scientists. Exodus members should begin to tell prospective clients the truth: Gay people are often happy, productive citizens and there are countless healthy, monogamous, lifelong gay relationships. They should admit that if one is in a monogamous relationship or practices safer sex, it is very unlikely one will contract HIV.

However, members should say, despite these facts, that Exodus still believes homosexuality is sinful. Being happy with gay life is irrelevant in their view because God disapproves. This message is still distasteful, but at least it is honest and not a reliance on disgraceful scare tactics.

Unfortunately, Exodus realizes that spooking people is a way to increase their membership roles. As with many of today's megachurches, Exodus focuses more on the "mega" and less on the "church." The group would rather brag about an increase in chapters than risk losing members by recruiting honestly. I suggest that Exodus reevaluates its methods and skewed interpretations of gay life. The group can begin by considering, "WWJD," or What would Jesus do?

5. Standardizing and sunshine. It is unconscionable that no standardized learning materials are offered by Exodus and many other ex-gay ministries. Each chapter is a hodgepodge of psychobabble, prayer, and experimental remedies usually offered by uneducated, unlicensed ministry leaders posing as therapists or charismatic saviors. There is no excuse, for example, why some ministries embrace Cohen's touch therapy as therapeutic, while others reject it as quackery. One ex-gay ministry may support spiritual warfare, including exorcisms, while other ministries may see these attempts at slaying Satan as a form of mystic barbarism.

The randomness of these programs often leads to self-styled leaders with self-serving agendas. For example, ex-gay leader Falzarano wrote a prayer request in his newsletter asking his flock to pray that "the Falzarano's house will sell quickly." This followed Falzarano's thanking God "that the Falzarano's have finally completed renovating their home."[11] What's next, the flock should pray that the Falzaranos get a George Foreman grill for Christmas?

Exodus, under Chambers' directorship, should move quickly to standardize all Exodus programs to ensure the more fringe practices are eliminated. Exodus should also set up a mandatory training program for all new ministry leaders—Ex-Gay University—to teach these budding leaders the appropriate ways to deal with clients. I believe it would help Exodus weed out potential sexual predators and limit the number of psychologically unbalanced people leading ministries.

In addition, Exodus also needs to enact a "sunshine policy" that allows reporters to come to all of the organization's meetings. When I visited the annual Exodus 2001 conference in North Carolina, I was told that I would be welcome to attend any of the sundry seminars they offered, but when I arrived, I was banned from more than three-quarters of the program and assigned a surly, overweight, ex-gay thug to follow me around to make sure I didn't walk into the forbidden seminars. Exodus was particularly diligent in making sure I didn't get to witness any of the behavior modification courses. In other words, Exodus wants critics to see only feel-good classes that are non-controversial. When it comes to the more objectionable material or Byzantine practices, Exodus quickly pulls the curtain to shield the painful truth. Fortunately, I slipped the rather tubby henchman shadowing me when he lumbered off toward the cafeteria-style buffet.

Without him blocking me, I was able to interview several Exodus leaders and attend many of the prohibited seminars. Exodus should drop this shadowing of journalists unless, of course, the group is unable to do so because members are ashamed of their product and have something to hide. If Exodus wants to avoid criticism it needs more sunshine and less darkness.

The Responsibilities of the GLBT Community

The ex-gay ministries have continued, in large part, because the GLBT community has not responded to their campaign of misinformation. The topic is taken seriously by the organized GLBT community only when there is a crisis, such as during the 1998 ad campaign. The way to avoid crisis, however, is to educate early and often, before disaster occurs. The ex-gay ministries had been around since the early 1970s, yet when the ads came out in 1998, some GLBT leaders were unfamiliar with them. When the campaign ended the political establishment once again buried its head in the sand and tried to forget the issue like it was a bad dream.

However, a few years later, Dr. Spitzer unveiled his tainted study and these disheveled leaders had to respond once more under fire. The lesson here is that this is a topic that is not going away. It will keep coming up, time and again, and be used as a dangerous political weapon that still resonates with many citizens and political leaders. So the question is, Will the powers that be continue to be reactive, or will they be proactive in launching far-reaching educational campaigns designed to counter ex-gay propaganda?

One problem is that many organizations see this issue as purely a religious one that should be addressed only when absolutely necessary, but they are fooling themselves with this deluded thinking. It is an incontrovertible fact that in the past five years ex-gays have been an integral part of the religious right's strategy to deny gay people equality. Ex-gays have spoken everywhere, from statehouses to school board meetings to Congress. Their message is that since change of sexual orientation is possible, GLBT people do not need equal rights. Until this message is soundly defeated, the political success of the GLBT community will remain spotty. This is not a peripheral issue, as conventional wisdom has it, but the central issue in GLBT politics. As long as a significant number of people believe gay people can become straight, they will not support the GLBT movement no matter how much money it spends or influence it wields.

When your average family discusses gay issues around the dinner table, they are not discussing legislation. They are talking about whether homosexuality is caused by nature or nurture. They speak of their confusion when they hear John Paulk tell Oprah that he has gone from gay to straight. If Paulk has gone straight, they wonder, than why can't Aunt Sally leave her life partner and become heterosexual too?

When a child comes out, the first inclination of many parents is to look for ways to "fix" that child. For many of these desperate parents, at first glance, Exodus, NARTH, or Homosexuals Anonymous may seem to be the answer. This delays the coming-out process, rips apart families, and tears at the spiritual, emotional, and political heart of the GLBT movement. Unfortunately, our community continues its Band-Aid approach to the matter, allowing the ex-gay ministries to impact negatively our families and our freedom.

Many things can be done to mitigate the efforts of ex-gay groups. We must approach this from religious, political, medical, and sociological perspectives. The following presents five ways I think the GLBT community can counter the toxic influence of the ex-gay ministries.

Embracing Gay Religious Institutions

The rise of the ex-gay ministries has a lot to do with the GLBT community's general aversion to religion. For years the GLBT community would argue for civil rights while studiously avoiding religious issues. Much of this has to do with the fact that many in the GLBT community were harmed by religion and the scars run deep. Some of this has to do with more secular leaders fearing they do not know enough about religion to discuss the topic.

But for the exception of a few spiritual gay activists, the realm of religion and spirituality has unnecessarily been ceded to reactionary forces such as Reverend Jerry Falwell. This all too often pits gays versus God in the media. Even for the best debaters, defeating God is a very tall order and puts our community at a disadvantage.

The reality is that millions of lesbian and gay individuals are people of faith, and many religious scholars disagree that homosexuality is sinful. The religious right does not corner the market on spirituality, yet, by our relative silence, the GLBT community has allowed people such as Pat Robertson to claim God as his ally in the unholy war to retain the right to hate and discriminate.

"The leaders of the GLBT movement need to take inclusivity more seriously," wrote Dr. Ralph Blair, a psychotherapist and founder of Evangelicals Concerned, a gay evangelical group. "There seems to be a not-so-subtle exclusion of conservative gays and lesbians as well as evangelical Christians—even in the GLBT religious movement."[12]

Within the past few years our community has been increasingly tolerant and supportive of religion, including gay evangelical Christians. Groups such as the Human Rights Campaign and the National Gay and Lesbian Task Force have recently taken steps to embrace communities of faith and have worked closely with moderate clergy. Our community has also become more accepting of gay churches. This is a very positive development that hopefully will continue. We must remember that ignorance and intolerance are the enemy, not religion.

"One thing [that we can do] is to celebrate these welcoming affirming churches," said author and spiritual activist Mel White, a former ghostwriter for Reverend Jerry Falwell. He explained that another way is to do outreach with people of faith so they can be part of the broader discussion.[13]

For many gay people who come out of the fundamentalist or ex-gay movement, the adjustment to a more secular life can be difficult. Often they enter a world that is scary and unfamiliar. The prayers, songs, and symbols they grew up with are nowhere to be found. Many of these individuals say they feel lost and alone.

"When a Christian leaves the ex-gay movement and he has to go to a typical gay community center or organization, he's not going to find a transition available to him," said White in our interview. "The first time I had tried to work in the community it was in a gay bar, and I had never been in a bar before. And to be in a bar was as traumatic as it was to be in a gay bar. . . . If you go to a bar they just caricature and stereotype the gay community," continued White. "They say, 'This is only about bars' and think, 'These preachers have been telling me right. This is an evil crowd.' Now that I know that bars are wonderful places, it's still not the transition that's going to help them."

Gay-affirmative churches often serve as a bridge between the two worlds, providing familiar symbols while helping conflicted individuals reconcile and integrate their faith with their sexuality. The more these people know about gay-affirmative churches, the less likely they are to run back to the destructive, but familiar ex-gay ministries.

"When I first went to [the Metropolitan Community Church] I began to cry from the moment I got in there to see gay people holding hands in church," explained White. "When you go to an MCC church, you can see who is new because they are just weeping. . . . When you go forward and take Communion with your gay friend, it is just liberating."

Missionary Work

The GLBT community must rise to the challenge and equal the fervor of the ex-gay ministries in terms of outreach. I have been to many ex-gay conferences across America where there was virtually no presence by the GLBT community. At these conferences ex-gay groups were free to disseminate their propaganda with no one present to offer an alternative point of view. Occasionally, groups such as Mel White's Soulforce are on hand to offer a counterbalance, but the GLBT presence at Exodus, NARTH, and Homosexuals Anonymous events is spotty and inconsistent. The GLBT community must marshal the resources and the will to take on these groups on their home turf.

This is not to say that Exodus conferences should be bombarded with obnoxious, screaming activists. This would be ineffective and appear to confirm what right-wing preachers have said about the GLBT community. Soulforce's tactics may work best with those ensnared in the ex-gay lifestyle.

"We don't preach or respond [at the conferences]," Soulforce founder Mel White explained to me. "They know who we are. And so we sit there and people come up and say, 'You know, I read your book. It's really a help to me, but I'm still not sure I can do this.' And we say, 'Hey, listen, we're gay Christians and we're in long-term, . . . healthy, loving relationships.'" White continued, "What we do is we hang around . . . and we talk to folks. . . . Gary [Mel's life partner] and I hold hands and the other couples . . . hold hands and go to their worship services."

I believe that GLBT religious organizations must go on a crusade to make sure every person involved in an ex-gay ministry is aware of an alternative point of view. Each member of Exodus should be aware that he or she can still be gay and Christian and that some interpretations of the Bible do not condemn loving same-sex relationships. "For every time they say, 'You can't be gay and lesbian and Christian,' we don't have to say, 'Yes, you can,'" said the Cathedral of Hope's Piazza. "We only have to provide a little bit of light to dispel an awful lot of darkness."

Although the national GLBT political organizations have the most financial resources to launch such a project, it is better left up to gay spiritual groups. Blair, of Evangelicals Concerned, correctly explains that the GLBT political groups don't "speak the same language" and "tend to see it in political terms": "I don't think the secular 'community' can reach out to those in the ex-gay ministries," wrote Blair. "That's because the secular GLBT movement does not experience the motivation of those who turn to ex-gay agencies for help. They don't get it. They don't have the same evangelical Christian concerns."

The schedules of ex-gay conferences can be obtained online, so we know where they are taking place months in advance. Therefore, we owe it to our struggling brothers and sisters to organize missionary teams to save their souls from the hell of the ex-gay ministries. One of the gay religious organizations should also consider starting a comprehensive, interactive Web site that deals exclusively with this issue. This Web site can offer spiritual advice, as well as an updated list of the ex-gay ministries' newest defections.

We cannot control the motivation or desire of people who elect to stay in these groups, but we can ensure that these struggling individuals are fully informed. I am a firm believer that once these people are educated and aware of alternative options, the majority will stay in these programs for much shorter periods of time.

Education Campaign

While in-person outreach is best left to gay and gay-friendly religious organizations, the secular GLBT community can have an impact as well. As we have discussed, much ex-gay propaganda revolves around portraying members of the GLBT community as hedonistic and diseased sinners. The best solution to combat these malicious fabrications is to show the truth. The lives of GLBT people are as respectable and diverse as those of any other Americans and can't be defined by shallow generalizations or simplistic stereotypes.

According to former ex-gay Clint Trout, images of happy gay couples are particularly useful for those in the ex-gay ministries. "The most helpful thing . . . our community can do is put our long-term couples out for people to see and let those stories come out," offered Trout. "When I was in the ministry I didn't believe [any long-term couples were possible]. I had a perception of a very lonely life." Continued Trout, "The most powerful weapon our community has is the truth that we can be happy and love each other."

A national, positive-image ad campaign is not a new idea, but it has been underutilized as a means to educate the public, although in recent years the need for one has diminished somewhat because pop culture has increasingly welcomed gay and lesbian Americans. Groundbreaking shows, such as *Ellen* and *Will & Grace,* have introduced gay and lesbian people to mainstream America, lifting the crippling veil of silence that had existed for so long.

Still, these advances are continuously threatened by the disingenuous work of the ex-gay ministries and their political partners. Through tours such as Focus on the Family's Love Won Out, misinformation is kept circulating through the public, with few efforts to counter it on the part of GLBT groups.

One or several gay organizations ought to come together to sponsor a major speaking tour that educates the public on the harm of the ex-gay ministries and reparative therapy. The tour could stop at churches, civic organizations, and universities nationwide. Speakers could include progay clergy, former ex-gays, mental health authorities, and sundry other experts.

Until steps are taken to educate the public, the dehumanizing theories pushed by NARTH and the ex-gay ministries will flourish and find audiences throughout the world. Sadly, our community now seems content to watch brush fires of ignorance spread and to react only when there is a full-scale conflagration. We must move forward with vision, wisdom, and perseverance, stamping out each brush fire before it can burn down the strong, but vulnerable foundation of truth.

Special Operations

One novel approach that I would like to see pursued is legal action against ex-gay ministries and reparative therapists. At least one organization—or a wealthy retired lawyer with a lot of spare time—could search for complaints filed against the various charlatans or quacks who run these abusive programs. I believe that many examples of "false memory syndrome," suicide, and fraud would be uncovered. Such a groundbreaking crusade would put enormous legal pressure on these groups and their "therapists." Hopefully, the future will provide us with the financial and human resources to embrace this worthy project.

If each of NARTH's members were thoroughly investigated and checked out, I think legal action could be taken against many of them. If enough of these therapists could be sued for damages, we might be able to put many of them out of business. Project "Sue a Quack" would be quite an extensive undertaking, but it would take only one great legal mind with commitment and determination to discredit the reparative therapy and ex-gay industries.

Another, extremely controversial way the GLBT community can precipitate the end of the ex-gay experiment is to dispatch undercover teams to catch ex-gay leaders engaging in not so ex-gay behavior. Imagine a team of young, attractive men and women outfitted with hidden cameras and tape recorders. Many of these contraptions are small enough to fit in a pen or notepad. These operatives could be dispatched to every ex-gay ministry in the nation to see whether the leaders try to seduce them. Simultaneously, a deal can be cut with a network or cable television show to air the juiciest parts of the videos.

Although this is a radical plan, I estimate it would put one-quarter to one-half of the ex-gay ministries out of business within a year. Sure, this is hardball, but if enough big leaders fell, this covert operation might have an outside shot at toppling the ex-gay ministries. And even if the results were disappointing and only ten ministries were exposed on television, it would still have a devastating impact.

I am a staunch proponent of covert operations to undermine Exodus or Homosexuals Anonymous, but many GLBT community leaders are adamantly against this, citing misplaced privacy concerns. For example, in our interview, Blair, of Evangelicals Concerned, said going undercover was "unethical." Comedienne Lily Tomlin also criticized undercover tactics by disparaging the sighting of Paulk as "righteous." According to her interview with notable gay writer Rex Wockner:

> I don't always agree with everybody's particular activist politics. I think people can get really righteous. Remember when the guy from Exodus was uncovered in the gay bar? I've argued with friends about it because even the people at the bar, they protected him from being photographed, which I thought was an honorable thing to do. Of course, everybody [in the activist world] is gleeful and excited over this [Paulk being caught in the bar] but in so many ways it's really kind of an activist, narrow point of view. It's like being a politician. It's partisan. They just want this to happen or they want that to happen.[14]

Of course, one would expect Tomlin to be a fierce defender of the closet—that is where she has resided during every important gay rights battle in the past three decades. (For the record, the staff at Mr. P's didn't "protect" Paulk. They didn't know who he was at the time they ejected me from the bar. As soon as they figured out who he was, they denied him an escape hatch and forced him to leave the saloon through the front door to face the music.)

In substance, the argument that undercover work is unethical and invades the privacy of ex-gay leaders is highly flawed. First, the ex-gay ministries have become a multimillion-dollar political industry that sells dangerous, faulty products and is protected by high-powered Washington lobbyists. Unmasking the ex-gay ministries is no different from *60 Minutes* setting up hidden cameras to catch shady companies that are bilking clients. To argue that the ex-gay ministries should be shielded under the guise of privacy is the equivalent of saying that *60 Minutes* is invading the privacy of the scoundrels it uncovers committing fraud.

The product sold by the ex-gay ministries is every bit as dangerous as the practices unmasked by *60 Minutes* and other investigative news programs. As I have pointed out, people have been known to commit suicide in ex-gay groups. Understanding this, how can it be coherently argued that these groups deserve more privacy than other companies that swindle the public? The public's *right to know* clearly outweighs any spurious privacy arguments, which do nothing but give rogue ex-gay groups a license to rip off unsuspecting clients.

I believe an activist's role is to serve the GLBT community's interests through a variety of tactics. Preferably this can be accomplished by negotiating in plush meeting rooms with reasonable people, but, when need be, it is important to lace up the combat boots and get down and dirty in the trenches. This includes going undercover to short-circuit the ability of ex-gay groups to harm desperate and vulnerable people.

Life is about making difficult choices. When people say they choose not to support undercover tactics because they are unethical, then they are choosing to allow vulnerable people to continue to be exploited by the ex-gay ministries. Faced with this choice, I feel it is unethical not to go undercover. Why would I allow GLBT people to suffer unnecessarily when I can do something about it? Why should the profitable and damaging interests of Exodus be placed above the well-being of young men and women who are struggling to accept their sexual orientation and may be contemplating suicide? To me, the issue is crystal clear. In a world of competing interests, my loyalties and concerns are decidedly with the people who are being manipulated, not the callous ex-gay profiteers who are engaging in cynical exploitation.

A More Supportive Community

The ex-gay ministries' contention that gay life is unhappy and destructive is nonsense, but we can't completely dismiss the negative experiences of ex-gays whose ill treatment in our community helped make them vulnerable to the empty promises of ex-gay groups. There is a grain of truth to some of their stories, and we ought to listen to what they are saying.

In fact, many people who enter the ex-gay ministries are not getting their legitimate needs filled by the GLBT community. They are treated poorly, cast aside, and by the time they cross paths with ex-gay leaders, they are truly receptive to their warm smiles and promises of unconditional love.

One particular group of GLBT Americans who get shortchanged are youth. The National Gay and Lesbian Task Force told the Associated Press that they estimate that 26 percent of gay youngsters are expelled from their homes because of their sexual orientation. The New York–based Streetwork Project, a group that helps homeless youth, estimates that 42 percent of homeless youth identify as lesbian or gay.[15]

One of the major reasons people join the ex-gay ministries is because they believe gay life is bars, drugs, and sex. This has more to do with their personal moral failings than those of the community, but the GLBT community also must continue to diversify its social outlets and move away from the bar as the central point of socialization. Don't get me wrong. I think the gay bars are incredibly exciting, and I've spent more time in these places than I care to admit. The GLBT community should be proud that it has developed the best network of nightclubs in the world, but there *is* more to life.

Every year the selection of places where GLBT Americans can find support and community grows. There is an ever-widening array of faith organizations, political groups, sports leagues, and music and dance clubs. The spiritual and social maturation of the GLBT community is a much-needed development that will greatly enhance the lives of gay Americans. It will also, in the long run, have a devastating impact on the ex-gay ministries, as people most susceptible to their propaganda will find rich and fulfilling lives in the GLBT community.

Finally, each GLBT individual can try being a little nicer. The turmoil of coming out should have made us more understanding and accepting of differences, but too many people have not learned from their experiences. I am ashamed when I hear people caught up in the ex-gay ministries say that at least they can get a "hug and a smile" at Exodus. Our community, especially men, should realize that it is no crime to be nice to a person who doesn't look like Brad Pitt.

It's not that straight people are friendlier. It is just that people who have suffered judgment and grew up fearing rejection should not be so fast to judge and reject other people. For those who don't fit in with the community, the ex-gay ministries can seem an attractive option, especially because they will accept anyone—except openly gay people—no matter how nutty, ugly, out of shape, goofy, or poor. It hurts me to say that we can learn an important lesson from the ex-gay ministries: Everyone deserves a warm embrace, a bright smile, and unconditional love. A little kindness can go a long way in improving peoples' lives and keeping them away from those who would take advantage of their insecurities and low self-esteem.

Accepting Limitations

One of the most frequent questions I am asked when I lecture on this topic is, "How much longer do you expect the ex-gay ministries to last?" The answer I give is that as long as gay people are stigmatized, discriminated against, and sometimes violently attacked, there will always be a market for the ex-gay ministries.

It is a natural inclination for people who are oppressed to try to change their situation. This is why we see skin bleaching in countries where lighter skin offers social advantages. It is why people living in areas where there is religious persecution change religions. The decision to forfeit a central part of oneself to circumvent social ramifications is as old as humankind.

No matter how much outreach the GLBT community does or how many people are educated to the follies and failures of the ex-gay myth, some individuals will attempt to change. The best that we can hope to accomplish is arming people with the information they need to make informed choices.

To illustrate this, I point to a recent encounter I had while visiting Miami Beach. I was tanning on the edge of the magnificent aqua water on a perfectly sunny afternoon when I looked up and saw an attractive young man. The tall redhead with pale skin looked nervous, as if he had never been to a gay beach before. It turned out that he had not. When he was confident there was no one he knew, he placed his towel beside mine and bluntly asked if I wanted to "hook up." I was turned on, but I had a boyfriend, so I set him up with a friend, Keith, who would be visiting Miami the following week.

Their date went well. It went so well, in fact, that the young man came out to his parents as soon as he got home from the date. Keith returned to Washington, DC, and tried to reach the young man via e-mail for several days but got no response. A week later, Keith found out that the young man, "Richard" (pseudonym) had enrolled in an ex-gay program and had cut off ties with all gay people. Here is the text of his letter:

Keith,

Sorry I took this long to get back to you. (Un?)fortunately, when I came home on Monday my mother was rather curious about my activities as of late. I quickly realized that she was going to ask me if I was gay, so I came out to her and my father. They were not angry, but very disappointed.

My father seemed appalled/flabbergasted that I don't know how good sex with a woman feels, and my mother believes that I am simply confused and not really gay. She outright told me that she would rather I at least behave as an asexual rather than a homosexual. Both my parents find this all very sinful. They are, of course, also worried about social effects on our family if I come out.

Anyway, it boils down to this. I have agreed to attempt therapy, and probably conversion. I admitted to them, myself, and now I guess to several friends that, socially and politically, my life would be *much* easier without having to deal with homosexuality. Hence, I plan to make a formal and full-fledged stab at conversion.

To do this, I am going to, at least for now, disconnect from *all* of my gay friends and the GLBT community.

This has nothing to do with you. If I was going to date a guy you would be him. You really are a great guy. I know this all sounds a bit weird, but if I can be straight my life will be easier. If none of this works and I am still gay in the end, my parents are going to be very hurt and I will probably leave Miami as to not cause problems in their social life and that of my siblings. If the therapy does not work, you'll be the first to know.

Best Wishes,
Richard

This letter shows the intense pressure people are still under to change their sexual orientation. The young man was afraid he was an embarrassment to his family and would have to move away from Miami. He also feared that he would never be able to run successfully for public office if he were openly gay, he told Keith during their date. To make life "easier" he felt he had to "change."

When the ex-gay ministries claim that people are unhappy being gay, what they fail to point out is that the unhappiness almost always stems from fear of *rejection*. Richard did not want to be rejected by his family. He did not want to be rejected in the city where he grew up. He did not want to be rejected, if he ran for office, by narrowminded voters who care more about his sexual orientation than his skills. In this case, and most others, the prejudice fostered in society by groups such as Exodus was the sole cause for unhappiness. If these groups would disappear, most of the unhappiness that Exodus disingenuously speaks of would subside.

The ex-gay ministries are insidious precisely because of their coercive nature. They would claim that it was Richard's choice to try to change, but was it really his choice? If he did not enter a conversion program, his parents would probably have rejected him and labeled him a quitter who would not make the attempt to change. Faced with such a painful situation, who can blame this young man for wasting part of his life in a useless endeavor that is destined to fail?

Richard's story also illustrates a macabre reality: There are limitations on what the GLBT community can do to stop people from joining the ex-gay ministries. After Keith received this e-mail we both tried to intervene, sending Richard a pile of information on the failure of these programs. Richard must now know about Colin Cook, Wade Richards, and John Paulk. He is aware of the medical and mental health establishment's rejection of these groups. Yet, because of familial and societal pressure, he feels compelled to continue down this dead-end path, and we have yet to hear from him.

We must do all we can but also realize that the promises made by these groups will continue to seduce vulnerable and impressionable individuals. Sometimes we must have the strength to let go and accept that some people must take dangerous roads before they reach their destination as out and proud individuals. I look forward to the day Richard and I shall meet again, in a place where he feels loved and accepted for who he is, not for who others want him to be.

Final Thoughts

The ex-gay ministries and reparative therapy will not last forever, and I am confident that one day we will celebrate their demise. As with all major prejudices, the passing of these groups and their heterosexual supremacist theories is inextricably linked to public opinion. The question is, What will cause public sentiment to change to the point at which these groups are no longer socially acceptable? Soulforce's Mel White believes the tide might turn if a major evangelical or fundamentalist religious leader repents for his antigay sins. According to White:

> I'm hoping for the kind of breakthrough, where a Jerry Falwell or a Pat Robertson will say, when he [finds out] his granddaughter is a lesbian, "You know, I've been wrong." Because I think that would bring it down.

I agree with White that this would have a significant impact, but I am less confident than he that a person with such moral courage and conviction will emerge. We would need another Jesus, Martin Luther King, or Gandhi to show such strength, and such transcendent individuals who change the way we think and live are rare gems. I certainly don't see avaricious theological tyrants such as Falwell or Robertson filling this hero role anytime soon.

There have also been some ill-fated attempts to find common ground between gay and ex-gay individuals. Most notably is a group called Bridges Across, an amalgam of well-meaning gays and ex-gays who admirably want to turn down the volume on this divisive issue. Unfortunately, such endeavors are bound to fail because gay people have nothing in common with ex-gays. It is difficult to form lasting friendships with people who disparage the most significant relationships in your life. It is also an unhealthy drain, both spiritually and emotionally, to spend time with people who believe you are sexually broken and not a whole and complete human being. Who would want friends like this?

Furthermore, whereas the premise of the entire gay rights struggle is that it is OK to be gay, the premise of the ex-gay ministries is that it is not OK. Therefore the ex-gay philosophy doesn't need to be accommodated, it needs to be vanquished. The best we can hope for is this:

- Ex-gays fully separate from the religious right and their campaign of persecution.
- Gay organizations and Exodus agree to disagree.
- When gay and ex-gay individuals interact on a personal level, they can treat one another with dignity and respect.

Any hope for a greater coming together of the minds is wishful thinking, if not naïveté. This is why the Bridges Across project has floundered. The participants simply ran out of things to say. If an ex-gay doesn't want to hear about the partner and child of a lesbian friend, what else, other than the weather, do they talk about?

The death of the ex-gay experiment most likely will not come as a result of a benevolent savior, reconciliation between factions, or even a major ex-gay scandal. Ultimately, the ex-gay ministries will be put out of business by good, old-fashioned, hard work by the GLBT community.

As society increasingly accepts lesbian and gay Americans, there will be less of a market for gay conversion. As demand decreases, the number of ministries will diminish. Furthermore, as antigay and ex-gay messages fail to resonate with the public, political preachers will need to find new targets to keep the money rolling in and financial support for ex-gay groups will dry up.

When it seems as if discrimination is an impregnable fortress or a wall too tall to scale, it is important to look at history. Time and again America has distinguished between traditional values and valueless traditions. Our nation has made horrible mistakes and participated in gross human rights abuses, such as the slaughter of Native Americans, black slavery, and the subjugation of women. In the end, though, America has taken the righteous path and turned its back on historic wrongs.

Fundamentalists such as Reverend Jerry Falwell will tell you that they will never change their religious convictions. They will swear on a towering stack of Bibles that their faith is one of unyielding absolutes, yet time and again they have changed their positions when public opinion has told them that their absolutes were absolutely wrong. When ancient prejudices become modern embarrassments, even the most intransigent people and institutions can miraculously change.

For example, in the past several years, Pope John Paul II has apologized to numerous groups, including women and Jews, for past mistreatment by the Catholic Church. In 1978, after protests, the Mormon Church overturned its long-standing policy of barring blacks from serving in the priesthood. Jerry Falwell, the beacon of tolerance that he is, also reversed his vocal support for racial segregation as public sentiment turned against his discriminatory position.

In all of these cases, the Bible was used to justify discrimination. Passages were plucked out of the Bible to support the prevailing prejudices of the day. The lesson here is that political preachers will never allow themselves to get burned by their own fire and brimstone. Obdurate and uncompromising absolutes are the rules by which *other* people are supposed to live. As soon as these preachers are negatively affected by their own application of scripture, they seem astonishingly adept at finding scriptural loopholes that maintain and protect their financial stability and social standing.

The same "miraculous" change in biblical interpretations that happened for other minorities will one day apply to gay people. As the GLBT community patiently slugs it out over the next two decades, progress will slowly continue unabated to the point at which programs such as the ex-gay ministries will seem embarrassing anachronisms. Political preachers, out of necessity, will once again renegotiate the once nonnegotiable rules they espoused. People will point to these relics in a few decades and say in amazement, "I can't believe this weird, hateful stuff used to go on. Wow, people sure were backward at the beginning of the twenty-first century."

Until this time arrives, however, thousands of families will be torn asunder by groups such as NARTH and Exodus. Like stage actors on Broadway, many sad people will play the straight role, only to wind up divorcing and creating broken homes for their children. Yes, in this day of discrimination, the ex-gay show must go on, but as with all shows, it someday must come to a close. For in the great drama of the ex-gay ministries, the final curtain always comes crashing down. The actors, at some point, must take off their costumes and be true to themselves once again.

"I've yet to meet one person who went through one of these programs who didn't end up coming back home," said Troy Perry, founder of the Metropolitan Community Church. "And when they do, we are there to welcome them."[16]

APPENDIX: RESOURCES

Affirmation
(United Methodists for Lesbian, Gay and Bisexual Concerns)
P.O. Box 1021
Evanston, IL 60204
<www.umaffirm.org>

Mission: Affirmation is an independent, not-for-profit organization that works for a Methodist church which acknowledges and affirms all of God's people are part of the body of Christ, including lesbian, gay, bisexual, and transgendered persons.

Dignity/USA
1500 Massachusetts Avenue, NW, Suite 11
Washington, DC 20005-1894
Phone: 800-877-8797
<www.dignityusa.org>

Mission: Dignity/USA envisions and works for a time when gay, lesbian, bisexual, and transgendered Catholics are affirmed and experience dignity through the integration of their spirituality with their sexuality, and as beloved persons of God participate fully in all aspects of life within the church and society.

Evangelicals Concerned
Phone: 212-517-3171
<www.ecwr.org>

Mission: Evangelicals Concerned is a nondenominational evangelical resource providing a community of fellowship that is a safe place for gay and lesbian Christians to reconcile their faith and sexuality, and to grow toward Christian maturity.

Human Rights Campaign
919 18th Street, NW, Suite 800
Washington, DC 20006
Phone: 202-628-4160
<www.HRC.org>
Mission: The Human Rights Campaign is the nation's largest national lesbian and gay political organization with members throughout the country. HRC effectively lobbies Congress, provides campaign support, and educates the public to ensure that lesbian and gay Americans can be open, honest, and safe at home, at work, and in the community.

Lutherans Concerned/North America
2466 Sharondale Drive
Atlanta, GA 30305
<www.lcna.org>
Mission: Lutherans Concerned helps people reconcile their spirituality and sexuality in an uplifting way and seeks to lead the church by example.

More Light Presbyterians
PMB 246 4737 County Road 101
Minnetonka, MN 55345-2634
Phone: 202-554-8281
<www.mlp.org>
Mission: More Light Presbyterians seeks the full participation of gay, lesbian, bisexual, and transgendered people of faith in the life, ministry, and witness of the Presbyterian Church (United States).

Parents, Families and Friends of Lesbians and Gays
1726 M Street, NW, Suite 400
Washington, DC 20036
Phone: 202-467-8180
<www.pflag.org>
Mission: Parents, Families and Friends of Lesbians and Gays (PFLAG) promotes the health and well-being of gay, lesbian, bisexual, and transgendered persons as well as their families and friends through support, to cope with an adverse society; education, to enlighten an ill-informed public; and advocacy, to end discrimination and to secure equal civil rights.

Seventh-Day Adventists, SDA Kinship International
P.O. Box 49375
Sarasota, FL 34230-6375
Phone: 866-732-5677 (toll-free)

Mission: This support organization is devoted to the spiritual, emotional, social, and physical well-being of current and former Seventh-Day Adventists who are lesbian, gay, bisexual, or transgendered.

Soulforce, Inc.
P.O. Box 4467
Laguna Beach, CA 92652
<www.soulforce.org>
Mission: Soulforce, Inc. is a network of friends learning nonviolence from the teachings of Gandhi and Martin Luther King Jr. to seek justice for God's gay, lesbian, bisexual, and transgendered children.

**UFMCC World Center
(Universal Fellowship of Metropolitan Community Churches)**
8704 Santa Monica Boulevard, Second Floor
West Hollywood, CA 90069
Phone: 310-360-8640
<www.ufmcc.com>
Mission: The Universal Fellowship of Metropolitan Community Churches helps thousands of gay, lesbian, bisexual, transgendered, and heterosexual people find hope and live the joy, reverence, and excitement of our fellowship and faith in God. UFMCC provides communities of faith that are places of healing and hope, places of reconciliation with family, with self-esteem, and with individual spirituality.

The United Church of Christ Coalition for Lesbian, Gay, Bisexual, and Transgender Concerns
PMB 230
800 Village Walk
Guilford, CT 06437-2740
Phone: 800-653-0799
<www.coalition.simplenet.com>
Mission: The United Church of Christ Coalition for Lesbian, Gay, Bisexual, and Transgender Concerns is an officially recognized interest group of the United Church of Christ, composed of justice-seeking individuals.

NOTES

Preface

1. For the unacquainted, those who say they have gone from gay to straight through a bizarre mix of therapy and religious programming designed to "pray away the gay" use the term *ex-gay*.

2. My parents are now very accepting and advocates with a Fort Lauderdale, Florida, chapter of Parents, Families and Friends of Lesbians and Gays (PFLAG).

3. Reparative therapy is a discredited psychological theory and practice that attempts to change a person's sexual orientation from gay to straight.

Candi's Bathroom Break

1. Accounts of this story are widely available on the Internet; see, for example, <http://www.washtimes.com/national/20021101-8683590.htm>; <http://www.gaytoday.com/world/110602wo.asp>; <http://www.baywindows.com/main.cfm?include=detailandstoryid=35711>.

2. Paulk, John (1998). *Not Afraid to Change: The Remarkable Story of How One Man Overcame Homosexuality.* Mukilteo, WA: WinePress Publishing.

3. Ibid.

4. Morphew, Clark (2000). Arden Hills church hosts conference of ex-gay group. *Pioneer Press,* August 12.

5. Paulk, *Not Afraid to Change,* p. 163.

6. Interview by Joel Lawson with John Mako, September 20, 2000, for the *Southern Voice.*

7. In May 2000, Window Media bought the *Washington Blade* and the *New York Blade,* making it by far the largest chain of gay newspapers in the nation's history.

8. Not surprisingly, the publication *In These Times* went on to label Paulk's alibi "Least convincing explanation of the month."

9. At Exodus's March 19-23 meeting, the board of directors voted unanimously to reinstate John Paulk as an active board member. Paulk would not be reinstated as

board chairman. Bob Ragan, who was appointed to replace Paulk, continues to serve in that position.

10. Bob Davies, who had been Exodus's executive director since 1985, resigned on September 30, 2001.

11. Exodus International (2000). Chairman disciplined for gay bar visit. Press release, October 3.

12. Goldman, David (2000). More fallout over ex-gay leader caught in gay bar. *Southern Voice,* September 28.

13. Ibid.

14. Exodus International, Chairman disciplined for gay bar visit.

15. Gorski, Eric (2000). Focus worker repents. *Colorado Springs Gazette,* October 4.

16. Gerson, Michael (1998). A righteous indignation. *U.S. News and World Report,* May 4, p. 22.

17. Re-igniting the hope for homosexuality (2000). *Focus on the Family.* Radio show, October 11.

18. Ibid., <http://www.family.org/resources/itempg.cfm?itemid=1884>. All quotes in the following material are from this show unless otherwise noted.

Undercover

1. On October 9, 2001, Exodus appointed Alan Chambers as the group's new executive director, replacing longtime leader Bob Davies. In early 2002, Chambers moved Exodus's headquarters from Seattle to Orlando, Florida.

2. Payne, Leanne (1993). *The Broken Image.* Wheaton, IL: Crossway Books, p. 53.

3. Paulk, Anne and John (1999). *Love Won Out.* Wheaton, IL: Tyndale, p. 126.

4. Consiglio, Bill (2000). *Homosexual No More.* Baltimore, MD: Regeneration Books, p. 90.

5. Davis, Natalie (1999). The other side of the rainbow: Part II. *Baltimore City Paper.*

6. Chin, Justin (1995). Our reporter survives the ex-gay ministries. *The Progressive,* December.

7. Kennedy, Dana (1998). Associated Press, January 3.

8. Chin, Our reporter survives the ex-gay ministries.

9. Eventually, I did speak to Worthen informally for about twenty minutes at the Exodus 2001 conference in Asheville, North Carolina.

10. Duin, Julia (1998). Ministries attracting criticism over attempts to change gays. *The Washington Times,* March 3.

11. Davis, Other side of the rainbow.

12. Potentials Unlimited (1988). *Gay and Unhappy.* Video.

13. Paulk and Paulk, *Love Won Out,* p. 47.

14. Paulk, John (1998). *Not Afraid to Change.* Mukilteo, WA: WinePress Publishing.

15. Bethell, Tom (1998). *The American Spectator,* October; WUSA (1999). Gordon Peterson, reporter, May 17; CNN (1998). *Talk Back Live,* June 17.

16. Interview with Alan and Leslie Chambers, taped, March 11, 2001. All quotes are from this interview unless otherwise noted.

17. Ybarra, Michael J. (1993). Going straight: Christian groups press gay people to take heterosexual path. *The Wall Street Journal,* April 21. Frank Worthen left Love in Action, which moved to Memphis, Tennessee. After traveling abroad, he returned to San Rafael to start New Hope Ministries.

18. Shepson, Bill (2001). Can Christians be gay? *Charisma,* July.

19. Kennedy, Associated Press.

20. Interview with Natalie Davis, taped, April 22, 2001. All quotes are from this interview unless otherwise noted.

21. Interview with John Napoli, taped, no date recorded. All quotes are from this interview unless otherwise noted.

22. See <http://www.stonewallrevisited.com/pages/john_s.html>.

23. Christian, Susan (1990). The last temptation. *Los Angeles Times,* April 5.

24. Interview with Brent Almond, taped, July 17, 2001.

25. Intervew with Scott Melendez, taped, July 17, 2001. All quotes are from this interview unless otherwise noted.

26. Chernin, Jeffrey F. (2001). Ex-gay: Born again queer. *Texas Triangle,* May 17.

27. Obejas, Achy and Lieblich, Julia (2001). Movement to convert gays grows, draws fire. *Chicago Tribune,* July 22.

28. For Bob Van Domelen's testimony and details on his sordid past, see, for example, <http://www.bridges-across.org/ba/intros/van_domelen_bob.htm>; <http://www.indegayforum.org/articles/pietrzyk1.html>.

29. Gold, Scott (2000). Healing for gays, or a new hurt. *Los Angeles Times,* July 19.

30. Comiskey, Andrew (2001). *Warring in Wisdom.* Desert Stream midyear report.

31. Goldberg, Michelle (2000). But I'm a queer leader. *Silicon Valley Weekly,* November 23.

32. Davis, Gode (2000). Inside the ex-gay scene. *The Guide Magazine,* February.

33. Crea, Joe (2001). What happens when they try to change us. *BPG and Mid-Atlantic Gay Life,* March 16, p. 4.

34. Stephen, Jerry (2000). *Out of the Closet and into the Light.* New York: Plume.

35. Phone interview with Reverend Jerry Stephenson, August 1, 2001.

36. Interview with Tracey St. Pierre, taped, September 21, 2001. All quotes are from this interview unless otherwise noted.

37. Payne, *The Broken Image,* pp. 51-52.

38. Paulk and Paulk, *Love Won Out,* p. 42.

39. Ibid., p. 198.

40. Ibid., p. 107.

41. To access testimonies, see <http://www.exodusnorthamerica.org>. Content of the Web site changes, so not all may be available at any given time.

42. Konrad, Jeff (1998). *You Don't Have to Be Gay.* Hilo, HI: Pacific Publishing House, p. 176.

43. The main reason the Mormon Church won't officially support Evergreen has to do with conflicting interpretations of Mormon theology. Although Evergreen

leaders believe homosexuality can be "healed," they do not believe that homosexuals choose to be gay. This is at odds with Mormon theology, which holds that homosexuality is a choice.

44. Miller, Mark (2000). To be gay and Mormon. *Newsweek*, May 8.

45. Comiskey, Andrew (1989). *Pursuing Sexual Wholeness*. Lake Mary, FL: Creation House, pp. 101-102.

46. Howard, Jeanette (2000). *Out of Egypt: One Woman's Journey Out of Lesbianism*. London: Monarch Books, p. 205.

47. Human Rights Campaign (2000). *Finally Free—Personal Stories: How Love and Self-Acceptance Saved Us from the Ex-Gay Ministries*. Washington, DC: Author.

48. Ibid., p. 170.

49. Interview with Clint Trout, taped, July 16, 2001. All quotes are from this interview unless otherwise noted.

50. Interview with Mel White, taped, July 17, 2001.

51. Paulk and Paulk, *Love Won Out*, p. 168.

52. Ibid.

53. Konrad, *You Don't Have to Be Gay*, p. 280.

A Trilogy of Tragedy

1. Interviews with Reverend Kent Philpott and John Evans, taped, 2001. The following scenario is based on these two interviews. All quotes are from these interviews unless otherwise noted.

2. Pennington, Sylvia (1989). *Ex-Gays? There Are None*. Hawthorne, CA: Lambda Christian Fellowship, p. 35.

3. Philpott, Kent (1975). *The Third Sex? Six Homosexuals Tell Their Stories*. London: Good Reading, Ltd. Hbk.

4. Pennington, *Ex-Gays? There Are None*, p. 38.

5. The one notable exception is Frank Worthen, who now runs a ministry called New Hope in San Rafael, California. Worthen's wife, Anita, ironically, has an openly gay son who lives next door with his male partner. Worthen is considered the grandfather of the ex-gay ministries and is still a leading figure in the movement.

6. The full text of McIntyre's suicide note appears in Pennington, *Ex-Gays? There Are None*, pp. 10-11.

7. A request was put in to interview Frank Worthen, but he declined to comment.

8. The following scenario is based on an interview with Jack Pantaleo, taped, July 9, 2001. All quotes are from this interview unless otherwise noted.

9. This passage and the following scenario are based on numerous discussions, on the phone and in person, and an interview with Wade Richards, taped, January 6, 2001. All quotes are from this interview unless otherwise noted.

10. Frank and Anita Worthen eventually moved LIA to Memphis, Tennessee. The ministry is still based in Memphis, but the Worthens moved back to San Rafael to run New Hope.

11. Moberly, Elizabeth (1983). *Homosexuality: A New Christian Ethic*. Greenwood, SC: The Attic Press, Inc.

12. Peter LaBarbera is well-known for his undercover trips to gay establishments and the stories he writes about these places. For typical LaBarbera stories, see <http://wnd.com/news/article.asp?ARTICLE_Id=26569>; <http://www.americans fortruth.com/CellucciPressRelease.html>.

Founding Follies

1. The following story is based on an interview with Michael Bussee, taped, April 20, 2002. All quotes are from this interview unless otherwise noted.
2. Christian, Susan (1990). The last temptation. *The Los Angeles Times*, April 5.
3. 3Z Hourglass Productions (1993). *One Nation Under God*. Video.
4. Ibid.
5. The following story is based on an interview with Jeremy Marks, taped, January 12, 2001. All quotes are from this interview unless otherwise noted.
6. Culver, Virginia (1995). Sessions with gays criticized. *Denver Post*, October 27.
7. Pietrzyk, Mark E. (1999). The ex-files: Not your usual gays. *Independent Gay Forum*, October 19.
8. Harkavy, Ward (1995). Come to Jesus: The love that dare not speak its name . . . in Kevin Tebedo's presence. *Denver Westword*, November 22.
9. Culver, Session with gays criticized.
10. Harkavy, Come to Jesus.
11. Japenga, Ann (1987). It's called change counseling. *The Los Angeles Times*, December 6.
12. Ibid.
13. Culver, Sessions with gays criticized.
14. Japenga, It's called change counseling.
15. Ibid.
16. Pietrzyk, The ex-files.
17. Japenga, It's called change counseling.
18. Culver, Sessions with gays criticized.
19. In the case *Romer v. Evans*, the Supreme Court ruled in 1996 that Amendment 2 was unconstitutional, giving the lesbian and gay community a historic victory.
20. Culver, Virginia (1995). Cook: "Emotional wounding" creates gays. *Denver Post*, October 27.
21. Culver, Sessions with gays criticized.
22. Harkavy, Come to Jesus.
23. Ibid.
24. Culver, Sessions with gays criticized.
25. Harkavy, Come to Jesus.
26. Ibid.

The Propagandists

1. 3Z Hourglass Productions (1993). *One Nation Under God*. Video.
2. Ibid.

3. Moberly, Elizabeth (1983). *Homosexuality: A New Christian Ethic.* Greenwood, SC: The Attic Press, Inc.

4. 3Z Hourglass Productions, *One Nation Under God.*

5. Nicolosi, Joe (1997). *Reparative Therapy of Male Homosexuality.* Northvale, NJ: Aronson Press, p. 105.

6. E-mail interview with Billy Bean, March 28, 2001.

7. Moberly, *Homosexuality: A New Christian Ethic,* p. 9.

8. Ibid., p. 32.

9. Ibid., p. 31.

10. Ibid., pp. 35-36.

11. See, for example, <http://www.biblebelievers.com/Cameron2.html> and <http://www.hatecrime.org/subpages/hatespeech/cameron.html>.

12. Harkavy, Ward (1996). Slay it with a smile: Paul Cameron's mission to stop homosexuality is hard to swallow. *Denver Westward,* October 3.

13. Walter, D. (1985). Paul Cameron. *The Advocate,* October 29, pp. 28-33.

14. Harkavy, Slay it with a smile.

15. Ibid.

16. Ibid.

17. Ibid.

18. Price, Kim (1982). Lincoln voters defeat gay rights issue. Associated Press, May 12.

19. Pietrzyk, Mark E. (1994). Queer science: Paul Cameron, professional sham. *The New Republic,* October 3.

20. Daniel, Leon (1985). The sideshow at a conservatives' convention. United Press International, March 1.

21. Gonnerman, Jennifer (1996). The anti-abortion stealth campaign. *On the Issues* 5(4)(Fall), pp. 20-23.

22. Daniel, Sideshow at a conservatives' convention.

23. Ibid.

24. Daniel, Sideshow at a conservatives' convention.

25. Rivera, Geraldo (1992). Gay youth who attend their high school proms. *Geraldo,* June 22.

26. Olsen, Walter (1997). William Bennett, gays and the truth. *Slate Magazine,* December 18.

27. Ibid.

28. Ibid.

29. ABC (1997). *This Week,* November 9.

30. Bennett, William (1998). Correspondence. *The New Republic,* February 23, p. 4.

31. Cimons, Marlene (1985). Dannemeyer hires AIDS quarantine advocate. *Los Angeles Times,* August 20.

32. Harkavy, Slay it with a smile.

33. Nebraska Psychological Association (1984). Minutes of the Nebraska Psychological Association meeting, October 19. See <www.psychology.ucdavis.edu/.../html/facts_cameron_sheet.html>.

34. Sociology group criticizes work of Paul Cameron (1985). *Lincoln Star,* September 10.

35. *Baker v. Wade*, 106 Federal Rules Decisions, 1985.

36. Church leaders shun gay dance hall, cite AIDS scare (1986). United Press International, January 24.

37. California originals 1: Bill Dannemeyer for beginners (1991). *The Hotline*, February 20; See also Reyes, David, and Cimon, Marlene (1985). Gays assail Dannemeyer for hiring researcher. *Los Angeles Times*, August 20.

38. Colker, David (1993). Videotape: Critics say figures on sex practices cited by doctor are not reliable. *The Los Angeles Times*, February 22.

39. Reed, Christopher (1993). Gay facts video has suspect origins. *Calgary Herald*, February 24.

40. Ibid.

41. Rivera, Gay youth who attend their high school proms.

42. Calhoun, Patricia (1994). This means war. *Denver Westword*, July 6; Harkavy, Slay it with a smile.

43. Paul Cameron moved his Family Research Institute headquarters from Washington to Lakespur, Colorado—near Colorado Springs—in 1995.

44. Harkavy, Slay it with a smile.

45. Harkavy, Ward (1998). Fact or friction? The ex-gay movement has its straight man—But ex-ex-gays may have the last laugh. *Denver Westword*, October 1.

46. Harkavy, Slay it with a smile.

47. Dreyfuss, Robert (1999). The holy war on gays. *Rolling Stone*, March 18.

Historic Injustice

1. NARTH (2000). Treatment: Impact and Change. Annual conference, Washington, DC, November 18-19.

2. Bob Knight currently works for Concerned Women of America.

3. Lewes, Kenneth (1988). *Psychoanalysis and Male Homosexuality*. New York: Simon and Schuster, pp. 19-20. Freud's use of the word *perversion* would today earn him a picket line in front of his office, and most certainly would keep him from receiving a Gay & Lesbian Alliance Against Defamation media award. In his day, however, this word was often used in its technical sense to mean a "disturbance in development earlier than the phallic Oedipal crisis." However, he believed this so-called disturbance was based on constitutional factors that were a natural part of psychological development for some people. Furthermore, Freud usually avoided calling homosexuality a perversion and took great care to call it "inversion," which gave it its own separate classification. Sadly, Freud's inconsistencies in areas such as these gave antigay "scientists" in later years ammunition to denigrate gay people.

4. Ibid., p. 22.

5. Interview with Jack Drescher, taped, no date recorded. All quotes are from this interview unless otherwise noted.

6. Lewes, *Psychoanalysis and Male Homosexuality*, p. 85.

7. Ibid., p. 137.

8. Ibid., p. 103.

9. Ibid., p. 134.

10. Ibid.

11. Ibid., p. 137.

12. Ibid., p. 183.

13. Ibid., p. 157.

14. Ibid., p. 102.

15. Ibid., p. 141.

16. Ibid.

17. Bieber, Irving (1962). *Homosexuality: A Psychoanalytic Study of Male Homosexuals.* New York: Basic Books.

18. Clendinen, Dudley and Adam Nagourney (1999). *Out for Good: The Struggle to Build a Gay Rights Movement in America.* New York: Simon and Schuster, p. 211.

19. CBS (1967). *CBS Reports,* March 7. "The Homosexuals." See also Ostrow, Joanne (1998). '67 fear, loathing revisited: Homosexuality topic of CBS show. *The Denver Post,* October 13.

20. This is the same Mike Wallace who is one of the stars of CBS's popular television show *60 Minutes.*

21. Alwood, Edward (1996). *Straight News.* New York: Columbia University Press, p. 73.

22. A-Pix Entertainment (1997). *Out of the Past.* Video.

23. In aversion therapy, a doctor will show erotic pictures to a homosexual and either shock him or her or use drugs to cause nausea when arousal occurs. The goal of this behavioral psychology is to create a negative association between a homosexual and the object he or she desires, thus putting an end to homosexual behavior.

24. Alwood, *Straight News,* p. 125.

25. Ibid., p. 126.

26. Clendinen and Nagourney, *Out for Good,* p. 209.

27. Charles Socarides's son, Richard, is gay and served as the gay liaison in the Clinton White House.

28. Clendinen and Nagourney, *Out for Good,* p. 216.

Nicolosi's Nonsense

1. Fox News Channel (2000). Is homosexuality a condition curable by therapy? *Hannity & Colmes,* August 8. Quoted material is from this show.

2. Heller, Matthew (1998). Getting straight. *New Times Los Angeles,* November 19.

3. The school, now based in Alhambra, California, is housed on four campuses throughout California, and its mission statement advocates "combating discrimination in all its forms, especially heterosexism."

4. Holland, Gale (1998). Seeking the heterosexual within. *LA Weekly,* August 21.

5. CNBC (1998). *Equal Time,* July 21.

6. Heller, Getting straight.

7. Ibid.

8. Ibid.

9. See <http://www.narth.com/docs/wanted.html>.

10. Satinover, Jeffrey (1996). *Homosexuality and the Politics of Truth.* Grand Rapids, MI: Baker Books, p. 194.

11. Lively, Scott (1995). *The Pink Swastika.* Keizer, OR: Founders Publishing Corporation, p. iv.

12. Weiss, Rick (1997). Psychologists reconsider gay "conversion" therapy: Group's proposal seeks to curb such treatment. *The Washington Post,* August 14.

13. Heller, Getting straight.

14. Ibid.

15. Interview with Tod LoRusso, taped, January 7, 2000. All quotes are from this interview unless otherwise noted. Also, the story of Inside Nicolosi's Lair, later in this chapter, is based on this interview.

16. Human Rights Campaign (2000). *Finally Free—Personal Stories: How Love and Self-Acceptance Saved Us from the Ex-Gay Ministries.* Washington, DC: Author.

17. Schlachter, Barry (1998). Breaking souls or breaking chains. *The Fort Worth Star-Telegram,* October 18.

18. Nicolosi, Joe (1997). *Reparative Therapy of Male Homosexuality.* Northvale, NJ: Aronson Press, p. 149.

19. Weiss, Psychologists reconsider gay "conversion" therapy.

20. Ibid.

21. Colbert, Chuck (1997). Psychologists take aim at conversion therapy. ANS News Service, August 20.

22. Weiss, Psychologists reconsider gay "conversion" therapy.

23. Roth, Catherine (2001). Amnesty says gay abuse rampant. Associated Press, June 22.

24. Pela, Robert L. (1997). Boys in the dollhouse, girls with toy trucks. *The Advocate,* November 11.

25. Schoofs, Mark (1998). Straight to hell. *The Village Voice,* August 11.

26. Duin, Julia (1998). Ministries attracting criticism over attempts to change gays. *The Washington Times,* March 3.

27. Nicolosi, *Reparative Therapy of Male Homosexuality,* p. 8.

28. Ibid., p. 9.

29. Ibid., p. 12.

30. Healy, Melissa (2001). Pieces of the puzzle. *Los Angeles Times,* May 21.

31. E-mail interview with Chandler Burr, May 7, 2001.

32. Interview with Simon LeVay, taped, no date recorded. All quotes are from this interview unless otherwise noted.

33. LeVay, Simon (1991). A difference in hypothalamic structure between heterosexual and homosexual men. *Science,* August.

34. Bailey, John M. and Richard Pillard (1991). A genetic study of male sexual orientation. *Archives of General Psychiatry,* December.

35. Hamer, Dean et al. at the National Cancer Institute (1993). A linkage between DNA markers on the X chromosome and male sexual orientation. *Science,* July.

36. Healy, Pieces of the puzzle.

37. Ibid.
38. Healy, Pieces of the puzzle.
39. E-mail interview with Tim Bergling, May 7, 2001.
40. Nicolosi, *Reparative Therapy of Male Homosexuality,* p. 165.
41. Ibid., p. 201.
42. Ibid., p. 33.
43. Ibid., p. 38.
44. Ibid., p. 37.
45. Ibid., p. 38.
46. Ibid., p. 39
47. Ibid., p. 104.
48. Ibid., p. 58.
49. Ibid., p. 238.
50. Lochhead, Carolyn (1997). Conservatives brand homosexuality a tragic affliction. *San Francisco Chronicle,* June 20.
51. CNBC (1997). *Equal Time,* December 30.
52. Nicolosi, *Reparative Therapy of Male Homosexuality,* p. 8.
53. Ibid., p. 98.
54. Ibid., p. 103.
55. Ibid., p. 100.
56. Ibid., p. 101.
57. Ibid., p. 243.
58. Ibid., p. 274.
59. Ibid., p. 193.
60. Ibid., p. 314.
61. Leland, John and Mark Miller (1998). Can gays convert? *Newsweek,* August 17.
62. Heller, Getting straight.
63. Interview with Jack Drescher, taped, no date recorded.

Radical Richard

1. Wesleyan Christian Community Church Web site, <http://fic.ic.org/cmag/92/3992.html>.
2. Associated Press (1977). January 6.
3. Ibid.
4. See <http://fic.ic.org/cmag/92/3992.html>.
5. United Press International (1983). July 15.
6. Interview with Richard Cohen, taped, March 15, 2001. All quotes are from this interview unless otherwise noted.
7. Cohen, Richard (2000). *Coming Out Straight: Understanding and Healing Homosexuality.* Winchester, VA: Oakhill Press, p. x.
8. Background information on Cohen was compiled from material in his book, *Coming Out Straight* (see note 7), our interview (see note 6), and from talking to people who knew him within the ex-gay ministries.

9. Ibid., p. 4.

10. Ibid., p. 5.

11. Ibid., p. 6.

12. Ibid., p. 7.

13. Ibid., p. 8.

14. Ibid.

15. Ibid.

16. Ibid., p. 9.

17. Ibid.

18. Ibid.

19. Ibid., p. 10.

20. Ibid., p. 11.

21. Ibid.

22. Ibid., p. 12.

23. Ibid., p. 13.

24. Ibid., p. 239. See also <http://www.gaytostraight.org>.

25. Ibid., p. 24.

26. CNN (1994). Can homosexuality be cured? *Larry King Live,* June 9.

27. Cohen, *Coming Out Straight,* p. 35.

28. Ibid., p. 45.

29. Ibid., p. 174.

30. Ibid., p. 114.

31. Ibid., p. 17.

32. Ibid., p. 78.

33. Ibid., p. 102.

34. Ibid, p. 49. During our interview, Cohen apologized for using Cameron's statistics. He promised to remove them from the next edition of *Coming Out Straight.* Let's hope this is a promise he keeps.

35. Franklin, Karen (1998). Study of 500 community college students, August 25. See <http://www.apa.org/ppo/issues/pfranklin.html> or <http://www.karenfranklin.com/> for a summary of her work.

36. MTV (1999). Hate crime study. Press release, April 6.

37. Who's Who Among American High School Students (1998). Poll, November 12.

38. Healy, Patrick (2001). Suicides in state top homicides. *The Boston Globe,* February 28.

39. Cohen, *Coming Out Straight,* p. 162.

40. Ibid., p. 128.

41. Paulk, John (1998). *Not Afraid to Change: The Remarkable Story of How One Man Overcame Homosexuality.* Mukilteo, WA: WinePress Publishing, p. 195.

42. Cohen, *Coming Out Straight,* p. 123.

43. Ibid., pp. 123-125.

44. Ibid., pp. 50-51.

45. Ibid., p. 52.

46. Phone interview with Harold Lief, April 10, 2001.

47. E-mail interview with Elizabeth Loftus, no date recorded.

48. E-mail interview with Pam Freyd, April 11, 2001.

49. NARTH (2000). Treatment: Impact and Change. Annual conference, November 18-19.

50. Cohen, *Coming Out Straight*, p. 153.

51. Ibid., p. 103.

52. Loftus, Elizabeth (2000). The most dangerous book. *Psychology Today* 33(6) (November 1), p. 32.

53. Ibid.

54. Cohen, *Coming Out Straight*, p. 160.

55. Ibid., p. 163.

56. Ibid., p. 128.

57. Ibid., p. 53.

58. Ibid., p. 139.

59. Ibid., pp. 197, 224, 59-60.

The Puppeteers

1. Gerson, Michael J. (1998). A righteous indignation. *U.S. News and World Report*, May 4.

2. Ibid.

3. On June 4, 1999, Clinton made a controversial "recess" appointment while Congress was out of session. Secretary of State Madeline Albright swore Hormel in at the State Department. By nearly all accounts, Hormel did a terrific job and served our nation admirably. Despite the warnings by the GOP senators who held his nomination, there is no evidence that Luxembourg is gayer today as a result of his ambassadorship.

4. America's Voice (1998). *The Right Side with Armstrong Williams*, June 15. Reaired as part of ABC (1998). Homosexuality, morality, and politics. *ABC Nightline*, July 30.

5. Boston, Rob (1999). The religious right's gay agenda. *Church and State*, October 1; Russell, Ron (1998). Gay-bashing for dollars. *The New York Times*, September 3; Schindehette, Susan (1998). Straight up. *People*, November 30.

6. Russell, Ron (1998). Gay bashing for dollars. *New Times Los Angeles*, September 3.

7. Kramer, Linda (1998). Straight up. *People*, November 30.

8. Heaton, Michael (1998). Onward Christian Folger. *The Plain Dealer*, November 8.

9. Folger, Janet (1999). Yes, stations that bow to the gay lobby are guilty of censorship and intolerance. *Insight on the News*, June 28.

10. Yearwood, Lori Teresa (1998). True believer: She's youthful and hip, but don't underestimate Janet Folger. As the architect of a national ad campaign urging homosexuals to change, this activist for the religious right is a force to be reckoned with. *Miami Herald*, August 12.

11. Goodstein, Laurie (1998). The architect of the "gay conversion" campaign. *The New York Times*, August 13.

12. Interview with Elizabeth Birch, taped, July 25, 2001. All quotes are from this interview unless otherwise noted.

13. Human Rights Campaign (1998). Coalition responds to anti-gay ad campaign with full-page ad in national newspaper. Press release, July 14.

14. Kornblut, Anne E. (1998). Boston doctor says ads distort his work on gays. *The Boston Globe,* August 4.

15. Interview with Joan Garry, taped, July 17, 2001. All quotes are from this interview unless otherwise noted.

16. For the full text of White's remarks before the Wisconsin State Assembly, see <http://my.execpc.com/~dross/aw/regwhite.html>. This site also provides directions on how to access the original document online.

17. Davis, James (2000). Gays, blacks rally against shared foes. *Sun-Sentinel* (Fort Lauderdale), July 22.

18. Ibid.

19. Dreyfuss, Robert (1999). The holy war on gays. *Rolling Stone,* March 18.

20. People for the American Way (1998). Press release, October 9.

21. Rousseau, J. (2000). The Pontiff, Pat Robertson, and G.W. Bush all need to get real about their racist sins. *Politics Today,* March 24.

22. Grant, George and Mark A. Horne (1993). *Legislating Immorality: The Homosexual Movement Comes Out of the Closet.* Chicago, IL: Moody Press, p. 4.

23. Kennedy, D. James and Jim Nelson Black (1994). *Character & Destiny: A Nation in Search of Its Soul.* Grand Rapids, MI: Zondervan, pp. 126-127.

24. Folger, Janet (1999). Reclaim America with the truth. *Coral Ridge Presbyterian Communicator* 9(2).

25. Folger, Janet (1998). Gay-rights activists don't permit same free speech they demand. *Sun-Sentinel* (Fort Lauderdale), August 3.

26. NPR (1998). *All Things Considered,* with Lynn Neary and Linda Wertheimer, July 17.

27. ABC (1998). Homosexuality morality and politics. *Nightline,* July 30.

28. Interview with Natalie Davis, taped, April 22, 2001.

29. The fantastic discrepancy in the cost of the television ad campaign comes from the fact that key members of the antigay coalition gave wildly different figures. Ex-gay Anthony Falzarano told the *Baltimore City Paper,* "They've [the Pro-Family Forum] raised $4 million and counting." In a meeting with ex-gays, according to an undercover source of mine, Phil Burress, president of Citizens for Community Values, based in Cincinnati, said between $1 million and $2 million was raised for the campaign. Janet Folger, later trying to downplay the fund-raising campaign, said that they planned to spend only $250,000.

30. Henderson was convicted and is currently serving two life terms. McKinney was also convicted on two counts of felony murder. McKinney could have received a death sentence, but the Shepards, in deference to Matt's views on the death penalty, in an amazing display of compassion, elected not to pursue capital punishment. McKinney was sentenced to life in prison without parole.

31. NBC (1998). *Today Show,* with Katie Couric, October 13.

32. See the HRC press release for October 15, 1998, at <http://www.hrc.org/newsreleases/1998/981015mattshepard.asp>.

33. Bull, Chris and John Gallagher (2001). *Perfect Enemies.* Lanham, MD: Madison Books, p. 274.

34. NBC, *Today Show,* October 13.

35. Rosin, Hanna (1999). Ads seeking to convert gays from lifestyle debut here. *The Washington Post,* May 11.

36. Ibid.

37. Benjamin, Jody A. (1998). Gay conversion theory sparks controversy, protest. *Sun-Sentinel* (Fort Lauderdale), September 7.

38. Pietrzyk, Mark E. (2000). Pathology of the ex-gay movement. *Gay and Lesbian Review,* Summer.

39. Pietrzyk, Mark E. (1999). The ex-files: Not your usual gays. *Independent Gay Forum,* October 19.

40. ABC (1998). Christian conservative ads. *Good Morning America,* July 14.

41. Falzarano, Anthony (1998). TCM and P-Fox receive two matching grants totaling $80,000!!! *P-Fox/Transformation Press,* October.

42. Falwell urges America's gay capital to walk away from homosexuality (1999). Associated Press, October 12.

43. Pietrzyk, Not your usual gays.

44. Buchanan and the fringe (1996). *Charleston Gazette,* March 30.

45. *Asheville Citizen-Times,* June 15, 1998.

46. Pietrzyk, Not your usual gays.

47. Interview with Alan Chambers, taped, March 11, 2001.

48. Thomas, Randy (1999). My response to Coral Ridge. See <www.justice. respect.org>.

49. Cole, Tom (1999). Anti-gay harassment must end. *Sun-Sentinel* (Fort Lauderdale), December 6.

50. Duin, Julia (2001). CUA cancels conference of ex-homosexuals. *The Washington Times,* June 8.

Political *Science*

1. Clendinen, Dudley and Adam Nagourney (1999). *Out for Good: The Struggle to Build a Gay Rights Movement in America.* New York: Simon and Schuster, p. 209.

2. Phone conversations with Robert Spitzer, no dates recorded. All quotes are from these conversations unless otherwise noted.

3. Spitzer, Robert (2001). Can some gay men and lesbians change their sexual orientation? 200 subjects reporting a change from homosexual to heterosexual orientation.

4. Duin, Julia (2001). New psychiatric study says gays can alter orientation. *The Washington Times,* May 9.

5. Ibid.

6. Adams, Henry E. (1996). Is homophobia associated with homosexual arousal? *Journal of Abnormal Psychology* 105(3), pp. 440-445.

7. Besen, Wayne (1999). HRC letter to Dr. Spitzer.

8. See <www.narth.com>.

9. Spitzer, Robert L. (2000). Letter to Dr. Joseph Nicolosi, March 15. A copy of this letter was mailed to this author by Spitzer.

10. Barlow, Gary (2000). Ex-gay flap at APA meeting orchestrated by antigay activists. *Dallas Voice,* May.

11. Ritter, Malcolm (2001). Study: Some gays can go straight. Associated Press, May 9.

12. Duin, New psychiatric study.

13. McFeeley, Tim (2001). NGLTF responds to flawed Spitzer study on so-called reparative therapy. National Gay and Lesbian Task Force press release, May 8.

14. Human Rights Campaign (2001). New conversion study is biased and unscientific. Press release, May 10.

15. Sheldon, Louis (2001). Noted psychiatrist says homosexuals can change! Traditional Values Coalition press release, May 9.

16. Falwell, Jerry (2001). Can "gays" really change? *Falwell Confidential,* May 10; Nicolosi, Joseph (2001). New research shows homosexuals can change. *Family Research Council Culture Facts,* May 11.

17. Talan, Jamie (2001). Study of gays flawed? Researcher: Therapy helps change orientation. *Newsday,* May 10.

18. Ibid.

19. APA statement in response to media articles regarding alleged changes in sexual orientation reported at APA annual meeting (2001). U.S. Newswire, May 9.

20. CBS (1995). Faith and politics: the Christian Right. *CBS Reports,* with Dan Rather, September 7; Hausman, Ken (2001). Furor erupts over study on sexual orientation. *Psychiatric News,* July 6.

21. Gay.com (2001). May 10.

22. E-mail interview with Robert Spitzer, May 16, 2001.

23. Bull, Chris (2001). Much ado about changing. *The Advocate,* June 19.

Future Follies and Failures

1. Exodus (2000). Exodus launches youth ministry. Press release, November 7.

2. Interview with Caitlin Ryan, taped, no date recorded. All quotes are from this interview unless otherwise noted.

3. See <http://www.scottlively.com/sevensteps/>.

4. Ibid.

5. American Family Association (2001). *Truth for Youth* bible evangelism. Action alert, August 9.

6. LeBlanc, Douglas (2002). Ex-gay sheds the mocking quote marks. *Christianity Today,* January 7.

7. Interview with Reverend Michael Piazza, taped, no date recorded.

8. Exodus International, <http://www.exoduseurope.org/index.html>.

9. For more on Mugabe's antigay policies, see, for example, <http://www.obv.org.uk/reports/2002/antigaymugabe.html>; for insight into Robertson's dealings with Taylor, check out King, Colbert I. (2001). Pat Robertson and his business buddies. *The Washington Post,* November 10.

10. For more information on discrimination in Saudi Arabia, see, for example, <http://www.gay.com/0175web/NewsBeheadings175.html> and <http://www.house.gov/lantos/caucus/TestimonyGreenwood060402.html>.

11. *Parents and Friends Press* (2001). 49(Spring), p. 3.

12. E-mail interview with Ralph Blair, October 25, 2001.

13. Interview with Mel White, taped, July 17, 2001.

14. Wockner, Rex (2001). Lily Tomlin comes out. *Windy City Times,* January 17.

15. Mason, Margie (2000). Concern for gay runaways in California. Associated Press, November 29.

16. Interview with Reverend Troy Perry, taped, no date recorded.

BIBLIOGRAPHY

Allen, C. (1958). *Homosexuality: Its Nature, Causation and Treatment*. New York: Citadel Press.

Alwood, Edward (1996). *Straight News: Gays, Lesbians, and the News Media*. New York: Columbia University Press.

Andre, Wayne and Balsiger, David (1993). *Face in the Mirror*. South Plainfield, NJ: Bridge Publishing.

Bagemihl, Bruce (1999). *Biological Exuberance: Animal Homosexuality and Natural Diversity*. New York: St. Martin's Press.

Bieber, Irving (1962). *Homosexuality: A Psychoanalytic Study of Male Homosexuals*. New York: Basic Books.

Boston, Robert (2000). *Close Encounters with the Religious Right: Journey into the Twilight Zone of Religion and Politics*. Amherst, NY: Prometheus Books.

Burr, Chandler (1996). *A Separate Creation: The Search for the Biological Origins of Sexual Orientation*. New York: Hyperion.

Chamberlain, Jonathan M. (1978). *Eliminate Your SDBs: Self-Defeating Behaviors*. Provo, UT: Brigham Young University Press.

Clendinen, Dudley and Nagourney, Adam (1999). *Out for Good: The Struggle to Build a Gay Rights Movement in America*. New York: Simon and Schuster.

Cohen, Richard (2000). *Coming Out Straight: Understanding and Healing Homosexuality*. Winchester, VA: Oakhill Press.

Comiskey, Andrew (1989). *Pursuing Sexual Wholeness: How Jesus Heals the Homosexual*. Lake Mary, FL: Creation House.

Consiglio, Bill (2000). *Homosexual No More*. Baltimore, MD: Regeneration Books.

Dallas, Joe (1991). *Desires in Conflict: Answering the Struggle for Sexual Identity*. Eugene, OR: Harvest House Publishing.

Davies, Bob and Rentzel, Lori (1993). *Coming Out of Homosexuality: New Freedom for Men and Women*. Downers Grove, IL: InterVarsity Press.

D'Emilio, John (1983). *Sexual Politics, Sexual Communities: The Making of a Homosexual Minority in the United States, 1940-1970.* Chicago, IL: The University of Chicago Free Press.

Dobson, Ed and Thomas, Cal (1999). *Blinded by Might: Why the Religious Right Can't Save America.* Grand Rapids, MI: Zondervan Publishing House.

Drescher, Jack (1998). *Psychoanalytic Therapy and the Gay Man.* Hillsdale, NJ: Analytic Press.

Duberman, Martin (1986). *About Time: Exploring the Gay Past.* New York: Meridian.

Gallagher, John and Bull, Chris (2001). *Perfect Enemies: The Battle Between the Religious Right and the Gay Movement.* Lanham, MD: Madison Books.

Grant, George and Horne, Mark A. (1993). *Legislating Immorality: The Homosexual Movement Comes Out of the Closet.* Chicago, IL: Moody Press.

Helminiak, Daniel A. (2000). *What the Bible Really Says About Homosexuality.* Tajique, NM: Alamo Square Press.

Hill, Jim and Cheadle, Rand (1996). *The Bible Tells Me So: Uses and Abuses of Holy Scripture.* New York: Bantam Doubleday.

Howard, Jeanette (2000). *Out of Egypt: One Woman's Journey Out of Lesbianism.* London, UK: Monarch Books.

Human Rights Campaign (2000). *Finally Free—Personal Stories: How Love and Self-Acceptance Saved Us from the Ex-Gay Ministries.* Washington, DC: Author.

Kirk, Marshall and Madsen, Hunter (1990). *After the Ball: How America Will Conquer Its Fear and Hatred of Gays in the '90s.* New York: Plume.

Konrad, Jeff (1998). *You Don't Have to Be Gay.* Hilo, HI: Pacific Publishing House.

Lewes, Kenneth (1988). *Psychoanalysis and Male Homosexuality.* New York: Simon and Schuster.

Liebman, Marvin (1992). *Coming Out Conservative: An Autobiography.* San Francisco, CA: Chronicle Books.

Lively, Scott (1995). *The Pink Swastika: Homosexuality in the Nazi Party.* Keizer, OR: Founders Publishing Corporation.

Medinger, Alan (2000). *Growth into Manhood: Resuming the Journey.* Colorado Springs, CO: WaterBrook Press.

Miller, Stuart H. (1999). *Prayer Warriors: The True Story of a Gay Son, His Fundamentalist Christian Family, and Their Battle for His Soul.* Los Angeles, CA: Alyson Books.

Moberly, Elizabeth (1983). *Homosexuality: A New Christian Ethic.* Greenwood, SC: The Attic Press, Inc.

Nicolosi, Joe (1997). *Reparative Therapy of Male Homosexuality: A New Clinical Approach.* Northvale, NJ: Aronson Press.

Paulk, Anne and John (1999). *Love Won Out: How God's Love Helped Two People Leave Homosexuality and Find Each Other.* Wheaton, IL: Tyndale.

Paulk, John (1998). *Not Afraid to Change: The Remarkable Story of How One Man Overcame Homosexuality.* Mukilteo, WA: WinePress Publishing.

Payne, Leanne (1993). *The Broken Image: Restoring Personal Wholeness Through Healing Prayer.* Wheaton, IL: Crossway Books.

Peck, Scott (1995). *All American Boy: A Memoir.* New York: Scribner.

Pennington, Sylvia (1989). *Ex-Gays? There Are None.* Hawthorne, CA: Lambda Christian Fellowship.

Philpott, Kent (1975). *The Third Sex? Six Homosexuals Tell Their Stories.* London: Good Reading Ltd. Hbk.

Piazza, Michael, S. (1997). *Holy Homosexuals: The Truth About Being Gay and Christian.* Dallas, TX: Sources of Hope Publishing.

Satinover, Jeffrey (1996). *Homosexuality and the Politics of Truth.* Grand Rapids, MI: Baker Books.

Signorile, Michelangelo (1993). *Queer in America: Sex, the Media, and the Closets of Power.* New York: Random House.

Stephenson, Jerry (2000). *Out of the Closet and into the Light: Clearing Up the Myths and Giving Answers About Gays and Lesbians.* Lincoln, NE: Writers Club Press.

White, Mel (1994). *Stranger at the Gate: To Be Gay and Christian in America.* New York: Plume.

INDEX

Abortion, political opposition to, 198-199, 224
Abrams, Kevin E., 137
Adams, Henry E., penile plethysmograph study, 230
Addiction, Exodus testimonials, 42
Adolescents
ex-gay ministries, 40
Exodus International, 246
GLBT support, 267-268
The Advocate, 9
Cameron, Paul, 106
Nicolosi, Joseph, 142
Richards, Wade, 78, 79
AIDS
Cameron's crusade, 108-109
crisis and Moberly, Elizabeth, 103, 104
fundamentalist view of, 99-100
religious healing, 47
Alcohol abuse, Exodus testimonials, 42
Alfie's Home, antigay children's book, 249
Almond, Brent, on orientation change, 37
Amendment 2, CFV campaign, 95-96
American Enterprise Institute, 110
American Family Association (AFA)
antigay cartoons, 248-249
Cameron's "studies," 112

American Medical Association, GLF action, 130
American Psychiatric Association (APA)
conservative psychiatrists, 145
and gay rights movement, 130
and homosexuality, 61, 130, 131
American Psychological Association (APA)
Cameron investigation, 110-111
on informed consent, 140-141
on reparative therapy, 152, 202
American Sociological Association, on Paul Cameron, 111
American Spectator, child molestation, 34
Americans for Truth, 77
Amnesty International report (2001), on reparative therapy, 142
Armey, Dick, 196, 197
Association for the Advancement of Behavior Therapy, GAA protest, 227-228
Audio tapes, orientation change, 32
Austin, Christopher, 182-183
Aversion, B-SADD, 175, 176-179

Bailey, John M.
biological causation, 147
homosexual traits, 149-150

Bakker, Jim, reordaining, 113
Bean, Billy
    gay athlete, 154
    on gender identification, 101-102
Bennett, William, Cameron's mortality
        statistics, 110
Bergler, Edmund, 125-126
Bergling, Tim, 150
Besen, Wayne
    coming out experience, *xiii-xv*
    Hannity & Colmes show, 133-134
    The Roseanne Show, 217, 218
    SALT show, 72-73, 77-78
Bieber, Irving
    American Psychiatric Association,
        130, 131
    CBS Reports, 128
    on homosexuality, 126, 127
Bioenergetics, B-SADD techniques,
        186
Birch, Elizabeth
    on Folger, Janet, 224
    HRC press conference, 211
    on opposition, 200-201
    on Shepard's death, 213, 214
Bizarre techniques, B-SADD, 175,
        184-189
Blackorby, Harold, 112
Blair, Ralph
    on GLBT community, 263
    on Moberly, Elizabeth, 100
    on religious inclusion, 261
Bless the Beast and the Children, 88
"Body image wounds," 173
Bridges Across, 272
The Broken Image, 26, 43-44, 184
Broken Yoke Ministries, leadership,
        38-39
B-SADD, therapy techniques, 175-189
Bull, Chris, 9
    Richards, Wade, story, 78
    on Shepard's death, 214
    Spitzer, Robert, interview, 241
Burr, Chandler, 146
Bussee, Michael
    background, 82-83

Bussee, Michael *(continued)*
    current life, 91
    and Exodus International, 81, 86-88,
        97, 99
    homosexual identity, 88-89
    marriages of, 84-85, 87, 89-90
    and Melodyland Christian Center,
        81, 83-84, 85-86

Cameron, Paul
    antigay rhetoric, 104, 105, 112
    antigay "studies," 105-108,
        110-112, 113
    attacks on AIDS victims, 109-110
    decline of influence, 114-115, 134
    and ex-gay ministries, *x,* 100
    investigation of, 110-111
    on sex, 115-116
Campus Crusade for Christ, antigay
        rhetoric, 104
Carter, Bob, Center for Reclaiming
        America for Christ, 215
Cathedral of Hope, gay church, 250
Catholic Church, on homosexuality, 51
Cendo, Rick, Tebedo attack on, 97
Center for Reclaiming America for
        Christ
    and Carter, Bob, 215
    Exodus International break, 220-221
    and Folger, Janet, 200
Chambers, Alan
    on antigay coalition, 215, 220-221
    and Exodus International, 245-246,
        250, 252
    on fundamentalist role, 50
    on honeymoon, 57
    on orientation change, 35
Chambers, Leslie
    on fundamentalist role, 50
    on honeymoon, 57
The Changing of the Guard, 207
Chibbaro, Lou, 9
Child Molestation and Homosexuality,
        107-108

Children
 antigay propaganda, 248-249
 antigay steps, 247-248
 and Exodus International, 246-247
 homosexual traits, 149-150
 reparative therapy, 142-143
 sexual assault, 162
Christian Coalition
 fratricidal power struggles, 101
 political influence of, 198
 Robertson's resignation, 234
Christianity
 antigay bias, 143
 and mental illness, 43-46
Church of the Open Door, 62, 66
Civil rights movement, and gays,
     205-206
Clendinen, Dudley, 228
Clinton, Bill
 Defense of Marriage Act, 198
 Hormel nomination, 196-197
 workplace discrimination ban, 197
Codependency, Exodus testimonials, 43
Cohen, Richard
 Alfie's Home, 249
 background of, 164, 167
 B-SADD therapy, 175-189
 homosexual causation theories,
     170-175
 and International Healing
     Foundation, 169-170
 marriage of, 166, 167, 169
 and NARTH, 159, 163, 164
 and NARTH conference, 120-121
 and PFOX, 223
 revelation of, 168
 sexual orientation, 164-166, 167,
     168
 on Socarides, Charles, 184
 and Spitzer, Robert, 232, 233
 SSAD, 171
 success rate, 190-192
 Wesleyan Christian Community
     Church, 163, 169
Cohn, Roy, and Anthony Falzarano,
     217

Cole, James K., on Paul Cameron, 107
Cole, Tom, on Coral Ridge, 222
Colmes, Alan, SALT show, 72-73
Colorado for Family Values (CFV),
     95-96
Colorado Springs Gazette, John Paulk
     story, 14-15
Comic strips, antigay, 248-249
*Coming Out Straight: Understanding
     and Healing Homosexuality,*
     35, 120, 163, 164, 171-172,
     176
Comiskey, Andrew
 on Desert Stream leadership, 39
 on "spiritual disfigurement," 52-53
Committee to Oppose Special Rights
     for Homosexuals, 106-107
Conner, Ken, FRC, 224
Connorton, Ellen, 179
Consiglio, Bill, *Homosexual No More,*
     29
Cook, Colin
 Amendment 2 campaign, 95-96
 background of, 93-94
 and HA, 94-95, 189
 at press conference, 96-97
Cooper, Gary
 and Exodus International, 81, 86-88,
     98, 99
 homosexual identity of, 88-89
 marriages of, 89, 90
 and Melodyland Christian Center,
     81, 85, 86
Coral Ridge Presbyterian Church
 criticism of, 221-222
 and Kennedy, D. James, 200,
     206-207
 and reconstructionists, 207-208
Courage, Catholic Church, 51
Courage, Exodus International
     ministry, 91-92
Couric, Katie, 213
Covert operation, opinions on, 265-267
Crain, Chris, 9-10

Dallas, Joe, on orientation change, 35, 37

Dannemeyer, William, and Paul Cameron, 113

Daughters of Bilitis, APA conference, 130

Davies, Bob, Exodus International, 16-17, 219, 245, 252

Davis, Natalie
on ex-gay ministries, 222
on obedience, 49
on orientation change, 35, 38

Davis, Sillman, on orientation change, 38

Defense of Marriage Act, 198

Defensive detachment
causation theory, 100-101, 149, 150
and Jesus Christ, 103

DeGeneres, Ellen, on Shepard vigil, 214

Denial, reparative therapy, 157

The Denver Post, Colin Cook, 96

Denver Westword
on Cameron, Paul, 107, 111
on Cook, Colin, 96

Desert Stream, lawsuit against, 39

Diagnostic and Statistical Manual of Mental Disorders, on homosexuality, 130, 131

Disassociation, B-SADD, 175, 179-181

Distraction, B-SADD, 175, 181-183

Dobson, James
political influence, 195-196, 197, 223
publications of, 135-136
right-wing empire, 18-19

Drescher, Jack, 123, 132, 159

Dunamis Ministries, 46

Eldredge, John, Focus on the Family, 115

Electric shock treatment, reparative therapy, 139

Ellen, 264

Ellsasser, Rick, 9-10

Equal Time, Joseph Nicolosi, 135, 155

Evangelicals Concerned, evangelical fellowship, 66-67, 261

Evans, John
LIA, 62-63, 64-66
LIA critic, 66-67, 79

Evergreen, Mormon Church, 51

Ex-gay Intervention Team (EXIT), 86

Ex-gays, description of, 30

Exodus International
AIDS impact, 99
antigay political activity, 192
and Bussee, Michael, 81, 86-88, 97, 99
Chambers' leadership, 215, 245-246, 253, 258
and Cooper, Gary, 81, 86-88, 98, 99
Davies' leadership, 16-17, 219, 245, 252
as ex-gay support group, 27-30
formation of, 81, 86-87
global expansion of, 250-252
in Great Britain, 91-93
incorrect phone numbers, 219
and Moberly, Elizabeth, 100, 254-255
ministerial testimonies, 55-56
ministry structure, 30
and NARTH, 254-256
orientation change, 31-33, 34-35, 38-39
participants, 40-42
and Paulk, John, 4, 16-17, 223
revised history of, 97, 98
Richards defection, 78
screening interview, 23-27
sexual misconduct, 39-40
southern expansion, 252
suggested reforms for, 253-259
2001 national conference, 35
Web site testimonials analysis, 42-47

Exodus Youth program, 246

FaithQuest Counseling Center, Inc., 95
False image (FI), LIA, 75, 76
False memory syndrome, 187, 265
Falwell, Jerry
    and Johnston, Michael, 218
    on religious convictions, 273
    and religious right, 18
    on Spitzer's study, 234
    on terrorist attacks, 223
Falzarano, Anthony
    criticism of political right, 221
    and ex-gay ministries, 217-218
    on former gay life, 217
    on gay orientation, 34
    hallucinations of, 44-45
    on orientation change, 32
    Parents and Friends Ministries, 223
    on Paulk, John, 17-18
    PFOX, 204, 223
    on *The Roseanne Show*, 217
    on Shepard, Matthew, 219
    and Spitzer, Robert, 236
    Washington Times, 229
Family constellations, B-SADD
        techniques, 188
Family Research Council (FRC)
    Cameron's "studies," 112
    and Falzarano, Anthony, 218, 236
    new policies of, 224
    Richards defection, 78
Family Research Institute (FRI), Paul
        Cameron, 112
Father, Nicolosi's view, 153, 154
*Finally Free—Personal Stories: How
        Love and Self-Acceptance
        Saved Us from the "Ex-Gay"
        Ministries*, 7-8, 54
Fiore, Edith, 188
Focus on the Family
    Cameron's "studies," 112
    description of, 18
    and Dobson, James, 195
    Glen Eyrie Resort conference, 115
    Homosexuality and Gender
        Department for Public
        Policy, 4

Focus on the Family *(continued)*
    immorality of, 21
    and Paulk, John, 14-15, 18-19, 22
    political influence, 198
    Richards defection, 78
    youth target, 247
Folger, Janet
    antiabortion activities, 198-199, 224
    antigay activities, 199-200, 205-206,
        207
    ex-gay ministries criticism, 220
    at HRC press conference, 211
    reconstructionist views of, 208-209
Ford, Jeff, on reparative therapy, 139
"Formers," ministries participants, 42,
        55
Foster, Darryl L., Exodus testimony, 46
Fowler, Raymond, on reparative
        therapy, 202
Fox, Earle, 223
Fraud, Paul Cameron, 111
Freud, Sigmund, 122, 123
Freyd, Pam, on intrauterine memories,
        185
Fringe Youth Outreach, Alan
        Chambers, 245
Fundamentalism
    antigay stance, *xi-xii,* 4
    authoritarianism of, 48
    as change requirement, 49-51
    and ex-gay ministries, 216-217
    ministries participants, 40-41
    third-world growth, 251

Gaffney, Mo, 155
Garcia, John, on Janet Folger, 199
Garofalo, Robert, on gay teens,
        203-204
Garry, Joan
    on ex-gay campaign, 225
    on "Gay for Life?," 204
Gay, Lesbian, and Straight Education
        Network (GLSEN),
        educational materials, 250

Gay, Lesbian, Bisexual, Transgender
    (GLBT) community
  ad campaign against, 201-207, 209
  community support, 267-268
  educational campaign, 263-264
  educational material, 249-250
  and ex-gay ministries, 259-260
  freedom of, 47
  limitations of, 269-271
  missionary work, 262-263
  political opposition to, 197-198, 200
  and religious institutions, 260-263
Gay Activists Alliance (GAA), protest
    activity, 227-228
The Gay Agenda, video, 113
Gay and Lesbian Alliance Against
    Defamation, *USA Today* ad,
    202
Gay and Unhappy, tape, *xiv-xv*
Gay liberation, role of, 61
Gay Liberation Front (GLF), AMA
    conference, 130
Gay men
  Exodus testimonials, 43
  Nicolosi's view, 154
Gay rights movement, mental health
    establishment, 130
Gay-Straight Alliances (GSAs) clubs,
    GLSEN, 250
Gender rejection, causation theory,
    101-102
Genesis Counseling, 35
Gerlott, Karl, 40
Gingrich, Newt, 195-196, 223
Gittings, Barbara, 130
Glen Eyrie Resort conference, 115
Glory House, LIA, 64
Gold, Ronald, GAA, 227-228
Grant, George, reconstructionist, 207,
    208

Haldeman, Doug, 141
Hallucinations
  Exodus testimonials, 43-46
  HRC letter, 231
  Spitzer 2001 study, 238

Hamer, Dean, genetic causation,
    147-148
Hannity & Colmes, Besen/Nicolosi
    debate, 133-134, 150
Harkavy, Ward, 107
Hartmann, Lawrence, on Spitzer study,
    235
Hefley Amendment, 197
Hellinger, Bert, 188
Henderson, Russell, 212
Herek, Gregory, 141
Herrschaft, Daryl, 3, 4
Hervey, Howard, on leadership
    misconduct, 39
Hillendahl, Louis, nude therapy,
    161-162
Hindman, Karen B., deliverance
    minister, 54
Homosexual No More, 29, 35
Homosexuality: A New Christian Ethic,
    100
*Homosexuality: A Psychoanalytic Study
    of Male Homosexuals,*
    126-127
Homosexuality
  biogenetic causation theories,
    146-150
  Cohen's theories, 170-175
  Falzarano's causation theory, 34
  LIA causation theory, 75, 76
  in the Middle East, 251
  Moberly's theories, 100-103
  and nonsexual touch, 119-120
  orientation change claims, 31-39, 64
  psychoanalytic theories of, 124-125
  and reparative therapy, 125,
    131-132
  as sin, 64
  and social policy, 127-128
  unbiased studies, 130-131
Homosexuality and Gender Department
    for Public Policy, John Paulk,
    4
*Homosexuality and the Politics of
    Truth,* 137

Homosexuals Anonymous (HA)
  AIDS impact, 99
  current status of, 97
  establishment of, 93-94
  orientation change, 37, 38
  revised history of, 97, 98
"The Homosexuals," *CBS Reports,*
  127-129
Hooker, Evelyn, 130
Hormel, James, opposition to, 196-197
Horne, Mark, 207
Howard, Jeanette, on battling Satan, 53
Human Life International conference,
  Paul Cameron, 109
Human Rights Campaign (HRC)
  budget of, 18
  and communities of faith, 261
  press conference, 211
  Shepard, Judy, 215
  Shepard vigil, 213-214
  Spitzer, letter to, 229-232
  Spitzer e-mail, 240
  on Spitzer study, 234
  USA Today ad, 202
Hypersensitivity, homosexual cause
  theory, 172-173

Independent Gay Forum, Anthony
  Falzarano, 217
Inner child work, B-SADD techniques,
  184
Inner healing, 161, 162
Institute for the Scientific Investigation
  of Sexuality (ISIS),
  establishment of, 107
International Healing Foundation,
  establishment of, 169-170
Intrauterine memories, B-SADD
  techniques, 184-186, 255

Jenkins, Sunny, on Satan, 53
Jews Offering New Alternatives to
  Homosexuality (JONAH)
  and fundamentalism, 50

Jews Offering New Alternatives to
  Homosexuality (JONAH)
  (continued)
  and NARTH, 144
Johnston, Michael
  at HRC press conference, 211
  as media star, 218-219
  Miami Herald, 203, 206
  at National Press Club, 210-211
  on overcoming homosexuality, 144
Johnston, Rebekah, Exodus testimony,
  46

Kameny, Frank, 130
Kardiner, Abram, homosexual
  stereotypes, 125
Karon, John, 110
Kaufman, Ben, NARTH, 136, 138
Kennedy, D. James
  criticism of, 220, 221-222
  on *Not Afraid to Change,* 4
  as televangelist, 200, 206-207
Kerusso Ministries, Michael Johnston,
  144, 218
King, Alveda, 206
Knight, Bob
  FRC, 224
  NARTH conference, 120
  and Nicolosi, Joseph, 136
  on Truth in Love campaign, 201
Konrad, Jeff, 48
Kopay, David, 154

LaBarbera, Peter
  Americans for Truth, 77
  FRC, 224
  on Richards, Wade, 78
Lawrence, Joan, on Janet Folger, 199
Lawrence, Patricia Allan, Exodus
  testimony, 53
Lawson, Joel, 9, 10, 11, 13
Lawson, Ron, Colin Cook
  investigation, 94, 96

Legislating Immorality: The Homosexual Movement Comes Out of the Closet, 207
Lesbians
  biological causation, 148
  Exodus testimonials, 43
LeVay, Simon, biological causation, 147
Lewes, Kenneth, 122
"Lifting the Fog" seminars, CFV, 96
Liuzzi, Peter, on Joseph Nicolosi, 136
Lively, Scott, 137, 247-248
Loftus, Elizabeth, on intrauterine memories, 185
LoRusso, Tod
  on reparative therapy, 139
  reparative therapy experience, 150-152
Lott, Trent, on homosexuality, 197
Love in Action (LIA)
  conversion program, 38
  establishment of, 62-63
  orientation change, 32, 36, 64
  Philpott leadership, 62-63, 65, 69
  program dropouts, 68-69
  Wade Richards, 74-76, 78
  Worthen leadership, 69, 70
Love Won Out, 29, 33
"Love Won Out" tour
  Paulk, John, 4-5, 247
  youth target, 247
Lucas, June, on Janet Folger, 199
Lumberger, Michael, Dunamis Ministries, 46-47

Mako, John, Mr. P's, 8
Manford, Jeanne, 109
Manning, John T., hand patterns, 148
The Map, 246
Marks, Jeremy, Courage ministry, 91-93, 222
Marmor, Judd, 131
Marriage, ex-gays, 56-57
Masculinity, Nicolosi's view, 153

Masturbation
  Exodus testimonials, 43
  fundamentalist view, 26
Matis, Stuart, suicide of, 51
McFadden, Dennis
  on gay genes, 146
  reaction to sound, 148
McIntyre, Jack, suicide of, 65-66
McKinney, Aaron, 212
Medical Consequences of What Homosexuals Do, 108
Medinger, Alan, on orientation change, 32
Melendez, Scott, on orientation change, 37
Melodyland Christian Center, 81, 83-84, 85-86
Mental health, gay rights movement, 130
Mental illness
  Exodus testimonials, 43-46
  and fundamentalism, 48
  homosexuality as, 123-127
  Nicolosi's view, 155-156
Metropolitan Community Church, role of, 71
Miami Herald, Michael Johnston, 203, 206
Military policy, Cameron's statistics, 113
Miller, Stephanie, 155
Minnery, Tom, 14
Mirin, Steven, on Spitzer study, 235
Moberly, Elizabeth
  Christian psychologist, 75, 76
  and Cohen, Richard, 170, 188
  Homosexuality: A New Christian Ethic, 100
  theories of, 100-103, 104
Monteith, Stanley, Cameron's statistics, 113
Morano, Ron, 62, 63
Mormon Church, on homosexuality, 51
Mother, Nicolosi's view, 153, 154
Mugabe, Robert, on homosexuals, 251

Mundy, Carl, 113
Murder, Violence and Homosexuality,
    108

Nagourney, Adam, 228
Nakas, Viktor, 223
"Name and claim theology," 83
Napoli, John, 36
National Association for Research and
    Therapy of Homosexuality
    (NARTH)
  antigay political activity, 192
  conference, 119-120
  and conservative psychiatrists, 138,
    145-146
  establishment, 136
  evaluation of, 254-255
  goal of, 137-138
  homosexual causation, 138, 146,
    148-149
  and intellectuals, 138, 144-145
  and Jews, 138, 143-144
  role of, 136-137
  and Spitzer, Robert, 232-233
  trade group protection, 138-143
National Gay and Lesbian Task Force
  and communities of faith, 261
  on gay youth, 267
  on Spitzer study, 234
National Press Club, National Pro-
    Family Forum campaign,
    210-211
National Pro-Family Forum
  opposition to GLBT movement,
    198, 200-201
  press conference, 210-211
National Public Radio, Janet Folger,
    208
Nebraska Psychological Association,
    on Paul Cameron, 111
The New York Times
  Exodus International phone
    numbers, 219
  Paulk, Anne, 3, 201, 207
  Paulk, John 3

Newsweek, "Gay for Life?," 204
Nicolosi, Joseph
  and Cook, Colin, 97, 152
  criticism of, 138-139, 158, 254
  on defensive detachment, 101
  description of, 152-153
  educational background, 134-135
  Hannity & Colmes show, 133-134,
    150
  "Love Won Out" tour, 247
  and NARTH, 121, 136, 138, 141
  religious views, 135-136
  and reparative therapy, 132, 135,
    156-158
  reparative therapy techniques, 140
  on Shepard, Matthew, 159
  social stereotypes, 153-155
  and Spitzer, Robert, 232, 233
  on Spitzer study, 234
  on urination, 156
Nightline, Sullivan/Folger debate,
    208-209
Nineteenth Avenue Baptist Church, 69
North, Gary, reconstructionist
    movement, 207
*Not Afraid to Change: The Remarkable
    Story of How One Man
    Overcame Homosexuality,* 4,
    34
"Not Natural," song, 206
Nude therapy, Wesleyan Christian
    Community Church, 161, 162
Nunberg, Hermann, 124

O'Donnell, Christine
  SALT leader, 76
  on Wade Richards, 78
Olsen, Walter, on Cameron's statistics,
    110
One Nation Under God, 90
Oprah, John Paulk, 260
Out for Good, 228
*Out of Egypt: One Woman's Journey
    Out of Lesbianism,* 53

Out of the Closet and into the Light, 41
Overcomers, orientation change, 38
Ovesey, Lionel, pseudohomosexuality
    theory, 125

Pantaleo, Jack
    on AIDS epidemic, 99-100
    Evangelicals Concerned, 68-69
    LIA infiltration, 69-71
Parents and Friends Ministries, 32, 223
Parents and Friends of Ex-Gays
    (PFOX), 204, 223
Participants, ex-gay ministries, 40
Paulk, Anne
    Exodus testimony, 45
    Love Won Out, 29, 33-34
    marital relationship, 57
    Mr. P incident, 3-4, 19-20
    The New York Times, 201, 207
    Newsweek, 204
Paulk, John
    appearance of, 254
    on Cameron's statistics, 115
    Colorado Springs Gazette, 14-15
    Evans' view of, 67
    and Exodus International, 4, 16, 22,
      223
    Exodus testimony, 45-46
    homosexual orientation, 15-16, 21,
      22
    at HRC press conference, 211
    "Love Won Out" tour, 4-5, 247
    marital relationship, 57
    marital therapy, 34
    at Mr. P's, 3-4, 7-8, 9, 11-13, 222
    The New York Times, 3
    Newsweek, 204
    on Nicolosi, Joseph, 136
    Not Afraid to Change, 182
    Oprah, 260
    Southern Voice story, 13, 14
    and Spitzer, Robert, 233
    talk show confession, 19-21
    20/20 newsmagazine, 15

Payne, Leanne, 24, 26, 43-44, 184
Penile plethysmograph test, 230, 237
Pennington, Sylvia, 65
Perfect Enemies, 214
Perry, Troy, on gay returnees, 274
Phelps, Fred, 214
Philpott, Kent
    Evans' view of, 67
    on homosexuality, 64
    interview of, 67-68
    later view of LIA, 69
    LIA leadership, 62-63, 65, 69
    The Third Sex?, 64, 81
Piazza, Michael, Cathedral of Hope,
    249-250, 263
Pietrzyk, Mark
    on Cameron, Paul, 108
    on Falzarano, Anthony, 217
Pillard, Richard, biological causation,
    147
The Pink Swastika, 137
Pollard, Robert, informed consent, 140
Polygraphy, ex-gay studies, 230, 237
Pornography addiction, Exodus
    testimonials, 43
Porter, Natalie, Cameron investigation,
    111
Portland Fellowship Ministries, Jason
    Thompson, 246
"Pseudohomosexuality," 125
*Psychoanalysis and Male
    Homosexuality,* 122
*Psychoanalytic Therapy and the Gay
    Man,* 123

Quest Learning Center, 94, 95

Ragan, Bob, orientation change, 32, 36
Reclaiming America for Christ
    conference, antigay
    publications, 208
Reconstructionist movement, views of,
    207

Reed, Ralph, on Janet Folger, 200
Regeneration Ministries, orientation
    change, 32
Relationships, Nicolosi's view,
    154-155
Religion, and GLBT community,
    260-262
Religious individuals, ministries
    participants, 41-42
Religious right
    and ex-gay ministries, 218-222
    immorality of, 21
    political influence of, 195-196, 223
    and reparative therapists, 192
Reparative therapy
    condemnation of, 141-142, 143, 202
    establishment of, 131-132
    religious right, 192
    techniques of, 139-140
*Reparative Therapy of Male
    Homosexuality,* 140, 145-146,
    156
Republican party, and religious right,
    195-196
Richards, Wade
    background, 73-74
    gay activist, 78-79, 222
    LIA group home, 74-76
    SALT program, 76-77
    talk show, 72-73
Rivera, Geraldo, 109-110, 114
Robertson, Pat
    on gay pride flags, 197
    on homosexuals, 206, 260-261
    Liberian business venture, 251
    and religious right, 18
    on terrorist attacks, 223-234
Rogers, Sy, 35
    on AIDS impact, 99
    appearance of, 254
    Asian missions, 251
The Roseanne Show, Besen and
    Falzarano, 217, 218
Rosenberg, Sam, 144
Rubber band technique, 29-30, 255
Rudiger, Larry, 237

Rushdoony, R. J., reconstructionist
    movement, 207
Rutherford Institute, Cameron's
    "studies," 112
Ryan, Caitlin
    on health provider education, 250
    on orientation change, 246

Sagen, Susannah, on Janet Folger, 200
Same-sex ambivalence, gay
    relationships, 102
Same-sex attachment disorder (SSAD),
    171
Same-sex friendships, as homosexual
    cure, 102-103
Satan, and homosexuality, 51, 52-53,
    236
Satinover, Jeffrey, NARTH, 137
Saudi Arabia, homosexual beheading,
    251
Saviors Alliance for Lifting the Truth
    (SALT), 72, 78
Sawyer, Forrest, *Nightline,* 208, 209
Schlessinger, Laura
    and Cohen, Richard, 163-164
    and NARTH, 144
    and Spitzer, Robert, 232, 238
Schneider, Yvette Cantu, FRC, 224,
    233
"Scientificization of stereotypes," 153
Seduction, B-SADD, 175-176
Self-mutilation, Exodus International,
    88-89
*Separate Creation, A: The Search for
    the Biological Origins of
    Sexual Orientation,* 146
The 700 Club, on terrorist attacks,
    223-234
*Seven Steps to Recruit-Proof Your
    Child,* 247-248
Seventh-Day Adventist church, and
    Colin Cook, 93, 94, 95
Sheldon, Lou
    NARTH conference, 120

Sheldon, Lou *(continued)*
    and Nicolosi, Joseph, 136
    on Spitzer study, 234
Shepard, Matthew
    death of, 158-159, 212-213, 214
    vigil for, 213-214
Sibling rivalry, homosexual cause
        theory, 172-173
Silverstein, Charles, 130
Sin
    antihomosexual bigotry, *x-xi*
    LIA position, 64
Sissyphobia, 150
60 Minutes, covert investigations, 266
Smid, John, 36, 40
Smith, David M., HRC, 215
Socarides, Charles
    and American Psychiatric
        Association, 131, 132
    Cohen's view of, 184
    on homosexuality, 128, 129, 130,
        138
    and NARTH, 136
"Social/peer wounds," 173-174
Society for Individual Rights (SIR),
        APA conference, 130
Soulforce, 56, 262
Southern Voice
    gay newspaper, 9-10
    Paulk story, 13, 14, 17
Spiritual warfare, use of, 54-55
Spitzer, Robert
    American Psychiatric Association
        conference, 131, 228
    early view of homosexuality, 227-28
    HRC letter to, 229-232
    right-wing connections, 232-233
    study clarification, 240
    study critique, 235-239
    study impact, 225, 233-235, 259
    study motivation, 241
    study research, 228-229, 232-233,
        238
Sports, gender identification, 101-102
Spring Life Ministries, *The Gay
        Agenda* video, 113

St. Pierre, Tracey
    failed deliverance, 54
    religious participant, 41
StandOut, Wade Richards, 78-79
Stephenson, Jerry, 41
Stonewall riots, 61, 129
A Strong Delusion, 35
"Sue a Quack," 265
Suicidal ideation
    Exodus International, 88-89
    Exodus testimonials, 43
    gay youth, 178, 179
Sullivan, Andrew, 110, 208-209
"Summer of Hate," 196
Sun Sentinel, Coral Ridge Church, 222

Talk Back Live, child molestation, 34
Taylor, Charles, 251
Tebedo, Keven
    and Cendo, Rick, 97
    CFV, 95
    and Cook, Colin, 96-97
The Third Sex?, 64, 67, 81
Thomas, Cal, on *Not Afraid to Change,*
        4
Thomas, Randy, of political right,
        221-222
Thomas Aquinas Psychological Clinic,
        reparative therapy, 135-136
Thompson, Jason, Exodus Youth
        program, 246
Tim Todd Ministries, antigay cartoons,
        248, 249
"Time to Stand" seminars, Amendment
        2 campaign, 95
Tomlin, Lily, on covert operations,
        265-266
Touch therapy
    B-SADD techniques, 189
    NARTH conference, 121, 163
Traditional Values Coalition (TVC),
        Cameron's "studies," 112
Trout, Clint, on representations of gay
        life, 55, 264

Truth for Youth bibles, antigay
    cartoons, 248-249
"Truth in Love" campaign, 3, 201,
    202-208
20/20 segment, 15, 76

Unification Church, Richard Cohen,
    166
The Unquiet Dead, 188
    GLBT ad, 202
    Reggie White ad, 202-203, 205
    USA Today, 202

Van Domelen, Bob, assault conviction,
    38-39

The Wall Street Journal, Robert
    Spitzer, 240
Wallace, Mike, "The Homosexuals,"
    127-128, 129
Washington Times, Anthony Falzarano,
    229
Waybourn, William, 9-10
"We're Standing for the Truth That
    Homosexuals Can Change,"
    3, 33, 34
Wesleyan Christian Community
    Church
    inner healing, 161
    sexual assault, 162-163

White, Mel
    on fundamentalism, 271-272
    on gay-affirming churches, 261, 262
    on ministerial leadership, 56
White, Reggie
    USA Today, 202-203
    Wisconsin State Assembly speech,
    205
Whitten, Clark, 48, 49
Wier, Terry, reparative therapy
    techniques, 139-140
Wildmon, Don, 206
Will & Grace, 264
Williams, Armstrong, 197
WITNESS! Freedom Ministries, 46
Wockner, Rex, Lily Tomlin interview,
    266
Wong, Melvin, on orientation change,
    32
Worthen, Anita, and Wade Richards,
    74-75
Worthen, Frank
    Asian missions, 251
    criticism of, 67
    LIA foundation, 65, 66
    LIA leadership, 69, 70
    and Marks, Jeremy, 91
    on orientation change, 32, 35
    and Richards, Wade, 74-75
Wulfensmith, Catherine, LIA
    conversion program, 3

You Don't Have to be Gay, 35, 48
Youth. *See* Adolescents; Children